# A Guide How To Start
# Dairy Farming

# A Guide How To Start

# Dairy Farming

Dr. Narender Kumar Vyas

AMIGA PRESS INC.

DELHI (INDIA)

**AMIGA PRESS INC.**
H.O.: 28-A, Indra Park, Chander Nagar
Delhi-110051 (India)
Tel.: 011-22504028, +91-98736-57000
E-mail: amigapub@gmail.com
Website : www.amigapress.co.in

This edition is published by Amiga Press Inc.

ISBN: 978-93-87295-01-8



First Published 2018



Printed and bound in India by Thomson Press Ltd. New Delhi

# Preface

Dairying is an important source of subsidiary income to small/marginal farmers and agricultural labourers. The manure from animals provides a good source of organic matter for improving soil fertility and crop yields. The gober gas from the dung is used as fuel for domestic purposes as also for running engines for drawing water from well. The surplus fodder and agricultural by- products are gainfully utilised for feeding the animals. Dairy farming is a class of agricultural, or an animal husbandry, enterprise, for long-term production of milk, usually from dairy cows but also from goats and sheep, which may be either processed on-site or transported to a dairy factory for processing and eventual retail sale. Most dairy farms sell the male calves born by their cows, usually for veal production, or breeding depending on quality of the bull calf, rather than raising non-milk-producing stock. Many dairy farms also grow their own feed, typically including corn, alfalfa, and hay. This is fed directly to the cows, or is stored as silage for use during the winter season. Additional dietary supplements are often added to the feed to increase quality milk production.

Dairy plants process the raw milk they receive from farmers so as to extend its marketable life. Two main types of processes are employed: heat treatment to ensure the safety of milk for human consumption and to lengthen its shelf- life, and dehydrating dairy products such as butter, hard cheese and milk powders so that they can be stored. Milk producing animals have been domesticated for thousands of years. Initially, they were part of the subsistence farming that nomads engaged in. As the community moved about the country, their animals accompanied them. Protecting and feeding the animals were a big part of the symbiotic relationship between the animals and the herders.

The book will meet the demands of not a vast majority of students and researchers, but also the policy-makers and all those interested in the livestock economy and dairy related products.

–Author

# Contents

# 1

# Introduction

Dairy farming is a class of agricultural, or an animal husbandry, enterprise, for long-term production of milk, usually from dairy cows but also from goats and sheep, which may be either processed on-site or transported to a dairy factory for processing and eventual retail sale. Most dairy farms sell the male calves born by their cows, usually for veal production, or breeding depending on quality of the bull calf, rather than raising non-milk-producing stock. Many dairy farms also grow their own feed, typically including corn, alfalfa, and hay. This is fed directly to the cows, or is stored as silage for use during the winter season. Additional dietary supplements are often added to the feed to increase quality milk production.

## WHY DO DAIRY FARMING

Dairying is an important source of subsidiary income to small/marginal farmers and agricultural labourers. The manure from animals provides a good source of organic matter for improving soil fertility and crop yields. The gober gas from the dung is used as fuel for domestic purposes as also for running engines for drawing water from well. The surplus fodder and agricultural byproducts are gainfully utilised for feeding the animals.

Almost all draught power for farm operations and transportation is supplied by bullocks. Since, agriculture is mostly seasonal, there is a possibility of finding employment throughout the year for many persons through dairy farming. Thus, dairy also provides employment throughout the year. The main beneficiaries of dairy programmes are small/marginal farmers and landless labourers. A farmer can earn a gross surplus of about ` 12,000 per year from a unit consisting of 2 milking buffaloes.

The capital investment required for purchase of 2 buffaloes is `₹ 18,223/-. Even after paying a sum of ₹ 4294/- per annum towards repayment of the loan and interest the farmer can earn a net surplus of ₹ 6000 - 9000/- approximately per year. Even more profits can be earned depending upon the breed of animal, managerial skills and marketing potential. World Bank estimates about 75 per cent of India's 940 million people are in 5.87 million villages, cultivating over 145 million hectares of cropland. Average farm size is about 1.66

hectares. Among 70 million rural households, 42 per cent operate upto 2 hectares and 37 per cent are landless households.

These landless and small farmers have in their possession 53 per cent of the animals and produce 51 per cent of the milk. Thus, small/marginal farmers and land less agricultural labourers play a very important role in milk production of the country. Dairy farming can also be taken up as a main occupation around big urban centres where the demand for milk is high.

### Scope for Dairy Farming and its National Importance

The total milk production in the country for the year 2001-02 was estimated at 84.6 million metric tonnes. At this production, the per capita availability was to be 226 grams per day against the minimum requirement of 250 grams per day as recommended by ICMR. Thus, there is a tremendous scope/ potential for increasing the milk production. The population of breeding cows and buffaloes in milk over 3 years of age was 62.6 million and 42.4 million, respectively (1992 census). Central and State Governments are giving considerable financial assistance for creating infrastructure facilities for milk production. The nineth plan outlay on Animal Husbandry and Dairying was ₹ 2345 crores.

### Financial Assistance Available from Banks/NABARD for Dairy Farming

NABARD is an apex institution for all matters relating to policy, planning and operation in the field of agricultural credit. It serves as an apex refinancing agency for the institutions providing investment and production credit. It promotes development through formulation and appraisal of projects through a well organised Technical Services Department at the Head Office and Technical Cells at each of the Regional Offices.

Loan from banks with refinance facility from NABARD is available for starting dairy farming. For obtaining bank loan, the farmers should apply to the nearest branch of a commercial or co-operative Bank in their area in the prescribed application form which is available in the branches of financing banks. The Technical Officer attached to or the Manager of the bank can help/ give guidance to the farmers in preparing the project report to obtain bank loan.

For dairy schemes with very large outlays, detailed reports will have to be prepared. The items of finance would include capital asset items such as purchase of milch animals, construction of sheds, purchase of equipments etc. The feeding cost during the initial period of one/two months is capitalised and given as term loan. Facilities such as cost of land development, fencing, digging of well, commissioning of diesel engine/pumpset, electricity connections, essential servants' quarters, godown, transport vehicle, milk processing facilities etc., can be considered for loan. Cost of land is not considered for loan. However, if land is purchased for setting up a dairy farm, its cost can be treated as party's margin upto 10% of the total cost of project.

## DAIRY FARMING AND CATTLE BREEDING

For the dairy production major, the love of cattle and of the land is usually very strong. Even though he finds himself working for a salary, he dreams of the day he can own his farm and his herd. This goal is attained sometimes, but not too often, for the simple reason it takes so much money to start dairy farming the average man, after paying income tax, supporting a family, owning a home and a car, hasn't much left.

The best way today to begin, for a young man who wants to be a dairy farmer, is to go right back home and go into partnership with his father and put his ambition and knowledge to work.

Another plan is to go into partnership with an old, established dairy farmer and gradually buy into the setup. Most of our dairy farmers are past 50 years old. Some very good herd owners are looking for the young man who loves cattle and the soil, to team up with.

Such jobs usually start with the young man acting as assistant manager. If he has the stuff he gradually becomes part-owner. There are more opportunities along this line than many people appreciate. Just consider the established herds in your own community. Who will carry on when the present owner no longer can "hit the ball"? (e) along with most established herds is the purebred cattle challenge and the pleasure of producing some seed stock, as well as milk. Today, we have too few constructive breeders. We need in our a.i. programme more proved sires, more good cow families and, industry wise, more good cattle. Due to our present income tax laws, and our farm labour picture, there is a declining number, and will continue to be, of wealthy herd-owner hobbyists.

These men, by virtue of sufficient capital, assembled many great animals. They bred some of our best cattle. They also purchased some of the top cattle from smaller breeders. In the future, farm-sized herds and the semi-commercial herd will, by virtue of a sound breeding and testing programme, produce much of our seed stock for the future. The farm-sized herd, where some individual cow attention can be given, will continue to be the leader in this area.

Going into business for himself will not for a long time have the glitter of a salary job. New cars, new suits, and a few of those things won't come too fast. An understanding wife is a must in this picture. Most fellows who choose this course won't be quitting at 5 p.m. And come in smelling like a rose for a 6 p.m. Dinner.

In the long run, however, they will amass more total capital, have more independence, more freedom of action and thought, be healthier, have a closerknit family life, be more appreciated in the community, and have less heart trouble than the classmate who chooses the humdrum city life and keeping up with the joneses.

**Herd Management Farm Superintendent**

It has long been said that "If you can't own your own herd the next best thing is to manage a good herd and farm for someone else." This is true today—but different than 25 years ago. There are fewer farms supported by some other business. Most farms today have to make money or at least pay interest on the investment. In America, there are vastly fewer jobs of estate managers than we once knew.

There will continue to be less! The hired dairy farm manager today will have to: Possess good business judgement and be able to handle large capital and to direct employees.

He will have to be an expert dairyman, as well as a farmer, and produce milk in large volume at low cost to meet competitive market demands. He will have to possess ingenuity and exert energy to keep his operation rightside-up in the face of the changing agricultural picture. He will also have to be a good salesman, to insure his employees and his stockholders that the future is sound and that his operations are equally sound. When one works for a Board or a corporation, he must always be prepared to defend his position.

It is my observation that to some extent good cow men and men capable of large-scale dairy operations are born with much of the potential. I have never believed it can be taught except by experience. I do believe sound teaching plus good experience can develop many men along these lines.

In the years ahead or see an acute shortage of capable managers who can handle a $500,000 to a two million-dollar dairy production setup. This is what we must face, because as suggested, have many more 200 to 2,500 cow herds, with the resulting capital, labour, feed, disease, and marketing problems. Men who can handle these jobs will always be few, but well paid. They should be well paid, as they are virtually, in the dairy field, what the economists call captains of industry.

**Dairy Procurement and Field Work**

There will continue to be increasing emphasis upon much procurement. As our dairy processes become fewer, with greater volume, greater overhead expenses, and tougher competition the importance of milk procurement increases. Plants are constructed to handle milk. They cost a lot of money.

Without sufficient volume they quickly become a liability. Procurement work involves direction of field staff, quality control, truck routes, and a score of problems that challenge the best of every worker in this field. It requires from the director to the newest fieldman a thorough understanding and appreciation of the problems of the producer and willingness to cooperate with him.

**Dairy Procurement and Field Work**

Our breed registry organizations are constantly adding men to serve as editors, advertising representatives, and field representatives in charge of registration and production testing. It is a good field and offers an opportunity to work with people and cattle.

*Artificial insemination:* This field is new. Starting just 21 years ago, the programme now embraces over seven million, or 37%, of our milk cows in America. There are roughly 12,000 employees in this field at present, but the number increases daily.

*Here are a few of the key jobs and their requirements:*

- **General Manager:** Requires a man capable of directing from 50 to 1,000 employees and heading a business with gross returns of $300,000 to as much as five million dollars a year. General Managers must be interested in cattle improvement, understand business management and finance, be good personnel directors, and be able to carry on a strong public relations programme.
- **Assistant manager :** Assists the manager in his varied duties. Requires same type of experience and training. Offers advancement to full managership.
- **Field Supervisor:** In charge of field operations. Includes supervision and working with technicians, selling the programme, public relations and, in some cases, trouble shooting. This is a type of extension work in many ways. Large organizations have a Director of Field Service, who directs the work of many field supervisors. Love of cattle and ability to supervise personnel is a must in this position.
- **Sire Analyst:** Every organization has a sire analyst, whose duties are to constantly evaluate sires in use and comb the field for improved sires that will improve the patron's herds. One or more assistants may also be employed. This job requires

a basic understanding of animal genetics, working knowledge of breed families, ability to analyse records, evaluate cattle for conformation, etc., and prepare copy for advertising sires in use.

- **Laboratory Supervisor:** This man must be scientifically trained. He has charge of semen collection, processing, storage, and shipping. His position is similar to that of Production Manager in many industries. A key job and one of the most vital. A man in this position must be research-minded, because he is constantly ferreting out weaknesses in his organization's operations that influence settling rate in the field.
- **Technician or Inseminator:** While mentioned last, by no means is the technician, whose job it is to inseminate cows, the least important in this field. In most eases he is the key man. He is usually well paid—if he is in a heavily populated cow area and wants to work. Many technicians are college graduates, though the majority are not. Working as a technician for a year or two is vital to the success of men in all positions in A.I. work. This is the place a college graduate should start his training for a more advanced position in this field.
- **Other jobs:** Most organizations publish a monthly or quarterly pamphlet, sent to all members. A part-time, or in some cases a% full-time, editor is employed. He also assists with publicity, sire catalogues, advertising, and public relations. Here is the field for the dairy production man who likes to write.

## NEW HEALTH PRODUCTS FOR FARM ANIMALS

Animal diseases cost U.S., agriculture $17 billion each year, according to the Congress Office of Technology Assessment. To help prevent these losses, animal scientists are using biotechnology to develop an array of products to diagnose, treat, and prevent disease in farm animals. An area where animal biotechnology has already had a profound impact is diagnostic testing. Many animal diseases are difficult to diagnose.

A veterinarian often has to wait hours or days for laboratory results to confirm a diagnosis. In the meantime, the veterinarian must either withhold treatment or risk using an inappropriate therapy. Using biotechnology, scientists are developing fast, accurate diagnostic tests for many of the most common farm animal diseases. In some cases, a veterinarian can conduct the diagnostic tests right on the farm and immediately start the best therapy.

Many of these new tests use monoclonal antibodies. Antibodies are proteins an animal's immune system produces in response to invasion by bacteria, viruses, or parasites. Each kind of antibody binds specifically with a characteristic part of a particular kind of invader. Scientists make monoclonal antibodies by fusing two kinds of cells. One is an immune system cell that produces antibodies, which bind to part of a particular disease-causing microbe; the other is a cancer cell. The cell that results from the fusion inherits from the immune system cell the ability to produce antibodies, and from the cancer cell the ability to reproduce indefinitely.

This new hybrid cell, or hybridoma, acts as an antibody factory. The antibodies are called monoclonal because they are produced by identical "clones" of the original hybridoma-all will bind with the identifying structure on the surface of the microbe in question. One application of monoclonal antibodies is as a test for brucellosis in cattle. This bacterial disease often causes cows to abort pregnancies, and it can be spread to farmers and people who drink milk from infected cows. Vaccines protect pregnant animals from abortion, but vaccinated cows may become carriers of the disease. Conventional diagnostic tests cannot distinguish between the disease-causing microbe and the vaccine, which is made from the microbe. Thus, these tests cannot help the farmer determine which animals are carriers of the disease and which are not. But diagnostic tests using monoclonal antibodies are so specific, they distinguish between cattle that carry the disease-causing bacterium and those that carry only the vaccine. With the aid of these new tests, farmers can isolate carriers to prevent the spread of infection. Diagnostic tests are not just for diseases.

A monoclonal antibody test to detect pregnancy in animals is so simple that a farmer can read the test right on the farm. Monoclonal antibodies are also used in a test to detect a disease called scours in piglets and calves. Scours is a bacterial disease of newborn animals that causes diarrhea. Many of the afflicted animals die of dehydration. By providing quick, accurate diagnosis, the monoclonal antibody test for scours permits immediate administration of therapy. The therapy for scours in calves is also based on monoclonal antibodies. Infected calves are fed monoclonal antibodies that coat the offending bacteria, preventing the microbes from causing diarrhea. Some other therapies for animal diseases are based on recombinant DNA technology. Genetic engineering allows scientists to insert one or more new genes into an animal, plant, or microbial cell. In developing treatments for an animal disease, for instance, an animal gene is inserted into a microbe or an animal cell that can be grown in a laboratory culture. The inserted gene is one that produces a natural disease-fighting protein. The microbes or animal cells become minute factories, producing large quantities of the therapeutic protein. For example, genetic engineering is used to produce interferons and interleukin-2, natural proteins that fight viruses.

Veterinarians long have used antibiotics against bacterial diseases, but they have had few drugs to treat viral infections. Interferons and interleukin- 2 not only kill viruses directly, they also stimulate the animal's immune system, improving the immune system's ability to fight disease naturally. One target of research regarding interferons and interleukin-2 is shipping fever, a disease of cattle caused by several viruses infecting an animal simultaneously. Although the animal's immune system normally keeps the viruses in check, outbreaks of the disease may result from stress during transport to feedlots or market. Shipping fever costs the beef industry more than $250 million a year. Injections of interferons or interleukin-2 before shipping may help to augment the cattle's natural immunity and prevent shipping fever.

**Better Vaccines to Prevent Disease**

In addition to producing new diagnostic tests and therapeutic proteins, animal scientists are using biotechnology to develop vaccines to prevent disease. A safe, effective vaccine for swine pseudorabies, a fatal herpes-virus, is already in use. An advantage of the swine pseudorabies vaccine, and other vaccines made through recombinant DNA technology, is that they use only a small portion of the original microbe. Conventional vaccines use killed or weakened forms of the disease-causing microbe.

Sometimes, when the microbes are not completely killed or sufficiently weakened, a conventional vaccine may cause the disease it was supposed to prevent. Disease-causing genes are not included in the genetically engineered vaccines. Therefore, the recombinant vaccines build up the body's immunity without the risk of causing disease. Another advantage of recombinant vaccines is the speed with which they can be developed. "Conventional vaccine development can take 20 or 30 years, maybe even 100 years," says

Karen Jacobsen, D.V.M., University of Georgia College of Veterinary Medicine.

"This is one reason why we don't have vaccines for a lot of animal diseases today". Recombinant vaccines are being developed for foot-and-mouth disease, a highly contagious viral disease that infects cattle, sheep, and other animals. Although this disease has been eradicated in North America, it still causes substantial livestock productivity losses elsewhere, particularly in developing countries. Infected herds must be slaughtered, and contaminated ranches must be left idle for months to prevent new outbreaks of the disease. Conventional foot-and-mouth vaccines are made by weakening the virus that causes the disease. These vaccines sometimes revert to the virulent state, and they have caused outbreaks of the disease in Europe.

The foot-and-mouth vaccine made with biotechnology cannot cause the disease because, as in other biotech vaccines, the disease-causing genes have been removed. The biotech vaccine does not need to be kept cold and, therefore, can be used in developing countries. In addition to being used in treating swine pseudorabies and foot-and-mouth disease, recombinant DNA technology is being used to develop vaccines against dozens of livestock and poultry diseases, such as scours and a variety of respiratory disorders. Some vaccines may be injected into eggs so that chickens are immunized before they hatch. Most vaccines protect against viral or bacterial infections, but using genetic engineering, researchers in New Zealand and Australia have developed a vaccine against a parasitic disease. Farmers must destroy the meat from sheep infested with a species of tapeworm common in those two countries. The new vaccine, which protects sheep from the tapeworm, may save farmers millions of dollars annually.

**Proteins for Animal Nutrition**

Natural proteins called somatotropins, or growth hormones, help animals convert feed into muscle or milk. Using recombinant DNA technology, scientists have been able to develop bacteria that produce commercial quantities of somatotropins.

They have found that administering small additional amounts of these proteins to animals helps to increase the animals' efficiency of feed conversion, thereby saving the farmer money. Porcine somatotropin (PST) may help improve human health, as well as lower the farmer's cost of production. PST improves feed efficiency in hogs by 15 to 20 per cent. It also reduces fat deposition, allowing PST-treated hogs to provide consumers with leaner cuts of pork. The ability to produce lean pork has enormous implications for improving human health by reducing dietary fat and cholesterol. Another growth protein, bovine somatotropin (BST), is being administered to make dairy cows more efficient, thereby lowering the dairy farmer's costs. Regular administration of small amounts of BST increases a cow's milk yield by 10 to 25 per cent. Although feed intake also increases, this feed increase is proportionately less than the increase in milk production.

Studies indicate that BST can improve the milk-to-feed ratio by 5 to 15 per cent. Extensive laboratory testing has shown that the meat and milk of treated animals contain no more PST or BST than the meat or milk from untreated animals. Other tests have shown that these proteins do not act on the human body, and therefore, they are safe to eat. Nevertheless, the use of BST remains controversial. Testing is under way to make sure that animals are not adversely affected by treatment with somatotropins. Another protein

that can be administered to animals to increase feed efficiency is called growth hormone releasing factor (GHRF). While not a growth protein itself, GHRF causes the animal to increase production of growth proteins.

**Improved Animal Breeds**

Long before anyone knew about genes or DNA, people were selectively breeding animals to produce desirable traits, such as strength, feed efficiency, and disease resistance. Selective breeding is a crude technology, because each cross between two animals mixes hundreds of thousands of genes, both desirable and undesirable. Recombinant DNA technology is now making it possible for scientists to breed animals with great precision.

One or more new genes can be inserted into an animal embryo without disturbing the rest of the animal's genes. The resulting animal with the new gene or genes is referred to as a transgenic animal. Despite the differences in technique, the scientist using recombinant DNA has the same objectives as the selective breeder: improving efficiency, disease resistance, and other desirable traits. But recombinant DNA provides a wider array of possible new traits, since, recombinant techniques allow animal scientists to insert genes not only from the same or closely related species, but also from distantly related animals, plants, and even microbes.

One possible application of gene transfer in animals is to develop dairy cows that produce more nutritious milk. Bottle feeding human infants with cow's milk is not an ideal substitute for breast feeding, because cow's milk differs from human milk in some important components. Scientists are looking for ways to transfer genes into dairy cows that will enable the cows to produce milk that more closely resembles human milk. Advances in Control of Parasitic Diseases Continue to Rely on Biotechnology Parasitic disease continues to be a major health problem worldwide in humans and domestic animals. Applying biotechnology has led to progress in prevention and control in many areas, particularly in regard to diagnosis.

Parasites, like most organisms, carry repetitive sequences in their genomes. These are sometimes tandem repeats (back-to-back in a chromosome), or they may be located at random throughout the genome. Often, repetitive sequences are intergenic and noncoding, and are thus far more subject to evolution and change, increasing the likelihood that they will be genus or even species specific. Since, detection of these sequences is not dependent upon gene expression, which may vary over time, repetitive sequence-based assays allow detection of the parasite at any life stage.

The effectiveness of repetitive sequence-based polymerase chain reaction (PCR) methods of identification has been demonstrated for parasites of several clinically important genera (1). A PCR assay has also been developed to differentiate two closely related nematode species that are virtually indistinguishable by morphologic examination (2), as well as for diagnosis of Toxoplasma and Cryptosporidium infections (3). Attempts to develop antiparasite vaccines have met with multiple failures. The problems often result from lack of post-translational modification by currently used vector-host systems and the inability to regenerate the secondary and tertiary structure of the native immunogens.

Antigen presentation in recombinant parasite vaccines has also been thought to be a problem resulting in failed efficacy. There is now some evidence to indicate that cloning of genes for antigens of interest to yield chimeric molecules expressed in the BCG strain of Mycobacterium bovis may provide improved antigen presentation to stimulate both humoral and cellular responses (4); however, it is unlikely that future applications of this technology will be simple. Nonetheless, work is proceeding on the application of biotechnology to the development of vaccines against parasites in most food animals.

A particularly striking exception to the marginal successes reported in other systems has been a recombinant vaccine for a parasitic helminth of sheep (5). This product yielded greater than 94 per cent protection in experimental work and is now available as a commercial product. A further possibility is the application of anti-idiotypic monoclonal antibodies. When monoclonal antibodies are prepared against a monoclonal antibody, it is possible to obtain, in a very small number of cases, an antibody which mimics the original antigen. Results of work with Cryptosporidium perfringens epsilon toxin suggest that animals immunized with anti-idiotype monoclonals can be protected against toxin challenge.

## MILK PRESERVATION METHODS

Cool temperature has been the main method by which milk freshness has been extended. When windmills and well pumps were invented, one of its first uses on the farm besides providing water for animals was for cooling milk, to extend the storage life before being transported to the town market.

The naturally cold underground water would be continuously pumped into a tub or other containers of milk set in the tub to cool after milking. This method of milk cooling was extremely popular before the arrival of electricity and refrigeration.

### Refrigeration

When refrigeration first arrived the equipment was initially used to cool cans of milk, which were filled by hand milking. These cans were placed into a cooled water bath to remove heat and keep them cool until they were able to be transported to a collection facility. As more automated methods were developed for harvesting milk, hand milking was replaced and, as a result, the milk can was replaced by a bulk milk cooler. 'Ice banks' were the first type of bulk milk cooler.

This was a double wall vessel with evaporator coils and water located between the walls at the bottom and sides of the tank. A small refrigeration compressor was used to remove heat from the evaporator coils. Ice eventually builds up around the coils, until it reaches a thickness of about three inches surrounding each pipe, and the cooling system shuts off.

When the milking operation starts, only the milk agitator and the water circulation pump, which flows water across the ice and the steel walls of the tank, are needed to reduce the incoming milk to a temperature below 40 degrees.

This cooling method worked well for smaller dairies, however was fairly inefficient and was unable to meet the increasingly higher cooling demand of larger milking parlours. In the mid 1950's direct expansion refrigeration was first applied directly to the bulk milk cooler. This type of cooling utilizes an evaporator built directly into the inner wall of the storage tank to remove heat from the milk. Direct expansion is able to cool milk at a much faster rate than early ice bank type coolers and is still the primary method for bulk tank cooling today on small to medium sized operations.

Another device which has contributed significantly to milk quality is the plate heat exchanger. This device utilizes a number of specially designed stainless steel plates with small spaces between them. Milk is passed between every other set of plates with water being passed between the balance of the plates to remove heat from the milk.

This method of cooling can remove large amounts of heat from the milk in a very short time, thus drastically slowing bacteria growth and thereby improving milk quality. Ground water is the most common source of cooling medium for this device. Dairy cows consume approximately 3 gallons of water for every gallon of milk production and prefer to drink slightly warm water as opposed to cold ground water. For this reason, PHE's can result in drastically improved milk quality, reduced operating costs for the dairymen by reducing the refrigeration load on his bulk milk cooler, and increased milk production by supplying the cows with a source of fresh warm water.

Plate heat exchangers have also evolved as a result of the increase of dairy farm herd sizes in the US. As a dairyman increases the size of his herd, he must also increase the capacity of his milking parlour in order to harvest the additional milk. This increase in parlour sizes has resulted in tremendous increases in milk throughput and cooling demand. Today's larger farms produce milk at a rate which direct expansion refrigeration systems on bulk milk coolers cannot cool in a timely manner.

PHE's are typically utilized in this instance to rapidly cool the milk to the desired temperature before it reaches the bulk milk tank. Typically, ground water is still utilized to provide some initial cooling to bring the milk to between 55 and 70 degrees F. A second part of the PHE is added to remove the remaining heat with a mixture of chilled pure water and propylene glycol. These chiller systems can be made to incorporate large evaporator surface areas and high chilled water flow rates to cool high flow rates of milk.

## HAND MILKING

Centralized dairy farming as we understand it primarily developed around villages and cities, where residents were unable to have cows of their own due to a lack of grazing land. Near the town, farmers could make some extra money on the side by having additional animals and selling the milk in town.

The dairy farmers would fill barrels with milk in the morning and bring it to market on a wagon. Until the late 1800s, the milking of the cow was done by hand. In the United States, several large dairy operations existed in some northeastern states and in the west, that involved as many as several hundred cows, but an individual milker could not be expected to milk more than a dozen cows a day. Smaller operations predominated.

Milking took place indoors in a barn with the cattle tied by the neck with ropes or held in place by stanchions. Feeding could occur simultaneously with milking in the barn, although most dairy cattle were pastured during the day between milkings. Such examples of this method of dairy farming are difficult to locate, but some are preserved as a historic site for a glimpse into the days gone by. One such instance that is open for this is at Point Reyes National Seashore.

### Vacuum Bucket Milking

The first milking machines were an extension of the traditional milking pail. The early milker device fit on top of a regular milk pail and sat on the floor under the cow. Following each cow being milked, the bucket would be dumped into a holding tank. This developed into the Surge hanging milker.

Prior to milking a cow, a large wide leather strap called a surcingle was put around the cow, across the cow's lower back. The milker device and collection tank hung underneath the cow from the strap. This innovation allowed the cow to move around naturally during the milking process rather than having to stand perfectly still over a bucket on the floor.

With the availability of electric power and suction milking machines, the roduction levels that were possible in stanchion barns increased but the scale of the operations continued to be limited by the labour intensive nature of the milking process.

Attaching and removing milking machines involved repeated heavy lifting of the machinery and its contents several times per cow and the pouring of the milk into milk cans. As a result, it was rare to find single-farmer operations of more than 50 head of cattle.

**Step-Saver Milk Transport**

As herd size began to increase, the bucket milker system became laborious. A vacuum milk-transport system known as the Step-Saver was developed to transport milk to the storage tank. The system used a long vacuum hose coiled around a receiver cart, and connected to a vacuum-breaker device in the milkhouse, allowing farmers to milk many cows without the necessity of walking increasingly longer distances carrying heavy buckets of milk.

## MILKING OPERATION

Milking machines are held in place automatically by a vacuum system that draws the ambient air pressure down from 15 to 21 pounds per square inch of vacuum. The vacuum is also used to lift milk vertically through small diametre hoses, into the receiving can. A milk lift pump draws the milk from the receiving can through large diametre stainless steel piping, through the plate cooler, then into a refrigerated bulk tank. Milk is extracted from the cow's udder by flexible rubber sheaths known as liners or inflations that are surrounded by a rigid air chamber. A pulsating flow of ambient air and vacuum is applied to the inflation's air chamber during the milking process.

When ambient air is allowed to enter the chamber, the vacuum inside the inflation causes the inflation to collapse around the cow's teat, squeezing the milk out of teat in a similar fashion as a baby calf's mouth massaging the teat. When the vacuum is reapplied in the chamber the flexible rubber inflation relaxes and opens up, preparing for the next squeezing cycle.

It takes the average cow three to five minutes to give her milk. Some cows are faster or slower. Slow-milking cows may take up to fifteen minutes to let down all their milk. Milking speed is only minorly related to the quantity of milk the cow produces — milking speed is a separate factor from milk quantity; milk quantity is not determinative of milking speed. Because most milkers milk cattle in groups, the milker can only process a group of cows at the speed of the slowest-milking cow. For this reason, many farmers will cull slow-milking cows.

The extracted milk passes through a strainer and plate heat exchangers before entering the tank, where it can be stored safely for a few days at approximately 42 °F. At pre-arranged times, a milk truck arrives and pumps the milk from the tank for transport to a dairy factory where it will be pasteurized and processed into many products.

## BULK TANK

In dairy farming a bulk milk cooling tank is a large storage tank for cooling and holding milk at a cold temperature until it can be picked up by a milk hauler. The bulk milk cooling tank is an important piece of dairy farm equipment.

It is usually made of stainless steel and used every day to store the raw milk on the farm in good condition. It must be cleaned after each milk collection. The milk cooling tank can be the property of the farmer or be rented from a dairy plant.

**Bulk Tank Types**

Raw milk producers have a choice of either open (from 150 to 3000 litres) or closed (from 1000 to 10000 litres) tanks. The cost can vary considerably, depending on manufacturing norms and whether a new or second hand tank is purchased.

Milk silos (10,000 litres and plus) are suitable for the very large producer. These are designed to be installed outside and adjacent to the dairy, all controls and the milk outlet pipe being situated in the dairy.

**Tank Construction**

A milk cooling tank, also known as a bulk tank or milk cooler, consists of an inner and an outer tank, both made of high quality stainless steel. The space between the outer tank and the inner tank is isolated with polyurethane foam. In case of a power failure with an outside temperature of 30°C, the content of the tank will warm up only 1°C in 24 hours.

To facilitate an adequate and rapid cooling of the entire content of a tank, every tank is equipped with at least one agitator. Stirring the milk ensures that all milk inside the tank is of the same temperature and that the milk stays homogeneous.

On top of every closed milk cooling tank is a manhole of about 40 centimetres diametre. This enables thorough cleaning and inspection of the inner tank if necessary. The manhole is covered by a lid and sealed watertight with a rubber ring. Also on top are 2 or 3 small inlets. One is covered with an air-vent, the other(s) can be used to pump milk into the tank.

A milk cooling tank usually stands on 4, 6, or 8 adjustable legs. The builtin tilt of the inner tank ensures that even the last drop of milk will eventually flow to the outlet.

At the bottom, every milk cooling tank has a threaded outlet, usually including a valve. All tanks have a thermometer, allowing for immediate inspection of the inner temperature. Most tanks include an automatic cleaning system. Using hot and cold water, an acid and/or alkaline cleaning fluid, a pump and a spray lance will clean the inner tank, ensuring an hygienic inner environment each time the tank is emptied.

Almost every tank has a control box. It manages the cooling process by use of a thermostat. The user can turn the system on and off, allow for extra and immediate stirring, start the cleaning routine, and reset the entire system in case of a failure.

New and bigger milk cooling tanks are now being equipped with onitoring and alarm systems. These systems guard temperature of the milk inside the tank, check the functioning of the agitator, the cooling unit and temperature of the cleaning water. In case of malfunctioning of any of these functions, the alarm will activate. The monitoring system will also keep a record of the temperature and of all malfunctions for a given period.

**Bulk Tank Manufacturing Norms**

Norms define among other criteria: insulation, milk agitation, cooling power required, variations in milk quantity measurement, calibration... Some are more demanding than others. ISO ISO standard 5708 published en 1983. Northern American standard 3A 13-10 updated in 2003. European Union standard EN 13732 published in 2003.

**Bulk Tank Outlet Standards**

Swedish outlet (SMS 1145), German outlet (DIN 11851), English RJT (BS 4825), IDF (ISO 2853), tri-clamp (ISO 2852), Danish outlet (DS 722).... can be found, not to mention different diametres. They vary from country to country. Non – standard outlets make the milk collection process difficult, as the operator needs to adapt to each different standard/ diametre.

**Cooling Systems**

There are two primary methods of cooling milk entering the bulk tank, each with its own advantages and disadvantages. The tank capacity and type will depend on herd size, calving pattern, frequency of milk collection, required milk quality, energy and water availability and future plans for development.

**Direct Expansion**

A bulk tank with direct expansion cooling has pipes or plates carrying refrigerant which are welded directly to the exterior of the milk chamber. A layer of insulation covers the exterior of the milk tank and the cooling lines, with an exterior metal shell over the insulation.

Direct expansion cooling cannot run when the tank is empty or the inside walls of the tank would freeze. Instead, the tank is rapidly cooled as warm milk first enters the tank, and then the tank is cooled slowly just to maintain a low storage temperature. The rapid cooling during milking requires very large refrigeration compressors and condenser radiators to quickly expel heat from the milk, and is better suited for very large farming operations where threephase electric power is available to operate the high-power cooling system.

**Ice Bank**

A bulk tank using an Ice Builder or Ice Bank immerses the bottom of the inner milk chamber in an open pool of water with copper tubes containing refrigerant suspended in the water. Between milkings, a small low-power cooling system slowly builds up a coating of ice around the copper tubes, and prevents icing of the pool over by continuously circulating the water in the pool. After the ice has achieved a thickness of 2-3 inches, the cooling system stops running.

During milking, the milk entering the tank is primarily cooled by circulating the water in the pool around the walls of the inner milk chamber, and the melting of the ice. After the ice has melted sufficiently the cooling system restarts to assist the ice bank and restart the ice building.

Ice bank bulk tanks are better suited for small family farm operations where only single-phase electric power is available, and high-power cooling systems would be either too expensive or difficult to install.

**Milk Pre-cooling**

For energy savings and quality reasons it is advisable to pre-cool the milk before it enters the tank using a plate or a tube cooler (shell and tube heat exchanger) supplied with chilled water from the well water, the ice builder or the condensing unit. The quicker milk is cooled after leaving the cow the better. This system achieves most of the cooling before the milk enters the tank, so that chilled milk, rather than warm milk, is being added to the already cooled milk in the tank.

### Cooling Temperature

Generic temperature for milk storage is 3 to 4°C. For raw milk cheese manufacturing, it would be advisable to keep the milk at 12°C, as milk characteristics will be kept in a better state. The milk cooling tank is usually not completely filled at once. A 2 milking tank is designed to cool 50% of its capacity at once. A 4 milking tank is designed to cool 25% of its capacity at once, and a 6 milking tank is designed to cool 16.7% of its capacity at once. The cooling performance depends on the number of milking it takes to completely fill the tank, the ambient temperature and the cooling time.

### Bulk Tank Cleaning Systems

There are two primary methods of cleaning bulk tanks, via manual scrubbing or automatic washing.

*Both methods generally use four steps to clean the tank:*

- Prerinsing with water to wet the surface and rinse off remaining milk residue
- Washing with hot soapy water
- Rinsing with water to remove the soap
- Final sanitizing rinse with an approved bulk tank sanitizer solution

### Manual Scrubbing

Manual scrubbing requires the bulk tank to have large hinged covers that can be lifted open to permit easy access to the interior surfaces of the tank. It tends to be much more thorough than automatic methods since, it permits the tank to be carefully inspected during the washing process. If the tank is not found to be cleaned well enough, a troublesome area can be given additional cleansing attention.

### Manual Scrubbing Limitations

This job is difficult to perform for very large tanks, and becomes more difficult as the overall cross-section or diametre of the tank increases, requiring either a longer brush or a raised work platform around the tank to lift the cleaning worker to reach over the side of a tall tank.

### Automatic Washing

Automatic bulk tank washing systems are used in closed tanks and are normally activated by the milk collection truck driver after each milk collection. The cleaning system operates similar to a consumer dishwasher and consists of one or more free-spinning high-pressure spray nozzles with tangential jets, with the spray nozzle mounted on the end of a flexible whip suspended down into the centre of the interior. As the cleaning solution sprays out of the jet, the force of the expelled water causes the jet to spin around and the whip to wildly swing back and forth, spraying the cleaning solution randomly all over the interior of the tank.

### Automatic Washing Limitations

Because no physical scrubbing occurs with automatic wash systems, the cleanser relies on surfactants and detergents to dissolve the fats left on the interior of the tank by the cream in the milk. However, this is not sufficient to remove milkstone buildup, and the tank may need to be washed occasionally with milkstone remover to remove this scale buildup that can harbour bacteria and contaminants.

Automatic scrubbing only cleans the interior of the tank. It is not capable of cleaning the exterior of the tank, and it does not do a good job of washing around the cover seals. While it is possible to just clean the interior and call it good enough, it does not provide the maximum sanitation of manually washing down the exterior of the tank following or during the automatic wash process. Also, some components that contact the milk such as the drain valve cannot be properly cleaned automatically without disassembling the valve and retaining washer and directly scrubbing in soapy water.

**Operating Costs**

Substantial reductions in running costs can be made when an ice builder is used in conjunction with off-peak electricity.

Pre-cooling milk using a plate or a tube cooler supplied with mains or well water can also reduce costs and add to the cooling capacity of the tank. Bulk tank condenser units, which are not an integral part of the tank, should be fitted in an adjacent, suitable and well ventilated place.

If at all possible, condenser units should not be fitted on a wall facing the sun. They should be installed in a way which allows them to draw in and discharge adequate quantities of air for efficient operation. Bulk tank should be easily accessible by large bulk collection tankers and positioned so that the tanker approaches can be kept clean and free from cow traffic at all times.

Although tanks have been calibrated when first installed, bulk tank miscalibration is not uncommon and in some cases it can result in significant loss of income. Milk tanks calibrated on the low side, can cheat raw milk producers by up to 22 litres on each shipment. It is therefore advisable to recalibrate a bulk tank.

**Other Usage of Bulk Tanks**

Stainless steel bulk tanks are also used to heat or cool a fluid or simply to keep it isolated and warm/cold. Because of the hygienical finishing of the inner and outer side of the tanks, almost any fluid can be stored: water, fruit juices, honey, wine, beer, ink, paint, cosmetics, aromatic food-additives, bacterial cultures, cleansers, oil, blood...

## MILKING PIPELINE

The next innovation in automatic milking was the milk pipeline. This uses a permanent milk-return pipe and a second vacuum pipe that encircles the barn or milking parlour above the rows of cows, with quick-seal entry ports above each cow. By eliminating the need for the milk container, the milking device shrank in size and weight to the point where it could hang under the cow, held up only by the sucking force of the milker nipples on the cow's udder.

The milk is pulled up into the milk-return pipe by the vacuum system, and then flows by gravity to the milkhouse vacuum-breaker that puts the milk in the storage tank. The pipeline system greatly reduced the physical labour of milking since, the farmer no longer needed to carry around huge heavy buckets of milk from each cow.

The pipeline allowed barn length to keep increasing and expanding, but after a point farmers started to milk the cows in large groups, filling the barn with one-half to one-third of the herd, milking the animals, and then emptying and refilling the barn. As herd sizes continued to increase, this evolved into the more efficient milking parlour.

### Milking Parlours

Innovation in milking focused on mechanizing the milking parlour to maximize throughput of cows per operator which streamlined the milking process to permit cows to be milked as if on an assembly line, and to reduce physical stresses on the farmer by putting the cows on a platform slightly above the person milking the cows to eliminate having to constantly bend over. Many older and smaller farms still have tie-stall or stanchion barns, but worldwide a majority of commercial farms have parlours.

The milking parlour allowed a concentration of money into a small area, so that more technical monitoring and measuring equipment could be devoted to each milking station in the parlour. Rather than simply milking into a common pipeline for example, the parlour can be equipped with fixed measurement systems that monitor milk volume and record milking statistics for each animal. Tags on the animals allow the parlour system to automatically identify each animal as it enters the parlour.

### Recessed Parlours

More modern farms use recessed parlours, where the milker stands in a recess such that his arms are at the level of the cow's udder.

Recessed parlours can be herringbone, where the cows stand in two angled rows either side of the recess and the milker accesses the udder from the side, parallel, where the cows stand side-by-side and the milker accesses the udder from the rear or, more recently, rotary, where the cows are on a raised circular platform, facing the centre of the circle, and the platform rotates while the milker stands in one place and accesses the udder from the rear. There are many other styles of milking parlours which are less common.

### Herringbone and Parallel Parlours

In herringbone and parallel parlours, the milker generally milks one row at a time. The milker will move a row of cows from the holding yard into the milking parlour, and milk each cow in that row. Once all or most of the milking machines have been removed from the milked row, the milker releases the cows to their feed.

A new group of cows is then loaded into the now vacant side and the process repeats until all cows are milked. Depending on the size of the milking parlour, which normally is the bottleneck, these rows of cows can range from four to sixty at a time.

### Rotary Parlours

In rotary parlours, the cows are loaded one at a time onto the platform as it slowly rotates. The milker stands near the entry to the parlour and puts the cups on the cows as they move past. By the time the platform has completed almost a full rotation, another milker or a machine removes the cups and the cow steps backwards off the platform and then walks to its feed.

### Automatic Milker Take-off

It can be harmful to an animal for it to be over-milked past the point where the udder has stopped releasing milk. Consequently the milking process involves not just applying the milker, but also monitoring the process to determine when the animal has been milked out and the milker should be removed. While parlour operations allowed a farmer to milk many more animals much more quickly, it also increased the number of animals to be monitored simultaneously by the farmer. The automatic take-off system was developed to remove the milker from the cow when the milk flow reaches a preset level, relieving the farmer of the duties of carefully watching over 20 or more animals being milked at the same time.

**Fully Automated Robotic Milking**

In the 1980s and 1990s, robotic milking systems were developed and introduced. Thousands of these systems are now in routine operation. In these systems the cow has a high degree of autonomy to choose her time of milking within pre-defined windows.

These systems are generally limited to intensively managed systems although research continues to match them to the requirements of grazing cattle and to develop sensors to detect animal health and fertility automatically.

## AUTOMATIC MILKING

They have been the topic of discussion for some time now, but as they become increasingly popular, Charlotte Johnston, TheCattleSite junior editor, looks at just how effective automatic milking machines are and evaluates their benefits.

A common myth regarding automatic milking machines is that they disengage the herdsman from the animals, and so neglect herd health. If this were true, the new Lely Astronaut A3 Next would not have won the 2009 Royal Association of British Dairy Farmers' Livestock and

Machinery Award at this year's Dairy Event. The award was presented on the grounds of economics, the welfare and close management of milking animals, the reduction of drudgery for family and employed staff, flexibility since, it applies to family run and larger units, and the longer-term needs of the dairy industry.

The Cattle Site spoke to four dairy farmers around the world to find out how automatic milking equipment changed their lives.

**How Does it Work?**

Very simply, a laser control will identify the location of the teats and a robust robot arm will attach cups individually to each teat from underneath the cow. Swift teat cup attachment is guaranteed even when milking cows with teats missing. Should a cup be kicked off, it is reconnected quickly.

**Cow Id System and Computer Management Software**

Each cow has an electronic tag, which is read when she enters the machine. This allows the computer system to identify each cow. Management through the computer tells the stockman specific data for each individual cow.

The MQC sensor system checks the milk colour, conductivity and flow to ensure maximum control of milk quality. Comparing individual cow data to the average allows problems to be identified.

Milk identified with blood is separated and either discarded or diverted into another holding place. Furthermore, if a cow is being treated with medicine, it is possible for her to remain in the milking herd. This does require strict attention to detail - as accurate information must be input into the computer system as to what the cow has been treated with, how long the withdrawal period is etc.

When the cow comes in to be milked next, her milk will be automatically diverted into a separate holding area or disposed of. The same can be done for colostrum, for example, when a cow has recently calved as it may be beneficial to retain the colostrum for a couple of days. Entering all information on the system will allow this milk to be stored separately and after two days, her milk will return to the bulk tank. By checking the computer twice a day, the stockman can identify cows that are overdue milking or can treat illnesses ident ified immediately and the accessibility to such detailed data can allow accurate management decisions to be made.

**Dynamic Feeding**

Dynamic feeding looks at an individual cow's feed requirements in relation to her yield. The programme takes into account milk yield, the cost of feed and the milk price received to work out the most economical feed rate for each individual cow. For Max Warren in Australia, this is particularly useful in a drought situation, where extra feed may have to be bought, but when milk prices are particularly low.

On average in the UK, for every litre of milk produced per cow, 0.3kg of dry matter is consumed, says Tim Gibson. This is standard regardless of whether they are high yielders. He believes he has saved one kilo of dry matter per cow per day, which with 140 cows equates to more than 51 tonnes of dry matter a year – in other words, a lot of money!

John Wolf and Doug Heintz from the US say that they now have the ability to feed a higher concentrate diet to higher yielding cows and they believe they have reduced feed costs.

The dynamic feeding programme allows optimum energy conversion efficiency. This unique and efficient system would not be possible without automatic milking machines.

**Labour Savings**

All four farmers have cut back labour units. In Australia, Mr Warren believes he would require double the number of staff to milk 300 cows on a rotary system. Mr Wolf is saving 200 hours of labour a week, whilst Mr Gibson and Mr Heintz have cut back by almost one labour unit each. Adding up the cost of current labour, it is not hard to see how much money can be saved.

Lely estimate that for every one machine milking 70 cows, half a labour unit is saved. Two robots would milk 140 cows and save three-quarters of a labour unit, whilst three machines would milk 200 plus cows and save one full labour unit.

"The biggest advantage by far is the labour saving. The flexibility has changed my life allowing me to spend more time with my family," says Mr Heintz.

**Building Space**

Mr Gibson recommends that an area of approximately 15ft by 12ft is needed. The machines, however, are only 15ft by 6ft; the extra space takes into account a clean area behind the machine. With so little space required per machine, customers have the opportunity to increase indoor housing.

**Controlled Grazing**

Both Mr Wolf and Mr Heintz keep cows housed all year round; only dry cows and heifers may be put to grass. Mr Gibson allows his cows to graze outside during the summer with controlled grazing. Unlike the other farmers, Mr Warren's cows are grazed outdoors all year around on a three-way grazing system.

Mr Warren operated a two-way grazing system, where cows moved paddocks every 12 hours. He found with this system that cows were hanging around the parlour and so he changed the process to a three-way grazing system. Now, cows move fields every eight hours, each time passing through the parlour.

Cows are fed a wagon mix in the shed and fed concentrates when milked. All pasture is irrigated.

**Training Herd to Use Machine**

Mr Wolf said that it takes about three to four days to train heifers to use the machines. However, when the machines were introduced, it took about three weeks before things were running smoothly.

He believes that there will be about 0.5 per cent of each herd that does not adapt. Mr Heintz says that he spent three weeks pushing cows up to the machines, but it probably took about three months until the machines were working at full efficiency.

Over in Australia, Mr Warren says that it took two to three weeks to train the herd to walk into the robots but he felt it was probably twelve months until he was fully trained to use the system, the technology including computers was completely new to him!

**Herd Benefits**

The Lely Astronaut has a refined udder preparation procedure. Teats are cleaned individually and sprayed. The machine also automatically washes three times a day as well as washing in between each cow.

At the Robotic Dairy in Australia, cows are lasting six lactations. Further improvements in herd health can be seen by Mr Gibson reporting an increase in lifetime lactations per cow. Mr Wolf and Mr Warren reported improvements in foot health and reproductive performance.

Mr Heintz, who believes he had high standards of animal health prior to the installation of the machines, has reported no significant improvements in herd health but said that previous levels had been easily maintained. He has also only been using the machines for just under a year.

Walking around Mr Gibson's yard, it was apparent that the cows seemed dramatically calmer and at ease than in an conventional dairy unit. In fact, all farmers mentioned that cows were a lot less stressed, which in turn they believed led to better health and increased yields.

Increased yields seemed apparent across the board but the improvement varied between farms. In the UK, Mr Gibson reported an increase of 1,000 litres per cow over the last eight years, whereas Mr Heintz reported an increaseof 10 to 15 pounds per day over the last ten months, which equates to 4562.5 pounds of milk per year or about an extra 2,000 litres per year.

**Service and Installation**

The same system operates in the US and the UK with Lely providing onsite support for the first 2-3 days of training cows. During the first two to three weeks, representatives will call in three or four times a week to help with the start-up. Chad Huyser, Director of Sales and Operations for Lely US, says that farm management support staff will visit a couple of times during the first few months to do a thorough review of the farm management process, which includes making slight adjustments to feed rations and robot performance settings. Mr Gibson, who completed farm management training in Holland with Lely, says that he goes onto clients' farms to help customers adapt to the new style of management and prevent problems.

Lely also offer web training events with the farm management support staff, providing information to farmers on how to use the T4C, which is the onboard management software on the robots. Mr Huyser says that one of the areas that Lely focuses on globally is providing on-going support to all their installations.

Speaking with Mr Warren, he feels that ongoing technical support is essential, and is more than pleased with the service Lely continues to provide. He thoroughly enjoys working with the company and together, they have made a number of changes to adapt to Australian grazing conditions.

The new Lely Astronaut A3 robotic milking system requires servicing three times a year. Mr Gibson says the older models require servicing every eight weeks. He says that information from each service is sent back to a database at the headquarters, which allows engineers to access a vast amount of data to refer to in the case of a fault.

Due to the relative newness of the machines, there is no guarantee how long they will last. Mr Gibson believes that the oldest one in place is approximately 17 years old and still going strong. There have been no reports of machines wearing out to date. Lely estimates that products with the correct service and care will last at least 30 years. Machines can be constantly updated with new software, which comes at no extra cost to the customer.

Some people may be under the impression that robotic milking systems require someone to be on call 24/7 in case of a breakdown. This is not technically true. If there is an error in the system, an alarm system rings a telephone to tell whoever is on duty. During the day, this is not a problem but during the night, it could be more than a nuisance.

Not one of the farmers complained about this. During the evenings, Mr Gibson and Mr Warren said their machines may go off once a week. With seven machines, Mr Wolf is called three or four times a week. Mr Wolf stressed that the system can be manipulated and managed to reduce these calls through only five minutes of maintenance per robot per day.

**How Much Does it Cost?**

The latest model, Lely Astronaut A3 Next, is around £110,000 for one robot. Opportunities for second-hand robots exist: all robots are refurbished at the Lely factory and come with a one-year warranty. Mr Gibson says that they often become available due to clients upgrading or retiring and cost approximately 75 per cent of the new price.

**Farm Benefits**

Mr Wolf explained that the introduction of robotic milking machines has allowed greater flexibility across the farm - particularly with regard to time schedules. "Having the robots in place means that I can now finish what I was doing in the field without rushing back to the parlour to milk the cows," he said.

Mr Wolf also stressed that the working environment has significantly improved with cleaner areas for both cows and employees. But by far the biggest benefit for him was the decreased costs of production.

When asked about the biggest benefit of installing a robotic milking system, Mr Warren said the fact he was still farming. "Without robots, I would have stopped milking years ago. I really enjoy working with automatic milking machines and Lely. I love the technology that is always improving. It makes my work so much more enjoyable and interesting."

**Who Supplies Automatic Milking Machines?**

If you are interested in robotic milking systems, Lely, BouMatic, Fulwood, DeLaval and GM Liberty are some of the suppliers.

**Management Tips**

*And finally, some tips from Mr Gibson, Mr Wolf, Mr Heintz and Mr Warren:*

- Run your cows numbers and cash flow and make sure that the operation and introduction of robots into your herd would be viable
- Design the layout of the facility to how you want to manage it

- When designing the layout, consider if you may want to expand the enterprise and make sure this is possible
- Be prepared for a change in management
- Make sure you are prepared to get involved with the robots, checking data and ensuring careful attention to detail
- Be sure that whoever is supplying the machines will provide longterm full technical support, and
- See as many farms as possible and speak to as many people as possible before making any rash decisions!

Despite the success in Australia, to date there are still only six units operating automatic milking systems, which Mr Warren finds unbelievable. Despite the excellent support from Lely, Mr Warren is disappointed in the lack of support from the local dairy industry in Australia. Robots have started to take off in America and Canada, as well as across Europe. In the UK, Lely is running 250 robots on over 100 units. Worldwide there are 9,000 Lely robots. So if you fancy reducing the drudgery of milking or simply improving herd management, whilst increasing milk yields and herd health, perhaps it is time for you to open your mind to automatic milking systems?

## PROCESS OF DIGESTING DAIRY MANURE

A variety of high rate anaerobic processes, which retain bacteria have been developed to treat soluble organic industrial wastes. These "high rate" digesters have reduced hydraulic detention times from 20 days to a few hours. They include anaerobic filters, both upflow and downflow, and a variety of biofilm processes such as fixed film packed bed reactors. Bacteria are retained in these reactors as films on carriers such as plastic beads, or sand, or on support media of all configurations. The waste washes past the retained bacteria. The bacteria convert the soluble constituents to gas but have little opportunity to hydrolyze and degrade the particulate solids, unless the solids become attached to the biomass. These reactors are not suitable for digesting dairy waste since, they are not effective in converting particulate solids to gas and tend to clog while digesting dairy manure slurries. These high rate reactors can treat the soluble component of dairy waste. But only a fraction of the available energy will be recovered.

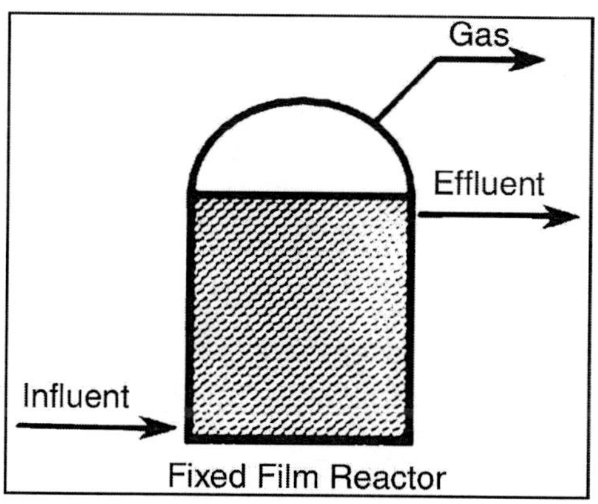


*Fig.1.1: Packed Fixed Film Reactor*

A widely used industrial waste anaerobic digester is the UASB or "Upflow Anaerobic Sludge Blanket", reactor. The process stores the anaerobic consortia as pellets, approximately the size of a pea. The upflow anaerobic sludge blanket reactor (UASB) is widely used in industrial treatment processes throughout the world. It is an extremely effective process for converting soluble organic materials, such as sugar to methane gas. It has not been used for processing dairy waste since, it is ineffective in converting solids to gas. It is primarily used to convert non-particulate or soluble waste to gas.

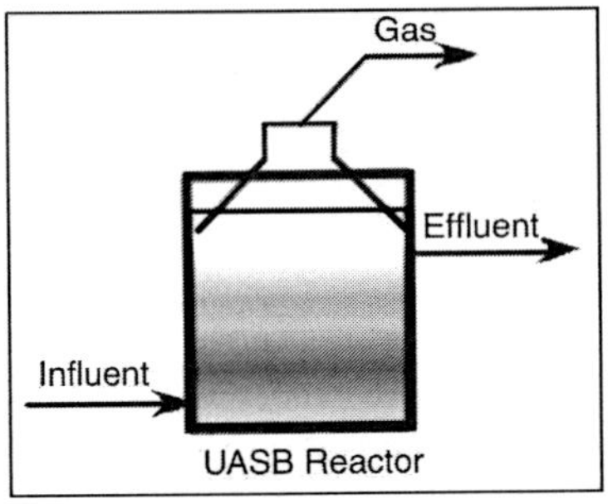


*Fig.1.2: Upflow Anaerobic Sludge Blanket Reactor*

The anaerobic baffled reactor is a horizontal version of the upflow anaerobic sludge blanket reactor. Both store large quantities of anaerobic bacteria as pellets approximately the size of a pea. Unfortunately, these very successful anaerobic reactors are not effective in digesting particulate waste.

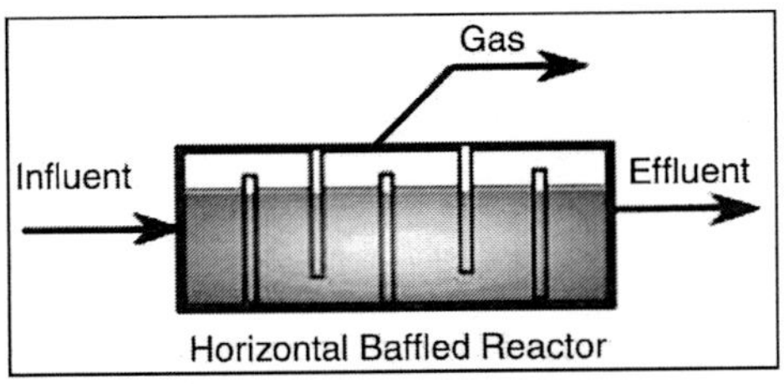


*Fig.1.3: Baffled Reactor*

Particulate solids tend to settle in the horizontal baffled reactor (HBR) while organic fibres will form a mat on the surface. There are no known instances of the HBR being used for the treatment of dairy waste. Unless the dairy waste was thoroughly screened and all particulate matter removed the HBR would tend to become clogged. The removal of solids by screening and gravity sedimentation will eliminate up to 80% of the energy generating potential from dairy waste.

## PROCESSES THAT CAN BE USED FOR DIGESTING DAIRY MANURE

The processes that have been used for digesting dairy waste can be subdivided into high rate and low rate processes. Low rate processes consist of covered anaerobic lagoons, plug flow digesters, and mesophilic completely mixed digesters. High rate reactors include the thermophilic completely mixed digesters, anaerobic contact digesters, and hybrid contact/fixed film reactors.

**Completely Mixed Digesters (Low Rate)**

The most common form of an anaerobic digester is the completely mixed reactor. Most sewage treatment plants and many industrial treatment plants use a completely mixed reactor to convert waste to gas. The completely mixed reactor is a tank that is heated and mixed. Most completely mixed reactors operate in the mesophilic range.

All of the initial anaerobic digesters used to treat dairy manure were completely mixed mesophilic digesters. The cost of mixing is high, especially if sand, silt, and floating materials, present in the waste stream, must be suspended throughout the digestion period. Some completely mixed reactors operate in a thermophilic range where sufficient energy is available to heat to reactor.

Highly concentrated readily degradable waste is required in order to generate sufficient heat for the thermophilic range of operation. Completely mixed thermophilic digesters are used in the EEC to treat animal manure. Recently, completely mixed thermophilic digesters were proposed in Oregon to treat dairy manure.

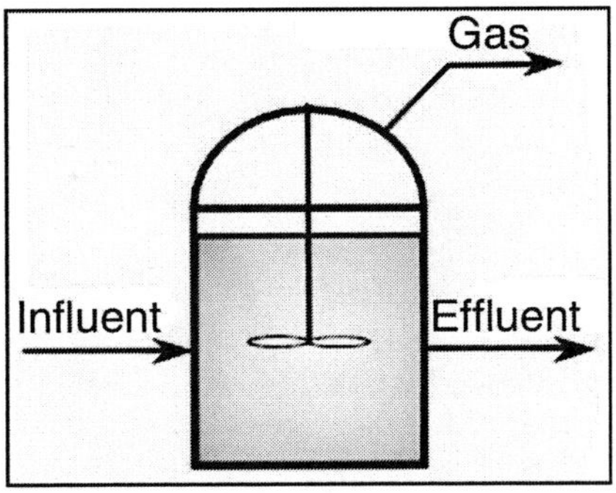


*Fig.1.4: Completely Mixed Reactor*

Most completely mixed reactors are heated with spiral flow heat exchangers. These heat exchangers apply hot water to one side of the spiral and the anaerobic slurry to the other. The spiral heat exchangers have proven to be a successful method of efficiently transferring heat. Completely mixed reactors can be constructed of a variety of materials. In the U.S., most completely mixed reactors have a low profile with a diameter greater than the height.

Some municipal digesters in the U.S., and most in Europe have an egg shape with a height much greater than the diameter. The egg shape enhances mixing while eliminating much of the stratification. Completely mixed reactors can have fixed covers, floating covers, or gas holding covers. Most municipal digesters have floating covers. Floating covers are more expensive than fixed covers. Mixing can be accomplished with a variety of gas mixers, mechanical mixers, and draft tubes with mechanical mixers or simply recirculation pumps.

The most efficient mixing device in terms of power consumed per gallon mixed is the mechanical mixer. Most municipal digesters are intensely mixed to reduce the natural stratification that occurs in a low profile tank. A large amount of evidence has been accumulated over the past 10 years indicating that intense mixing may inhibit the bacterial consortia. But, intense mixing is required to keep sands and silts in suspension. The advantage of the completely mixed reactor is that it is a proven technology that achieves reasonable conversion of solids to gas. It can be applied to the treatment of slurry waste such as dairy manure.

The disadvantage of the completely mixed reactor is the high cost of installation, and the energy cost associated with mixing the digester. The completely mixed conventional anaerobic digester is a biomass growth based system. The process requires a constant conversion of a portion of the feed solids to anaerobic bacteria rather than gas. Since, anaerobic bacteria are constantly wasted from the process, new bacteria must be produced to replace the lost bacteria.

If the bacteria are retained, the portion of the waste that would have been converted to new bacterial cells will be converted to gas. For this reason, bacterial growth based systems are not as efficient as retained biomass systems. The advantage of the completely mixed thermophilic reactor is the rapid conversion of solids to gas and biomass. Some claim that the rate of conversion is three times greater with thermophilic reactors. Consequently, the HRT can be lower and the gas production greater. The disadvantage of the thermophilic reactor is the energy required to heat cold dairy manure to thermophilic temperatures.

Additional costs are incurred in tank insulation and heat exchangers. Sufficient heat may not be available from the gas produced unless the solids are highly concentrated. Thermophilic digestion of dairy manure cannot be used with manure diluted with parlor or flush water since, sufficient energy will not be available to meet the heat requirements. In addition, the higher temperature thermophilic reactors increase end product inhibition, especially ammonia and organic acids.

**Anaerobic Lagoons (Very Low Rate)**

Anaerobic lagoons are covered ponds. Manure enters at one end and the effluent is removed at the other. The lagoons operate at psychrophilic, or ground temperatures. Consequently, the reaction rate is affected by seasonal variations in temperature.

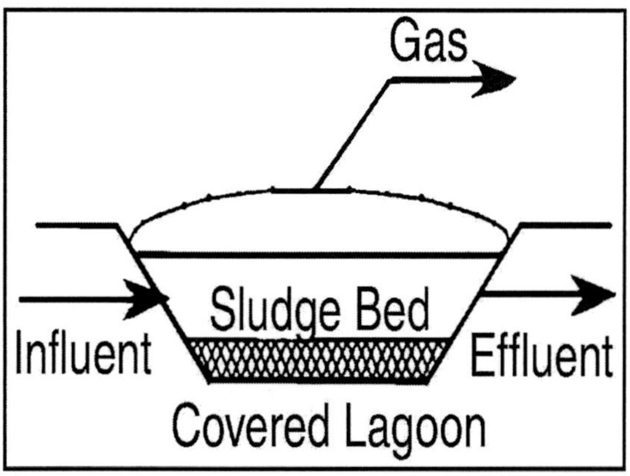


*Fig.1.5: Anaerobic Lagoons*

Since, the reaction temperature is quite low, the rate of conversion of solids to gas is also low. In addition, solids tend to settle to the bottom where decomposition occurs in a sludge bed. Little contact of bacteria with the bulk liquid occurs. The biomass concentration is low, resulting in very low solids conversion to gas (High F/M ratio with poor growth rates at low temperatures). Little or no mixing occurs. Consequently, lagoon utilization is poor. Anaerobic lagoons have been used to treat parlor and free stall flush water. Gas production rates have been low and seasonal. Solids may be screened and removed prior to entering the lagoon.

A considerable amount of energy potential is lost with the removal of particulate solids. The advantage of anaerobic lagoons is the lowcost. The low cost is offset by the lower energy production and poor effluent quality. Periodically the covered lagoons must be cleaned at considerable cost. Nuisance odours may be generated while cleaning the lagoons.

**Plug Flow Digesters (Low Rate)**

The plug flow anaerobic digester is the simplest form of anaerobic digestion. Consequently, it is the least expensive. The plug flow digester can be a horizontal or vertical reactor. The waste enters on one side of the reactor and exits on the other.

Since, bacteria are not conserved, a portion of the waste must be converted to new bacteria, which are subsequently wasted with the effluent. Since, the plug flow digester is a growth based system, it is less efficient than a retained biomass system. It converts less waste to gas. Plug flow systems are subject to stratification wherein the sands and silts settle to the bottom and the organic fibres migrate to surface. The stratification can be partially inhibited by maintaining a relatively high solids concentration in the digester. Periodically, solids must be removed from the plug flow reactor. Since, there is no easy way of removing the solids, the reactor must be shut down during the cleaning period.

The cost of cleaning can be considerable. Since, the solids concentration must be maintained at high levels, dilute milk barn waste is normally excluded from the digester. Plug flow reactors are normally heated by a hot water piping system within the reactor. The hot water piping system can complicate the periodic cleaning of the reactor.

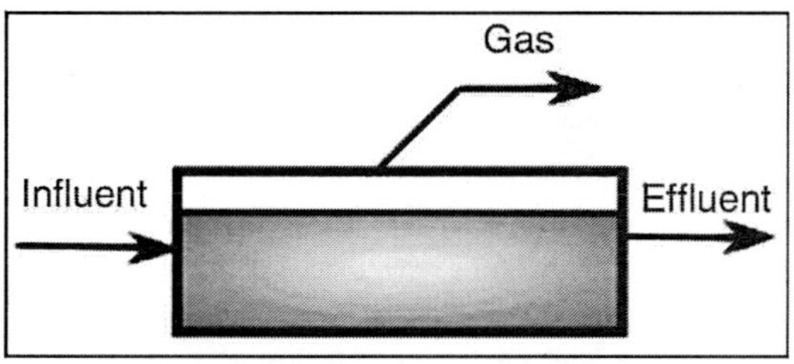


*Fig.1.6: Plug Flow Reactor*

The plug flow reactor is a simple, economical system. Applications are limited to concentrated dairy manure containing a minor amount of sand and silt. If stratification occurs because of a dilute waste or excess sand, significant operating costs will be incurred.

**Contact Stabilization Reactors (High Rate)**

The anaerobic contact stabilization process is a more efficient contact process. Burke used the anaerobic contact stabilization process for the digestion of both dairy manure and potato waste. The process has the advantage of efficiently converting slowly degradable materials such as cellulose in a highly concentrated reactor. Organic materials, which can be degraded rapidly, are digested in the contact reactor. The bacteria and slowly degradable organics are removed and degraded in a highly concentrated reactor.

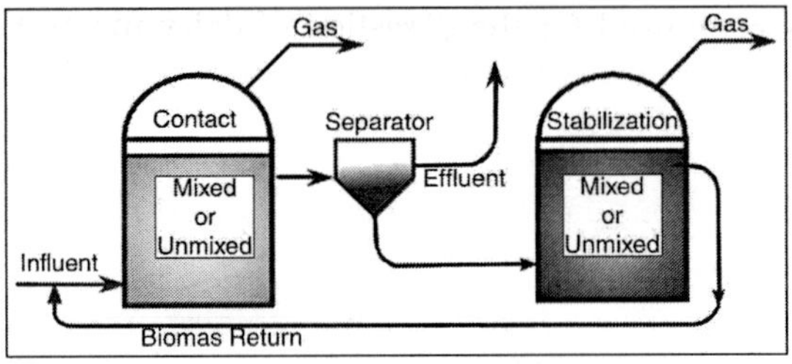


*Fig.1.7: Contact Stabilization Reactor*

**Sequencing Batch Reactors (High Rate)**

A sequencing batch reactor is a contact digester, which utilizes the same tank for digestion as well as separation. In a sequencing batch reactor the same tank is used to digest the waste and separate the biomass from the effluent liquor.

Generally, two or more tanks are used. The tanks are operated in a fill and draw mode. The separation is accomplished by gravity. Consequently, a more dilute, screened waste is treated. Laboratory scale sequencing batch reactors have been used to digest dairy manure.

**Contact Digesters (High Rate)**

The contact reactor is a high rate process that retains bacterial biomass by separating and concentrating the solids in a separate reactor and returning the solids to the influent. More of the degradable waste can be converted to gas since, a substantial portion of the bacterial mass is conserved. The contact digester can be either completely mixed or plug flow. It can be operated in the thermophilic or mesophilic range. The contact reactor can treat both dilute and concentrated waste provided the separator can concentrate the digester effluent solids sufficiently to enhance the process.

A wide variety of separators have been tested over the past 30 years. Initially gravity separators (settling tanks), or solids thickeners were used. It was soon discovered that the solids could not be sufficiently concentrated in a gravity separator without degassing to remove the gas bubbles attached to the solids. Actively fermenting digester effluent containing gas bubbles floated rather than settled in the separator.

Lamella or plate separators have also been used to concentrate the biomass after degassing. Both of these gravity-settling techniques are not effective for concentrated digester solids. Gravity separation techniques are effective with dilute waste following a completely mixed reactor. Separation requires several days of detention. The completely mixed digester will prevent stratification. The effluent is then allowed to separate by gravity in the separation reactor. The digester solids concentration should be less than 2.5% for gravity separation to be used. Long separator detention times are required. Mechanical separation devices have been tested to reduce the detention time required by gravity separation. Centrifuges, gravity belts, membranes, and other mechanical separators have been used with limited success. These disruptive devices have been shown to inhibit the bacterial consortia and thus limit the effectiveness of the contact process. Burke used gas flotation to separate and concentrate the digester effluent for the efficient and tranquil recovery of the anaerobic consortia.

The process has been used for the digestion of dairy manure, sewage sludge, and potato waste. It has been shown to be effective for concentrating the biomass from actively fermenting digester liquors without the need for degassing. The process has been referred to as the AGF or "anoxic gas flotation" process. Gas flotation can achieve significantly greater biomass concentrations than gravity separation without the adverse consequences associated with disruptive separation techniques.

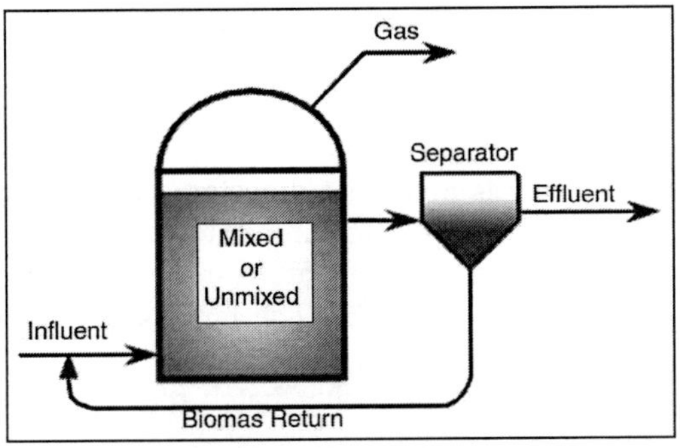


*Fig.1.8: Contact Reactor*

Gas flotation can also remove enzymes, organic acids, and other products of digestion that cannot be removed through settling or other mechanical means. Finally, gas flotation can be performed in a non-mechanical manner, which is simple to operate and maintain. During the contact process, refractory organic and inorganic solids accumulate within the system.

The accumulated sands, silts, and non-degradable organic fibres dictate the rate of solids wasting. Wasting the nonbiodegradable solids causes the loss of bacterial mass and reduced process efficiency. The anaerobic contact process can utilize mechanical separating devices to remove refractory solids from the digestion system.

**Phased Digesters**

Both acid phased and temperature phased digestion have been used to convert municipal sludge to gas. Acid phased digestion takes advantage of the fact that the acid forming bacteria have a much higher growth rate than the methanogens. Consequently, the initial reactor can be much smaller than the subsequent methane producing digester.

Acid phased digestion offers greater efficiency in the size of the anaerobic digesters. Acid phased digestion has not been applied to dairy waste. Temperature phased digestion has been applied to the digestion of sewage sludge. The initial digester is operated in the thermophilic mode followed by a second digester, which is operated in the mesophilic mode.

In the first thermophilic digester, pathogens are destroyed. In the second mesophilic digester, the mesophilic bacteria consume the organic acids created in the thermophilic reactor. Consequently, the odours associated with a thermophilic effluent are eliminated while achieving the desired pathogen destruction.

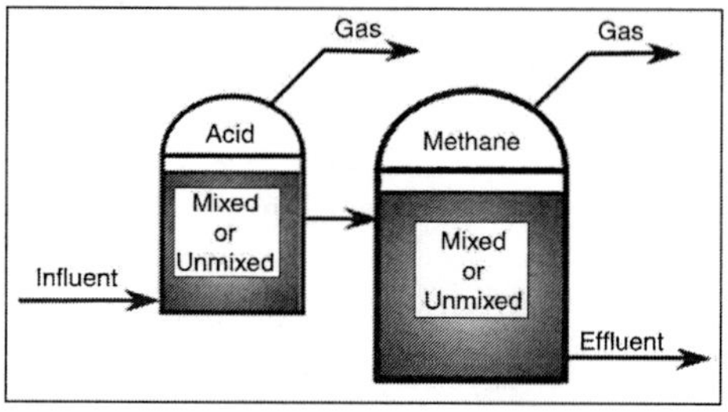


*Fig.1.9: Acid Phased Digester*

Temperature phased digestion has been used to digest dairy manure. In addition it must be pointed out that completely mixed reactors are not completely effective in removing pathogens.

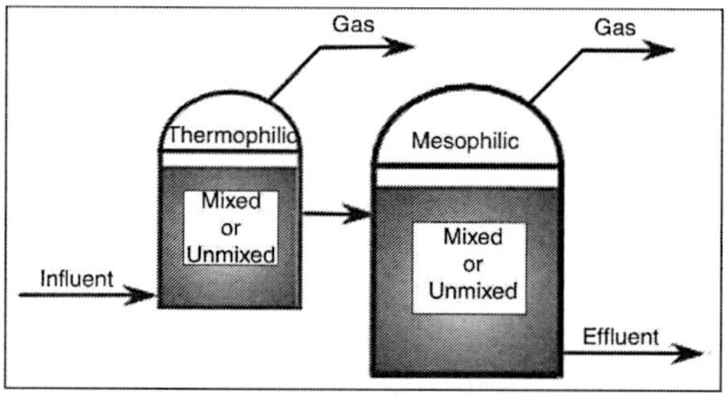


*Fig.1.10: Temperature Phased Digester*

**Hybrid Processes**

A number of hybrid processes have been developed and applied to many different kinds of waste materials. The hybrid processes incorporate a combination of the previously described configurations.

## FINANCIAL RISK IN DAIRY FARMING

The financial risk these farmers were prepared to accept affected the rate and extent of growth. Farmers A, B and E were prepared to accept increased financial risk. Each reduced their equity in the business to around 20 per cent at the time of major growth. One of the reasons they did this was that they perceived the size of their business put them at more risk of not surviving in the future than did the financial risk from increasing leverage to expand.

Farmer C was the only farmer in this study who was especially wary about expanding 'too fast' and increasing the financial risk. Farmer C had foregone the opportunity to purchase more land. The rate of growth of Farmer C's business was slower than the rate of growth for the other farmers in this study. For Farmers A, B, E the risk of failure because of inability to service debt increased once they had expanded their businesses.

Farmer A said at the second interview: You do not get a chance to come back if you over-step the mark – it is not like if you put on too many cows, it is easy to remove the extra cows, rather if you over-borrow it is very difficult to come back. Farmer A would not allow his equity to fall to 20 per cent again. He believed that attitude to equity depended on the stage of farming career and family life.

He now has more capital invested in the business and would only let his equity fall to 50 per cent. Having expanded their businesses, Farmers B and E were not prepared to borrow again to the same extent. This was because they now had more of their own capital to lose. As well, the risk of their business not surviving is lower than before growth. Both the need and desire for growth had diminished.

**Consumption**

The decision of a dairy farmer to use more of the annual cash surplus for consumption results in less cash surplus available for debt servicing and investment. This slows the rate equity, or the business, grows. During expansion, Farmer A, B, D and E lived in old farm houses and invested on farm for greater future consumption, rather than use surplus cash flow for present consumption. The farmers who had gone without a new house and extras in the years prior to growth, wanted to consume more after growth. They felt they had invested for future consumption and that it was now the time for some modest increase in consumption.

**Infrastructure**

The capacity of infrastructure on farm was found to be both a constraint to growth and a motivation for growth. One of the most challenging issues for the farmers prior to, or during, an expansion phase was the question of when to replace capital infrastructure. The farmers considered their financial position and the economics of replacing the dairy. At the time of major growth Farmer B decided they would not replace their existing dairy.

Their existing shed with current employees would be suitable. Two things happened after major growth. First, milking the increased herd took 11 hours a day. These farmers and their employees could barely do the other essential farm work. Farmer B had no time to contemplate other business opportunities. The situation was exacerbated because he had to manually change irrigation throughout the night.

Second, higher than normal milk prices occurred. The unexpected cash surpluses earned from high milk prices meant they were able to pay for half the cost of a replacement dairy. Farmer E replaced the dairy when he was milking 250 cows in a shed and yard designed for 150 cows.

Like Farmer B, Farmer E waited until the labour required to operate the older equipment increased and the price of labour increased.

Milking more cows than the existing infrastructure efficiently allowed reduced the time Farmer E could put into other business activity. Farmer D replaced their dairy when milking was taking five hours a day, which was more time than initially budgeted. Farmer C also found that the size of the current infrastructure was stopping them from increasing the size of the milking herd at the rate that they wanted. They replaced the infrastructure before they experienced any significant increase in the time of milking the cows, unlike the other three farmers.

This change was instigated by receiving an interest rate subsidy through the Productivity Enhancement Programme of the Rural Finance Corporation. For four out of the five case study farmers, the capacity of the existing capital equipment prevented further growth for a time. In contrast, Farmer A replaced the dairy within the first few years of farming with a dairy that had a much larger capacity than required by the herd at the time. Consequently the capacity of capital infrastructure became an inducement for further growth for Farmer A. Farmer A was in a different situation to the other four farmers because at the time of replacing the dairy he was a sharefarmer. The owner of the farm business paid for the replacement dairy.

The impact that the capacity of capital infrastructure has on business expansion is related to other factors than the dairy. Farmer B installed a labour intensive feed system in the dairy when they first began farming. This feed system involved manually taking the feed to troughs. They fed the cows like this for five years.

With this system it was difficult to feed more cows. Their milk company offered an interest rate subsidy for a loan that was used to upgrade the feed system in the dairy. Comparing the costs of the two systems, the replacement technology was better. Upgrading capital infrastructure changed milking time and the quality of milk. In this study, it was repeatedly seen that when the farmers bought extra land, the whole farm needed improvement. Farmer E for example, found that on all the properties he bought, the fences and other infrastructure were dilapidated and the pastures and the farm layout needed improvement. On these properties the previous farmers had decided not to replace capital infrastructure preceding the time of 'shut down'. Eventually over many years it gets to the stage where all infrastructure needs to be 'replaced'.

Farmer E not only had the capital cost of buying the land, but also the capital cost of improving that land. The farmers considered that it would have been more economical if they had started with a 'green-fields' site, rather than becoming a large dairy farm business by buying adjoining but run-down dairy farms.

## DAIRY FARM BUSINESS

Growth increased the profitability of the businesses studied. Growth affected the skills required of management and labour. Major growth involving significant changes to infrastructure, labour and land in a relatively short time affected the profitability, financial viability and management of the farm business. In contrast, minor growth did not significantly affect management and labour.

### Major Business Expansion Resulted in Adjustment Costs

Immediately following expansion, the farmers of case studies A, B, D and E experienced unplanned adjustment costs. For all these farmers the adjustment costs were in management and livestock. The farmers of case studies A and D, who expanded to a new region, had additional adjustment costs relating to the difficulty of finding and training skilled labour.

Case studies B and E expanded the area of the home farm. They had additional adjustment costs relating to infrastructure and land. In each case the adjustment costs were exacerbated by external factors such as unexpectedly low milk price and unfavourable climatic conditions. During this transition period, where the businesses had to deal with unanticipated adjustment costs, the case study businesses faced increased risk of business failure. This was because the amount of milk produced per cow declinedii at the same time their costs increasediii.

Further, external factors that decreased cash flowiv also reduced the amount of cash surplus available for reinvestment back into the farm. This slowed the gains from growth and exposed these businesses to greater periods of risk. Added to this business risk, each of the farmers had decreased their equity in the business significantly - by up to 30 per cent in a couple of the cases - which consequently increased their financial risk.

**The Adjustment for the Farmer**

The farmer in this study who expanded his business through minor growth had to develop new skills; this farmer had time to adjust and found learning new skills did not slow growth. Farmer C took growth slowly and found the changes required were 'evolutionary'.

Pursuing minor growth, Farmer C increased the herd size by a small percentage each year, or took on more adjoining land, and slowly improved that land whilst waiting for their own replacements to utilise that land. The skills required for this growth were needed in the early years of Farmer C's farming career. Farmer C applied those same principles to more cows or more land over time. For minor growth, few new skills are required quickly. Rather, minor growth required fine tuning of technical farm management skills.

Farmers A, B, D and E not only had to fine tune technical farm management skills but also had personal adjustment costs immediately after embarking on the major growth phase. As the expansion process was implemented, the work efficiency of each of these farmers decreased as they had to manage unexpected circumstances.

Farmers A, B and E all felt, to differing degrees, stress, depression, and some disbelief that the expansion was not delivering all the benefits they had expected. They had expected that by expanding, they would have more time off, would not need to do night work, and would be able to employ more people, which would give them more time with their family. It did not happen this way – not for quite some time. Once time had passed and they had developed the necessary skills, and learnt to accept that others could do their work, and had updated the infrastructure that was needed, then efficiency increased.

The extent growth affects the new skills a farmer requires depends on the rate of growth. Farmer A doubled business size at once, rather than over a few years. The difficulty with rapid expansion was the new knowledge and skills the manager and his employees needed to acquire rapidly. These challenges were exacerbated because the manager on the second farm soon left.

Unlike Farmer A, Farmer E experienced little extra pressure and few difficulties. This was partly because he anticipated the problems, but also because major growth occurred over a number of years.

Farmer E bought a property and spent the next two years upgrading it. He employed someone at the start of the major expansion phase who stayed with the business for the entire major expansion phase. Farmer B also purchased a dairy farm that needed improvement. He spent a year improving farm layout and building a new dairy. The slower growth rate for Farmers E and B reduced the rate and extent of personal adjustment required.

**The Adjustment for the 'Management Team'**

Growth affected the management team adversely when new personnel were recruited and had to perform well almost immediately. This happened when Farmer A had to find a replacement manager for his second farm when his manager left shortly following expansion. It also happened when Farmer D took on a third farm and they were relying on finding a person who could quickly develop the skills needed to manage that third farm.

Further, when a business gave an employee time to 'develop' within the business before taking on a role as manager, the adjustment costs of expanding the management team were reduced. Farmer E expanded the management team at the same time as he began the four year expansion path. The rate of growth affects the degree of impact the growth has on the management team.

### The Affect of Expansion on the Economic and Financial State of the Business in the 'Steady State'

Expansion increased capital efficiency and revenue generation and cost control, and therefore increased the return on capital.

Return on assets was increased by increasing operating profit and increasing the asset turnover ratio. Operating profit was increased by spreading fixed costs over more output; by lower prices for inputs through volume purchases; and by higher prices for milk for increased volume. Four of the case study farmers increased their asset turnover by making greater use of resources. Since, expanding, all the farmers had increased their net worth.

### The Change in Role of the Farmers

The specific areas of the businesses that were highlighted as changing as a result of major growth were: labour management, financial management, office management, owner/manager's role, technical management and young stock management. Skills in herd management and logistical management also needed to improve. In the following, the requirements of management in each of these areas are described.

### Labour Management

As these farmers expanded their businesses, their role became more specialised and less directly involved with the daily operations of the farm. There was less physical work and more management work. After a major growth step, Farmers A, B and E were not able to do all the jobs on the farm themselves and had to pass responsibility to others.

All the case study farmers who were managing large farm businesses experienced difficulties caused by the quality of the first farm labourers they employed. When managing larger dairy farming businesses they needed to recruit better calibre employees than their present employees. Each of the case study farmers in this study had strategies for recruiting quality labour.

One employed a sharefarmer, another a family friend, another promoted a farm labourer to manager and employed an existing employee to be manager on the home farm. The farmers also employed contractors for specific tasks.

The farmers found they needed good negotiating skills and communication skills in order to manage labour successfully. Building strong relationships with the managers was important; involving them in decision making and encouraging them to attend discussion groups and to undertake further training was also important.

### Financial Management

The dairy businesses with high equity and around the average size had rudimentary requirements for financial management, compared to the expertise needed for the larger operations. Financial management became more important as the farmers expanded the business. The farmers had borrowed and reduced their equity percentage to finance growth. Farmer B, for example, reduced the equity percentage from 50 per cent to 20 per cent in order to expand the business.

It was at this time that financial risk was great, and the farmers needed to monitor their cash flows closely, and to enhance skills in managing their finances. High gearing ratios meant the farmers needed high-level negotiating skills in the financially difficult years. Farmer A explained that it was important to communicate regularly with the people who had a major share in the business to let them know what was happening during the difficult years.

**Office Management**

For a farmer managing 100 to 200 cows, the extent of office management was writing cheques, with some cash flow control. As a farm expanded, office management became a greater proportion of the farmers work and the farm became a more complex business to manage.

*Office management on a large farm involved:*

- Researching new ideas;
- Organising the jobs that needed to be done and setting priorities;
- Organising time off for employees;
- Planning what jobs were needed on the farm;
- Analysing and dissecting the events on the farm;
- Implementing decisions;
- Paper work associated with employing labour;
- Financial management;
- Keeping track of the set goals (one of the farmers said that it was very easy to become disillusioned when you have such a huge debt. He said that you almost feel as though you are working to pay the bank back. But he said the key was to keep your mind on the end goal); and
- Juggling the different demands of the farm.

The time available to devote to office management was significantly less than the farmers had anticipated. Thus, time management was another skill these farmers had to develop.

*The farmers dealt with issues of time management by:*

- Delegating jobs to their employees;
- Using contractors (however, they found that they needed to build up a relationship with contractors so that they would show up when they said they would and so that they did not need to be there to supervise the contractors work.); and
- Being flexible on the number of days spent in the office and the number of days on farm. One of the farmers, who expanded to another spatially separate farm, spent six months planning for growth. This involved thinking through what changes needed to be done on the property, the labour required and his own change in role. Farmer E explained that a lot of planning went into replacing the dairy. Farmer D spent a lot of time planning new business activities. Farmer B spent every Wednesday planning.

**Owners Role**

The owner's role on a 500 plus cow farm involved spending some days in the office and some days helping on the farm. Farmer E described himself as filling in when someone is away or helping at the busy times on the farm.

This gave more time doing other activities, such as increased involvement with research bodies. Farmer B also found that after the initial phase expansion gave time to explore other ventures.

**Technical Management**

Technical management – the management of the pastures, the herd, feeding, and so on was crucial no matter what size the business. However, as the business expanded, technical management became more complex and difficult. This was partly because the farm was on a much larger scale, which meant that problems were amplified. It also meant new problems and complexities evolved.

**Young Stock Management**

The farmers found that to expand the business they had to remove young stock from the home property. They found that the land adjoining their property was best used for their milking herd. They either had to contract rear their young stock or they had to lease/ buy a run-off block.

**Herd Management**

With around 100 to 200 cows, the farmers knew cows individually. As the number of cows in the herd increased the management of the herd changed. Before expansion, the farmers did not fully appreciate the added work specifically associated with increasing stock numbers. The farmers had considered the implications of milking more cows and the infrastructure requirements. However, they generally had not considered sufficiently the detailed logistics associated with moving more cows, joining more cows, feeding more cows, calving more cows, looking after more dry stock and rearing more young stock.

The additional problems associated with managing more cows related to wear on the tracks, more cows to fit into the yards, more cows to go through the milking shed, and more cows to obtain access to water. These factors had major implications for feed management, the use of out-paddocks, contract rearing and so forth.

**Logistics Management**

The degree of improvement required in logistical management skills depended on the rate of major growth. The dairy farmers in this study who rapidly doubled their herd size did not have sufficient time to develop adequately the required logistical management skills for managing a herd of twice the original size, and experienced additional problems for this reason.

Expanding the area of their home farm rapidly without replacing the old dairy caused further logistical problems. Some of the farmers at the time of expanding did not have the capital to replace their existing shed. They also doubted whether it would be economically sensible to replace the shed at that time.

They believed that by dividing the herd into two, and then having two milkings in the morning and two milkings in the evenings, the current shed would be a viable solution. However, the logistics associated with organising two herds and the time involved meant that this 'solution' was inefficient and the farmers ended up spending much more of their day in the dairy shed than planned.

The dairy farmers that expanded their businesses geographically experienced added complexity with managing the logistics of the human resources. These farmers had more people to manage, which were on two spatially separate farms.

❒

# 2

# Fish Farming

## INTRODUCTION

Fish farming is an activity which is mostly done under natural conditions following the natures law though subjected to variations due to different agroclimatic conditions. According to the nature of the biomass generation in the pond, fish types being reared, feeding habits, space requirement for the fish, the soil of the place, the water, management operations to be done, etc., some basic principles can be enunciated for the benefit of those who want to start a fish farm.

Fish production is a complex process that involves interaction between various eco-biological factors such as soil, water, air, light, heat, microorganisms, micro flora and fauna, plants, animals and human beings. Basically it is a biomass production which takes place in a pond or aquatic ecosystem. In the fish production it is mainly the interaction between the fish reared and the pond ecosystem which is organised by human beings.

The success in fish farming depends on how best one can organise these interactions between the variations of each of the eco-biological factors in such a way that maximum production of fish takes place in a given pond system. The complex process in the fish production involving combinations of many things living, non-living and environmental factors results in unlimited variations in management practices. Therefore, no single practice can be considered the ideal one and the management practices should be decided at times on the spur of the moment according to the variations resulting from the above mentioned combinations. However we can reduce most of the practices in the fish farming into few principles which if followed will ensure success and satisfaction.

At the time of planning for fish farming if one is mindful of all these principles he can establish the fish farm in such way that all the operations during fish farming can be carried out with least expenditure in terms of time, labour and energy.

## OPERATIONS OF FISH FARMING

Once the farmer has found out the place for the pond the next step is to decide what kind of fish culture is possible with the space available. He must also decide whether his resources will allow him for starting a fish farm. This planning is necessary to determine the number of fish ponds to be constructed and the kind of fish culture one wants to take up.

A range of ideas are presented in this section of the booklet concerning the kinds of fish farm operations whether raising fish or breeding fish, whether raising carps, tilapia or catfish, whether prawns or shrimps, etc. He also gets an idea on the type of ponds small or big, grow in one pond or in more ponds, advantages of small and big ponds, advantages of mixing or separating different breeds of fish and sexes, etc.

A farmer who prepares himself to start fish farming should keep in mind that a certain percentage of fish introduced into the pond will die however much we try to take care of them.

In the nature many fishes never reach their adult size because they are eaten by other animals or big fishes or they die of diseases. "Survival of the fittest" is the law of nature. In the artificial rearing of fishes in the ponds the farmer tries to provide maximum growing and development conditions for getting maximum number of fishes and thereby maximum number of fishes reach marketable size.

**Kinds of operations**

As already mentioned once the site is identified the farmer has to decide whether he wants to go for breeding and production of fry and fingerlings or rear them till they attain marketable size. For breeding he needs more number of small ponds. The number of ponds may be more if he is trying to breed several breeds of fishes and in the same breed several sets of breeders (one set of breeders consists of two males and one female). If the farmer is planning to rear the fish only he needs big ponds. Depending on the number of fishes he wants to rear he may need one or more ponds. He also should consider whether he is raising the fish for the family usage or tor marketing purposes and whether he wants it as a main business or as a subsidiary business.

*Questions like these have to be considered so that he can construct*

- The right kinds of ponds,
- The right number of ponds and
- Stock the right kinds of fishes.

**Types of Ponds**

The types of pond a farmer can build depend upon water supply, soil and topography. Generally, two types of ponds are built -barrage ponds and diversion ponds. The main difference between these two types of pond is the water source though in many aspects the construction details are the same.

**Barrage Ponds**

In barrage ponds the water source is the rain run-off water or a spring forming into a small stream running down the valley. The site is marked by a valley type of topography and the pond is constructed by building a wall across the valley and store the running water through the valley. The area where water is collected is called the pond area.

The barrage pond requires only one wall at the lower side of the pond area. By building a number of walls at suitable intervals the farmer can make several ponds successively one after the other forming a chain of ponds. The water enters first into the pond which is at the highest elevation among all the ponds and then passes on to the next pond lower in elevation. In other words the drained out water from the higher pond is collected by the lower one through a drainage pipe and then to the next lower till we reach the last one. From the last one the water is drained out safely. When ponds and the water inlet and outlet are arranged in such a way that the water flows from one pond to the other it is called ponds in series or rosary system.

Water can also be directed independently into each pond from a channel running along one side of the pond and drained out into another channel at the other side of the pond. This is the best system of water supply to the fish ponds. Arrangement of ponds in this way is called ponds in parallel system. The channel that supplies water is called inlet channel and the channel that collects water from each pond is called drainage channel.

The drainage outlet may be fixed at the bottom side of the pond if the pond is to be drained out completely. Besides this drainage outlet there should bean outlet at a height beyond which the farmer does not want to accumulate the water in the pond. This is for the protection of the build which will be broken if water gets accumulated beyond certain height. The excess water is drained out from the pond through this drainage which acts as an overflow channel. The drainage and the overflow channel should be constructed in such a way that the water should be drained out safely without eroding the soil and causing damage to the pond. In barrage ponds, flow channels are fixed at a suitable height in order to drain out the excess water that may be accumulated during the rain. There are many variations of overflow channel system from which the farmer can choose the most suitable one. The drainage and overflow channel can be joined together just before they join the common big drainage channel.

Barrage ponds should not be built where the flow of the water is high. The walls will not be able to withstand the force of rushing water especially during the rainy season.

**Diversion Ponds**

Diversion ponds are those which receive water from river or stream through a diversion channel. One diversion channel takes water to the pond and another diversion channel act as a drainage. The drainage channel may be taking the water into the same river or stream from which the water came in or to a farm where it is used for irrigation or the water may be drained out into any other outlet. If more than one pond are constructed they are connected with the inlets and outlets in series or in parallel design. Diversion pond can be made in a number of ways de- pending on the ingenuity of the farmer. It can be built anywhere provided water can be taken to it from a water source by channel or pipe. If the pond is built on a flat ground there should be walls all around to prevent the collapse of the sides. Sometimes the ponds are constructed by deepening an area which is lower than the surroundings. If there is enough space and water supply is assured there can be several ponds successively constructed to use the overflow of water from one diversion pond to a second one and from the second to the third and so on, till the last.

Whatever may be the type of pond being constructed there will always be some advantages and disadvantages. The farmer has to consider both the advantages and disadvantages and make his decision most beneficial to him. However, diversion ponds are better than barrage ponds because they are less likely to overflow and the water source is more dependable. But barrage ponds are cheaper in construction. Similarly parallel system of pond construction is better than the se- ries or rosary system. One can have a mixture of barrage ponds and diversion ponds arranged in series (rosary) or parallel system. The art of planning and constructing fish ponds is very much an individual thing. There are many ways of using land and water resources. But the exact shape, number and size of the ponds have to be decided by the farmer.

**Number of Ponds**

The number of ponds usually depends on the number of functions the farmer wants to perform and also the number of times he would like to repeat a single function within a given period of time. The functions related to the fisheries are holding a breeding stock, breeding, hatching, raising fry, raising fingerlings and rearing for marketing. Normally these functions are better done in different ponds or water bodies.

At the same time it should be remembered that several functions can be performed in the same pond or water body. For example, breeding and hatching and raising fry can be done in the same pond. However, for breeding large number of breeding stock we require more than one pond. Similarly, the number of ponds also depends on the number of breeds or kinds of fish the farmer wants to breed. For example, if the farmer wants to breed several breeds of fish, different ponds may be required, or several sets of the same breed is to be maintained. In the same way if the frequency of breeding is more (eg. once a week, once in two weeks, a month, etc.) the number of ponds required will be more. At least two ponds are required for rearing for market purposes. If the farmer cannot make more than one pond he can also breed and hatch the fish in an enclosure of inverted mosquito-net fixed inside the pond.

**Size of the Pond**

The size of the pond also depends on topography, water supply, and the need or volume of production one intends to have. However, the nursery ponds will be smaller than the rearing ponds. Apart from this the size of the rearing pond itself can be varying. The advantages of small ponds are, function like harvesting, draining, refilling, treatment for diseases, etc., can be done quickly and easily. But the cost of construction and the land area required for the small ponds will be more compared to large ponds. But for the small and marginal farmers few small ponds are better than having large ponds.

**Depth of the Pond**

The depth of the pond also depends on several factors such as breeding, fry raising, fingerling raising, rearing for marketing, etc. Least depth is required for breeding and fry raising and maximum depth is required for rearing for marketing. Normally for breeding and fry raising the pond depth ranges from 0.5 to 1.0 m while for raising fingerlings a depth of 1.0 to 1.5 m is recommended. For rearing fish to market size the recommended pond depth varies from 1.2 to 2.0 metre. Normally, sunlight does not reach deeper than two metres and the growth of the planktons will be restricted.

At the same time too shallow pond will heat up the water or too much vegetative growth may occur and consequently the available oxygen to the fish will be much less than the required especially during the night hours. But in commercial farms breeding and raising of fry is done in plastic tubs, basins, glass jars or even in big mud pots. Glass vessels are better for this purpose because we can observe the fertilization, hatching and the conditions of the fry well.

### Single Pond Operation

If the farmer can have only one pond he could purchase or collect fry and fingerling and rear them to market size. For this there should be regular supply of fry and fingerlings. He can also breed fish inside a netted area in the same pond.

The farmer who is having single pond can go for culture of single breed or a mixture of several breeds. The former is called monoculture and the later polyculture. Both have advantages and disadvantages.

### Monoculture

Monoculture is the fish culture of only one species. It is intensive in caring, feeding and other management practices. It is easier to perform all the management practices since, only one type of fish is involved. In monoculture the farmer has greater control over the size, age and sex.

In mono culture fish can be harvested selectively by using nets of different mesh size. In monoculture diseases and pests are easily controlled at the same time there is a possibility of complete elimination of the whole lot by some epidemic type of diseases and pests if they go out of control.

### Polyculture

In polyculture different breeds of fish are mixed together in fixed proportion or at random. Polyculture is more closer to the natural method of growing fish and under this situation only the fittest ones will survive. Several small fishes may be eaten by the bigger ones or they could not compete with the bigger ones for food and space. This problem is more in the case of poly culture in which both carnivorous and herbivorous fishes are reared together.

At the same time a farmer can have a polyculture with proper combinations (in number) of selected breeds of fishes. The selection is done on the basis of feeding habits. Such polyculture is called composite fish farming. For example, a farmer can rear a mixture of Indian carps such as catla, rohu, mrigal and Chinese carps such as silver carp, common carp and grass carp.

The catla and silver carp normally takes feed from the upper layers of the water body, the rohu and common carp from the middle layers, while the mrigal and grass carp takes feed from the bottom layers of the pond. All are herbivorous in their feeding habit. In the composite fish culture full utilisation of the pond is possible.

If the breed introduced are naturally fast multiplying like tilapia and their number is a problem in the pond, another fish breed like catfish which is carnivorous can be introduced. The catfish will feed on the organisms at the bottom as well as the fry of tilapia keeping the population of tilapia under control.

Introducing some grass carp among other breeds of fish that are being reared is the best method of controlling the weed growth in the pond. For farmers who have only one pond and do not have facilities like regular supply of fry and fingerlings nor he is unable or unwilling to breed them and those who cannot feed and care in the scientific and intensive ways, it is advisable to go for polyculture with fishes that naturally breed in the pond.

### Monosex Culture

In monosex culture either male or female fish of the same breed or more than one breed is reared. The advantage is faster growth of the fish since, all the energy is concentrated on the growth and development. No energy is used for the reproduction. Sexes can be separated individually during the breeding season or by noting the difference between the male and female in a breed of fish. In the cross breeding of some fish the off springs produced are sterile by nature or produce hundred per cent male fish.

For example, if we cross male tilapia of *Tilapia macrochir* with female of *T. nilotica*, the male of *T. mossambica* with the female of *T. nilotica* and male of *T. hororum* with female of *T. mossambica* the off springs will be completely male. There are no crosses in which 100 per cent off-springs produced are female. Monosex culture is valuable but difficult for ordinary farmers to carry out the breeding and rearing. Therefore, it is not recommended generally to the small scale fish farms unless there is a steady supply of male fry or fingerlings.

### More than One Pond Operation

If the farmer has more than one pond then, he can rear fry or fingerlings for marketing in all the ponds or he can take up the breeding in one, raise fry or fingerlings in another and can rear fish up to marketable size in another pond. If he still has more ponds he can replicate the same functions in more than one pond. With three ponds a farmer can go for breeding and raising of fry for his own farm. The smallest one is used for breeding while the others may be used for rearing till they attain marketable size. The major difference between a large farm operation and a small farm operation is the number of ponds and the fry or fingerlings reared. In big fish farms all the input requirements will be more so also the greater output can be expected in terms of production as well as income.

## SPECIFIC TYPES OF FISH FARMS

Within intensive and extensive aquaculture methods, there are numerous specific types of fish farms; each has benefits and applications unique to its design.

### Fish Rearing in Cages and Pens

As fish necessarily requires water, most people tend to think that for fish rearing they should have their own fish pond which may be situated near the streams, rivers, lakes, permanently flooded areas or reservoirs but do not have the ownership of any portion of any of them, or he may be having a water body which is linked with a lake, reservoir or river. Under such conditions one can go for rearing of fishes In cages and pens. The idea is to rear fish in a common and unbounded water body. This booklet explains the basic methods employed on cage and pen fish farming. Many poor farmers may get benefit from this method, at least partially meet their food and finance requirement.

If a farmer is living near a huge water body, such as canal, river, stream, lake, permanently flooded area or reserviors which does not belong to him or he has a water body which is linked with some other huge water bodies (rivers with lakes or sea, streams with big rivers or flooded areas) he can rear fishes in cages and pens. Of course under this system only a limited number of fishes or a specific type of fish may be reared. However, the number will depend on the size of the cage or the pen used. Those who are able to establish bigger pens and cages will be able to rear proportionately large number of fish provided he can feed them.

Feeding of fish reared in cages and pens is very important among the management practices. Therefore the main thing one should consider is the sufficient availability of feed for the fish reared in the cages and pens. Of course the type of feed depends on the type of the fish being reared Some fish are carnivores, some herbivores and some others are omnivores. For more details about feeding of fish please consult Booklet No. 525 on "Fish Feeding". Generally, a mixture of oil cakes and rice polish is a very good feed for most of the species of the fishes that are being reared by people.

The cages and pens can be constructed with any material conveniently available at the local level provided it is durable at least for one year. However, more the durability of the material greater will be economic benefit from this system of fish rearing though the initial cost may be more.

This type of fish rearing has been practiced since, long in certain parts of the Asia. Perhaps this system of fish culture is originated with the view to control retrieval of the stocked fish. Its application is more relevant for those people for whom the suitable water supply and land for fish culture are becoming less and less available. Further to intensify this system of fish culture, scientific methods are being evolved for increasing the production of fish in cages by forced aeration or by using different types of filters and better feeding and management practices. In India this system can be practiced in the low lying and permanently flooded areas of Kerala, West Bengal, Orissa, Andhra Pradesh, Karnataka, Goa, Gujarat, North Bihar, Assam, Manipur, etc., though much work needs to be done still to perfect and standardise this system.

**Structure of Cages and Pens**

The cages are structures which are covered and secured from every sides and the fishes are kept inside. They can be fixed stationary, suspended, partially or fully immersed, or floating, depending on the convenience. The cages are fitted with a door which can be opened in order to introduce the fishlings, to feed and care them and to harvest them at the end of the rearing season.

The best positioning of the cages is to fix them in such a way that the top portion of the cage is exposed to air and sunlight so that the fish can breath air whenever it is necessary. Also due to the constant contact with the atmospheric air the amount at oxygen dissolved into the water will be more to the benefit of the fishes.

On the other hand, the pens are fixed as fencing structures or enclosures covering an area of the water body. They are made by fixing the fencing material into the ground at the bottom and rising right through the water column and make them stand at about 1-2 ft above the water. The pens are open at the top and exposed to atmosphere. They cover much larger area than the cages. In a way pens are enclosed areas.

Pens also give the idea of several sections of an enclosed area each harbouring a certain number of fishes of different type, size, and age. For breeding purpose the breeding stock may be kept in small pens. Similarly for spawning and hatching also separate pens are required.

The pen looks like a fenced area. Wooden reapers, bamboo splits, reeds or any other suitable material can be used for the construction of the fence. The fencing material is fixed vertically on the ground, under the water and held very close to each other by ropes. Horizontally fixed fencing material is so closely arranged that the gap between them is reduced to the minimum required space, that would not allow the fish to come out and also they will remain safe from predators.

Enclosed area denotes a larger area than the pen area. A portion of large water bodies such as lakes, reserviors, flooded areas, etc., is fenced around in order to rear large number of fish for commercial purpose as is practiced by some people living near the Chilka lake in Orissa.

The pens and enclosures are established only in shallow waters whereas the cages can be used even in deep water areas.

**Material for Construction**

There are a number of materials that can be used for making the cages and pens for fish rearing. Depending on the ingenuity of the farmers and availability of the things a farmer can use any type of material to construct the cages and the pens. Some of the common ones are mentioned here.

**Bamboo and Coir Rope**

Mature and seasoned bamboo splits tied closely using firmly twisted coconut fibre rope perhaps is the best material for making cages and pens in the rural areas where other commercially produced materials are not usually available. Both these materials are durable in submersed conditions. Thin bamboo splits of half inch thickness and width are held together closely by inter-twining them using thin coconut fibre ropes. The main frame of the cage is made of bigger bamboo splits or wooden reapers.

**Nylon Threads**

Strong nylon threads are better than any other material for making the cages and pens though this may be quite costly for an ordinary farmer. Nets are made out of this nylon thread. The mesh size of the net depends on the size of the fishlings which will be reared in the cage. For fry (up to 15 days old) the mesh size should be very small, for the fingerlings (15 to days) the size will be bigger, while for the growing or stocking fishes (reared for market size) the mesh size will be still bigger (half to one inch size).

**Plastics**

Tubes, sheets, ready made meshes made of strong plastic material can be used as cage and pen material. However the plastic should be very strong and non- degradable. Now-a-days very strong and non- degradable type of plastics are available in the market. One has to search and find out the most suitable material for his own purpose.

**Wire Meshes**

Wire mesh is another important material for the construction of cages and pens for fish farming. The mesh as already mentioned could be of any size depending on whether the farmer wants to keep the fry or fingerlings or fish grown for market purpose. It is highly advisable that the mesh is made of galvanised wire in order to reduce the possibility of rusting. Rust can be also controlled by coating with water proof paints on the wire mesh.

**Wood**

Wood can be used as a caging. or penning material. There are several types of wood which can withstand the submersible condition. There could be many other materials which are locally available and could be used for the construction of the cages and pens for fish rearing. The size and shape of the cage or pen is decided by the farmers. Those who have large space and want to rear fish in large number will need bigger cages and pens. But they could be made in any shape and size. Depending on the space available the cages and pens may be constructed big, medium or small, long or short. The shape may be rectangular, square, triangular, irregular or any other: The size of the cage and pen too vary a lot tram very big which harbours hundreds or thousands of fish, to very small in which only one or two fish may be kept.

**Others**

There may be several other materials which may be available locally or commercially for the construction of the cages and pens. It is for each one to look for the appropriate material available at cheaper rate and to use them for the construction.

There may be ready made modular type of material in the form of parts of the cage or pens. Using them we can construct, dismantle and reconstruct the cages and pens. Such materials may not be possible at the farmer's level in the case of cage construction but it is possible in the case of pen construction.

## FISH PRODUCTION IN INTEGRATED FARMING SYSTEMS

Guided by major findings on livestock-fish farming published in a preliminary set of principles defining the various aspects of the culture technology and promotion of fish production in integrated farming systems is suggested and outlined, as a basis for further deliberation.

*Principles pertaining to technology of livestock-fish farming are:*

- Fish production in integrated systems is more complex than the conventional separate aquaculture system, requiring more knowledge and better management inputs
- Integrated farming systems may vary in the degree of intensification of the livestock and fish subsystems, varying from extensive, semiintensive to intensive subsystems.
- Extensive subsystems utilise natural feed produced without international fertilization; semiintensive subsystems require fertilization to produce natural feed and/or supplementary feed but with a significant component of diet supplied by natural feed; and in intensive subsystems all the nutritional requirements are provided by artificial feed given to fishes with natural feed contributing little or no nutrition.
- Fish cultured in an integrated farming system with livestock (especially duck; Edwards, 1986) benefit from a significant amount of the nutrition derived from natural food, which develops in the pond due to the fertilization by organic manures. This suggests the important role of pelagic algal-based food web which cultivates in fish biomass.
- The largest contribution of the manure to fish nutrition therefore, appears to be due to its fertilizing effect in the pond. Bacteria, breaking down the organic matter in the manure, release nutrients which lead to the production of phytoplankton and zooplankton.
- In a manure-fed fish pond, fish nutrition may also be derived from direct consumption of the manure. However, a detritus food web has a secondary role in fish biomass production biomass production, as compared with the algalbased food web.
- The direct nutritional value of manure for fish is by its content of spilled animal feed. A large proportion of the nutrients in livestock feed are not assimilated, but are voided in the excreta, particularly pig excreta (Edwards, 1985).

- Over-fertilization with manure may lead to poor water quality of fish pond, particularly leading to depletion of dissolved oxygen and fish kills.
- Management of water quality is needed to overcome fish kills due to oxygen depletion and extreme fluctuation of dissolved oxygen levels. The strategy is to promote a growing biomass of phytoplankton which will generate sufficient oxygen to maintain relatively high dissolved oxygen have on a 24-hr basis. It is essential to maintain a positive net photosynthesis
- The criteria for selection of fish species for stocking into manurefed fish ponds should be based on the ability of fish species to:
  - Filter and feed on plankton (bacteria, phytoplankton and zooplankton)
  - Tolerate low levels of dissolved oxygen (< 2mg/l minimum as defined by "Criteria for the Protection of Aquatic Life")
- An optimal stocking density of fish species is critical in attaining high cumulative fish yields and in reaching the upper carrying capacity of a manure-fed fish pond.
- Determination of and recommendation of the optimal stocking density of fish consider differences in local circumstances such as the fish species, manure-type and inputs to the pond, addition of other off-farm feed, and water quality of the pond.
- Ways to intensify fish production from integrated farming systems involve management inputs to:
  - Stock a higher initial fish biomass, followed by
  - Harvesting the fish intermediately when the growth curve of stocked fish starts to slow down
- There is a need for a more complex marketing system to handle the inputs and products from two subsystems as opposed to a single subsystem.
- Integrated farming on the one hand, enables the distribution of risk (both biological and economic), since, two subsystems are involved as opposed to one in a single-commodity farming system; on the other hand, the failure of one subsystem can adversely affect the other.

## TYPES OF ANIMAL-CUM-FISH FARMING

Rearing of each animal is a system by itself which becomes more complex when we add the dimensions of rearing, feeding, disease control, breeding, management, etc., of any animal. In the fish-cum-animal stock system two complex systems are being combined to take advantage of the complementary nature of the animal rearing systems and the fish culture systems.

Therefore the planning and layout of the fish cum animal structure should be done meticulously. Prior making any structure it is necessary to make a layout and a blue print of the available land, locating each pond and the animal unit in the proper place. Sometimes one has to relocate the units and see how the time and movement for doing all the operations can be reduced to the minimum. Marketing is an important aspect for the success of any enterprise. Depending on the market the type of fish, the extent of fish culture, the type of the animal and the number of the animals, etc., should be determined.

Based on the type of animal rearing we can have systems like cattle cum fish, horses and donkeys cum fish, pigs cum fish, goat and sheep cum fish, ducks cum fish, geese cum fish, poultry cum fish, quails cum fish, guinea fowls cum fish, turkeys cum fish, ostriches cum fish, rabbits cum fish, guinea pigs cum fish or any other animal cum fish. Depending on the place, climate, availability of inputs and marketing facilities anyone or few of the animal units can be established along with the fish rearing ponds. Some of the most important ones among them are described here for providing basic ideas and information.

**Cattle-Cum-Fish Culture**

By cattle we mean cows, bulls, she and he buffaloes. Normally every farming family has got a cattle shed with a few animals. On an average 15-30 kg of cow dung and 40-60 litres of urine is excreted per day per cattle. Besides there will be the cattle shed wash. Normally in one year about 5500 to 11,000 kg fresh dung is produced per cattle. This amount varies with the size of the animal and the quantity of feed given per day per head. At the same time it should be remembered that the dung requirement based on the fresh weight for the fish pond varies from 5500 to 10,000 kg per hectare/ year. For the low fertility ponds as much as 10,000 to 12,000 kg (fresh weight basis) dung per hectare pond is required whereas in high fertility status the amount may be reduced to half of the amount required for the low fertility ponds.

This means the, dung from one animal in one year is sufficient to fertilize one hectare of fish pond provided there is no wastage or other use of the dung. Theoretically speaking, a farmer can have as many hectares of fish pond as he has adult animals with him. The urine is an additional source of fertilizations In other words he should maintain at least one cattle per hectare of fish pond provided he uses all the dung, urine and shed wash in the pond.

After the initial dose of 2000 kg cow dung per hectare pond area, every month 1000 kg cow dung per hectare pond area is to be provided into the fish ponds for about 8 to 10 months. This dosage varies with soil fertility variation of the pond. Depending on the number of animals and the fertility of the soil, one call determine the area of the pond required to utilise the full amount of dung and urine.

The dung can be fed to the biogas plants and its slurry can be used directly into the fish ponds. Under this condition there should be a slurry retention tank from which we can divert the slurry into each pond or plot after diluting it four times with shed wash or by adding fresh water. Slurry if it is too thick it will not give a smooth and 'complete flow through the channels. The urine and cattle shed wash also can be stored into the slurry retention tank. They are also useful for diluting the slurry.

If there are many ponds, channels are constructed to reach the mixture of the cattle shed wash and urine to each of the ponds separately. The cattle shed and the fish pond are constructed in such a way that the dung and the urine can easily be transferred to the ponds through channels or some other conveyances. Cattle dung should be used only after decomposition whereas the urine and shed wash can be used directly into the pond. But over dosage should be avoided. By over dosage the pond gets too much algal growth which will upset the oxygen content in the water during the night. By experience one will be able to judge the optimum dosage.

The suitable designs of cattle housing and fish ponds are explained in Booklets 198 and 520 respectively. For further details the reader is requested to refer literatures published by the same institute about various topics on cattle rearing (Book-lets Nos., 197,202, 198, 41, 200, 201, 199). Anyone who would like to start any type of fishery cum animal unit, he should first of all master the theoretical knowledge at least in these booklets about the type of fish culture and the types of animal rearing. Afterwards he should refine his theoretical knowledge with his own well observed and documented experience.

The layout of the cattle sheds and the fish ponds should be such that all the works can be carried out easily and without much cost. The requirement of labour for doing various operations should be kept minimum. The layout for each farm should be made separately depending on the shape and size of the land and the various inputs available at the local level.

**Horses and Donkey**

Horses and donkeys farms are very rare in our country. Private stud (farms for horse breeding) farms are yet to become a practice in our country. Indian Army maintains several stud farms but they are not interested to have fisheries along with their stud farms. However, this is an idea which can be practiced by private as well as public horses and donkeys farms. Hence, this portion is included in this booklet. Anyone who would think of starting such an enterprise this portion of the booklet will be helpful to him. The sheds of the horses and donkeys have to be designed and built as per recommendation. What is important is that every bit of horse/donkey dung and every drop of urine should be collected and should be utilised either in the fish ponds or for the cultivation of fodder for the horses and donkeys.

The manure value of the horse dung is higher than that of the cattle and hence, more area can be fertilized by the same amount of horse dung as compared to cattle dung. However it should be composed before the dung is used in the fish pond or in the fodder cultivation field. It can also be used in the biogas plant and the slurry is used in the fish ponds after dilution. Under this circumstance we can also mix the urine and shed wash also into the slurry collection tank. By this we can dilute the slurry to some extent. The sheds for the horses and the donkeys and the fish ponds are constructed in such a way that the dung can be transferred to the compost boxes and the urine and shed wash into the collection tank and from there to the fish ponds and to the fodder cultivation fields. For this the ponds, sheds, compost boxes and urine and shed wash collection tank should be linked with roads, paths and channels. The management should be specially careful about the general sanitation and cleanliness of the complex. Regarding the rearing of the horses and donkeys the reader is requested to collect information from reliable people who have both theoretical and practical knowledge about the rearing of horses and donkeys and reinforce it with one's own experience.

**Pig-Cum-Fish Culture**

Pig dung is a very good manure. On an average one adult pig excretes 5 to 8 kg of dung and 10 to 20 litres of urine per day. The dung is used better after decomposing it in compost boxes as mentioned earlier. The urine can be collected along with the shed wash in a tank and the mixture can used for fertilizing the fish pond or to irrigate and to fertilize the fodder plots. In some cases the dung, urine and shed wash are mixed to form into a thin slurry which can be used to fertilize the pond. However this practice is to be discouraged since, the harmful effects of decomposition may occur.

The pig dung also can be used in the biogas plants for the production of gas and the slurry that comes out of them can be used directly into the fish ponds. The piggery is constructed in such a way that all the shed wash can be directed to different ponds through a net work of channels. Depending on the number of pigs and the amount of dung available a farmer can decide the area of pond, and whether to use all the dung and urine into the fish pond or to use partially only. Use the pig dung after decomposition only, whereas the use and shed wash may be used directly into the pond. As already mentioned in the case of cattle cum fish culture, one has to arrive at the optimum dosage of the pig manure and urine to be used in the fish ponds for the fertilization. For details about the construction of pig housing and: management of pigs, refer Booklets on various topics prepared under the same.

**Goat and Sheep-Cum-Fish Culture**

Goat is known as the poor man's cow and they are reared by small and marginal farmers for their domestic needs as well as additional income generating unite. Wherever convenient they can also include a fish pond, which may differ in size. The floor and the drainage line of the goat house is made in such a way that the shed wash is diverted into the pond directly in the case of small amount or collected into a small tank in the case of large amount. The goat droppings need time to decompose and hence, it is necessary to give enough time to compost it before using in the pond.

The details about the construction of the goat house in relation to the fish pond depends on the ingenuity of each farmer who adopts the practice of goat cum fish farming.

Similarly we can have sheep rearing with fish ponds. For details about sheep rearing refer Booklets on sheep. There can be differences in the construction of shed for and management of the sheep.

**Duck-Cum-Fish Culture**

Ducks are aquatic birds and they fit in well with fish farm though, they pray on the fishes and eat on fry or fingerlings. By not letting the ducks into the ponds in which fry and fingerlings are raised, we can avoid this problem. After certain age and size the fish can escape from the ducks.

The dropping of the ducks are excellent manure for the fish ponds. About 100 to 200 ducks per hectare may be kept in the fish ponds providing each about 50 to 100 square metre for movement and feeding. The number of ducks may be increased or decreased depending on the feed availability for the ducks from the natural growth in the pond or by the supplementary feeds given to them. The amount of organic manure required for the maintenance of the pond fertility is also a criterion to decide the number of the ducks to be reared in areas attached to the fish pond. Over fertilization is as harmful as under fertilization.

The duck house can be constructed on the bank of the pond or over the pond. In the first case the droppings are decomposed first and then applied into the pond. In the second case the droppings fall directly into the pond. In that case the harmful effects of over dosage of duck droppings cannot be controlled. Therefore it is better that the house is made on the bank of the pond in such a way that the droppings can be collected and decomposed before they are utilised into the pond. The house should provide minimum two square feet area per duck. The ducks are kept on a platform or floor of the duck house is raised by two or the three feet from the ground. For the self cleaning purpose the platform is made of one inch square welded wire mesh, fixed strongly on a wooden or iron frame. The rest of the portion of the cage can be made according to the suitability. However every cage should be properly enclosed for security reason and should also have a door. The cage should protect the ducks from inclement weather conditions. The cage is fixed on four pillars up to a height of two or three feet. The floor below the cage should be cemented with a slope towards the pond so that the duck dropping can be washed down into the pond

The duck house also can be constructed in a floating manner and the cage may be left floating in the pond. The structure of the cage may be same and the bottom of the cage is maintained about two feet above the water and is made of one inch square wire mesh as already mentioned. The drop- ping of the duck will automatically fall into the pond through the wire mesh. For details about duck housing and management refer Booklets on various topics under "Ducks".

**Geese-Cum-Fish Culture**

Geese are also aquatic birds and can be reared just like ducks along with fish ponds. The geese house can be constructed similar to that of the duck house, one inch square welded wire mesh fixed firmly at the bottom. But the geese require at least tour square feet area per bird in the cage. The height of the cage also should be increased to 3-4 feet.

The geese cage can be constructed by the side of the pond or above the pond or kept floating in the pond water. The last two forms of housing allows the droppings to fall into the pond directly. Under such situation the decomposition takes place inside the pond and there are chances that the pond water gets contaminated and the fishes may be affected. Therefore for commercial rearing of fish along with geese it is highly recommended that the cage is built by the side of the pond and the droppings are decomposed in the compost box before using. About 30 to 60 geese can be kept per hectare of pond area. Geese are voracious grazers and hence, the grasses on the sides of the fish ponds serve as feed for them. They can also be fed with fish waste generated from the fish ponds.

**Poultry-Cum-Fish Culture**

Like the ducks, poultry can be maintained in association with a fish farm. Depending on the size of the pond and the number of fish reared, the number of birds reared may be adjusted. We can also adjust the area of the pond and the number of fish reared depending on the number of birds reared. The size and number of the one influences the other.

The poultry house may be constructed in such a way that it is projecting into the pond and the droppings may be falling directly into the pond or it may be constructed on the side of the pond and the dropping are first decomposed in the compost boxes and then used in the pond. Hence, it is highly advisable to use the poultry dung after the decomposition only. For details about poultry rearing refer Booklets on various topics in poultry rearing.

**Quail-Cum-Fish Culture**

Quails are very small birds that are reared for eggs and meat. They lay on an average 300 eggs per year. Though the eggs are small they are more in weight compared to the eggs of desi chicken. These birds require comparatively less feed and are hardy in nature so that they are less prone to diseases.

The quail houses may be built by the side of the pond, over the pond or floating in the pond as already mentioned in the case of poultry and ducks. In the last two cases the droppings will fall directly into the pond. Under this condition there is no control of the amount of the manure applied in the ponds. Beside all the droppings fall in one place which results in over fertilization of the particular spot. For the commercial rearing of the fish it is advisable to build it by the side of the ponds. The housing should be built in such a way that each quail should get a minimum of one square foot space for movement. If they are left out they will escape and live in the wild stage. Therefore they have to be totally hand fed inside the cage. Inferior millets and poultry feed are suitable for the quail.

**Guinea Fowls-Cum-Fish Culture**

Guinea fowls are reared for egg and meat purpose though they are not as popular as the chicken and duck. They require on an average 3 to 4 square feet caged area. They can be kept on cemented floor slightly slopping towards the fish ponds.

This means the guinea fowl housing is situated on the bank of the fish pond. They can also be kept on the welded thick wire mesh fixed as a floor of the cage of the guinea fowl.

At night they like to perch on the branches of trees. In order to satisfy this natural tendency their houses are built on high altitude on bamboos or poles which may be placed across the room so that they perch on them at night.

Along with the housing, an enclosed run may be also made for the guinea fowls to move around. Inside the run bushes are maintained to provide some sort of natural setting for the guinea fowls.

Heaps of dry leaves and twigs of plants may also be placed here and there inside the enclosure. These leaves and twigs are used by the guinea fowls to make nests to lay their eggs. In general it is difficult to train them to lay eggs in laying boxes placed inside the cage or in the enclosures.

By placing a lot of grass, straw and twigs inside the cage or the enclosures we encourage the birds to make their nest by themselves to lay the eggs inside.

The dropping of the guinea fowls are collected composed or digested in a biogas plant and only decomposed manure should be applied into the pond according to the requirement.

Guinea fowls are omnivorous and can be fed with cereals, millets, pulses, vegetable and fruit wastes.

They are also good grazers and the grasses growing on the bunds and sides of the ponds can also utilized as supplementary feed for them. They can be let out for grasing but they should be brought back to the house. Otherwise they may stay around any where in the open or in the bushes growing near the pond area.

**Turkeys-Cum-Fish Culture**

Turkeys are valued for their meat and eggs. In Europe turkeys are essential part of the food during the christian celebrations. Other times of the year also commercially the fine tasty meat of turkey is very important.

Turkeys are omnivorous and hence, they can be reared on any kind of crop wastes and organic byproducts. The adult male grow up to 10 kg and a female up to 5 to 6 kg in size. Each female turkey lays about 8 to 15 eggs at one stretch and are hatched in 28 days. The young one are called poults. Turkeys prefer wood land with water and hence, fish ponds with turkey rearing plots is an ideal combination. Depending on the number of turkeys and the number of fish ponds the unit may differ in size. The fish waste is also feed for the turkeys while the droppings of the turkeys will be good manure tor the fish pond.

Besides the meat and eggs the feathers of the turkey are also commercially valuable. They are used for making feather meal, feather matresses, etc., The render is advised to look for further information if he has a plan to start a turkey farm.

**Ostrich-Cum-Fish Culture**

Ostriches are very big birds which are valued for their meat, eggs and feathers. Though originally from Africa they spread to all other parts of the world. An adult male can grow 2.5 metres tall and 155 kg in weight. The eggs are about 15 cm long and 12.5 cm in diameter. The males are black but have white plumes in the wings and tail. The females are mostly brown. The head and most of the neck is reddish to brown in colour. The head is small and bill is short but wide. The eyes are brown and big with thick black eye lashes. The legs and the thighs are naked.

They live in flocks of 5 to 50 and move around with other grasing animals. They can run as fast as 65 km per hour, though the average speed may be around 40 km per hour. When disturbed they can kick strongly to inflict harm on others. They too are omnivorous and good grazers of grasses and other vegetation. They grow fast and attain an average weight of 40 kgs in 6 to 8 months time.

One male can serve 3 to 5 female ostriches which lay eggs in a common nest on the ground. The number of eggs range from 15 to 60 per nest. The eggs are hatched in 40 days and for hatching the male sit on the eggs during the night and females sit during the day. Within one month after hatching the young ones can keep up with the adult in moving around and in foraging. Ostrich plumes are very valuable from ancient times. They are used for decoration and ornamental purposes. Hence, ostrich farm are being establishedin many parts of the world especially in South Africa, USA and Australia.

The hide of the ostrich provide good quality and well tanned leather. They do well in captivity and grow up to 50 years. In less rain fall and dry areas along with fish ponds one can go for commercial rearing of ostriches. The dung from the ostriches is excellent manure to fertilize the pond and the slaughter waste is excellent feed for the fish while the fish waste will serve as feed for the ostriches.

**Rabbit-Cum-Fish Culture**

Rabbits dropping are similar to the goats dropping in size, shape and hardness. It is a very good manure for the fish pond. Hence, rabbit rearing can be associated with the fish pond.

The rabbit housing as in the case of the other animals can be built close to the fish pond and all the urine and the shed wash are directly allowed to flow into the pond. The dropping should be decomposed well before it is used into the pond. For details about rabbit housing and management refer Booklets on various topics on rabbit rearing (Nos. 45, 203, 204, 205, 206, 207 and 401).

**Guinea Pigs-Cum-Fish Culture**

Guinea pigs are native of Central and South America. They were domesticated by the Indians in Peru and Equador and Columbia for meat, long before the arrival of the Spaniards who introduced this animal to Europe. Initially they were reared in Europe for meat but later they were mainly reared as pets.

Besides for meat, skin and as pets they are now extensively used in the laboratories for biological, medical and other experimental purposes. They are cute little animals existing in various colours and patterns that they look admirably beautiful. Hence, there are people who are interested in breeding them into intricate combinations of colours and patters. They grow on an average 25 cm long and weigh not more than one kilogram. They have four toes on the front leg and three on the hind legs. The legs are short, the body is stout, the head is large compared to the body size. They attain sexual maturity in two months and have a gestation period of 60 to 70 days. The young ones are born fully developed and with hair and are able to move around within hour of their birth. On an average 6 to 8 young ones are born in one litter. In a year 4 to 5 litters could accomplished. One male is enough to serves to 6 females.

The housing for the guinea pigs rue similar to that of the rabbits. The most important thing in the construction of the housing for the guinea pigs is to ensure quick cleaning, watering and feeding.

The house should be clean, dry and odourless. The layout of the guinea pig house and the ponds should be such that the dung could be easily transferred to the compost boxes and the urine to the collection tank. For more details about the housing of guinea pigs the reader is requested to refer the booklet No. 568 on Guinea Pig.

## DUCK-CUM-FISH FARMING SYSTEM

Usefulness of livestock wastes such as cowdung, poultry and pig excreta, goat and sheep pellets, in fish culture to enhance the production of fish food organisms, as well as, in cutting down the expenditure on costly feeds and fertilizers have been well documented (Kapur, 1981, 1984; Kapur and Lal, 1986; Yadava, 1987).

Cowdung is at present, the most widely used manure in fish culture while other animal excreta like poultry, pig, sheep and goat pellets have been tried effectively. No systematic and scientific based studies have been done till now on duck excreta and its utilisation for fish-culture. At present our knowledge regarding the suitability and in different combinations with other livestock wastes, rate of mineralisation under varying physico-chemical characteristic of the medium, their toxic and 'safe' levels for autotrophs, zooplankton and fish and the specific food requirements of the carp fry and adult fish under integrated system, is very meagre. Therefore, the present investigations have been taken up keeping above lacunae in view.

### Material and Methods

Test organism, viz., fish fry (C. carpio) and zooplankton (Daphnia longiremis) were collected from the fish farm ponds, Department of Zoology, H.A.U. Hisar, and transferred to the fisheries laboratory. Fish fry were acclimated to the laboratory conditions in an aquarium, and fed on zooplankton. The test organisms were subjected to the Static Bioassay procedure following APHA (1976) using 500 ml conical flasks for zooplankton and 10 1 glass aquaria for fish fry. In order to work out the LC50 of duckery wastes, concentrations of duck waste ranging from 0.001 to 0.1 percent were initially tested. Suitable test concentrations from the above broad-range of concentrations were investigated, with respect to the mortality of treated carp fry after 24 to 96h (sample size = 20). To find out the suitability of the estimated 'safe' concentration of duck waste in the aquatic medium, levels of gross primary productivity (GPP) and dissolved oxygen (DO) were conducted in a screen house under semi-field and field conditions. Some experiments were conducted at the animal sheds of the College of Animal Sciences, HAU, Hisar, in the duck cage house of the Department of Livestock Production and Management. Eight duck birds of different age groups ranging between 1 year to 1.5 years and having different body weights ranging between 2.0 and 2.5 kg were taken. The process of feeding the birds, recollection of left-over food and the collection of excreta from each bird's pen was repeated after every 24 hrs.

Field experiments were conducted at the fish farn of the Department of Zoology HAU, Hisar, for 96 days, to study GPP and DO levels in waters treated with duck and duck-cowdung wastes combinations as well as secondary productivities (Zooplankton no/ litre). The methods of estimation were those from APHA (1976). The tested fish fry (C. carpio) with an average length of 5.9 cm, were stocked in all the experimental ponds at a density of 8000 fry/ha. Gross doses of duck, duck and cowdung combinations at 'Safe' concentrations were estimated as per ha per yr. These doses were further split into six equal doses and applied at intervals of 15 days in the experimental ponds. Survival and growth of test fish (C. carpio) were studied in relation to some physicochemical characteristics, primary productivity and secondary productivity (Zooplankton) of the waste-treated waters. Correlations were also drawn between growth (based on length and weight) of fish and various factors given above, of the treated waters.

**Results**

Data from the present studies on the survival of fish (C. carpio) and related physico-chemical characteristics of duck waste-treated waters, which depicts only mean levels of physico-chemical characteristics during the observation time (0-96 h) vis-à-vis fish survival after 24 and 48 h. The later data was utilised for calculating the 'Safe' concentration of the wastes.

No mortality was observed between 0.005 and 0.015 per cent concentrations of duck wastes up to 96h, possibly due to the existence of favourable hydrological conditions like dissolved oxygen, pH, BOD, hardness, conductivity, etc., for the survival of fish. It has been clearly indicated during the present studies that with the increase in concentration of duck wastes from 0.005 to 0.07 per cent, DO gradually decreased, while on the contrary, BOD, conductivity and chloride contents gradually increased, whereas pH and hardness fluctuated between 7.6 and 8.3, 58.4 and 61.9 mg/1 respectively.

During the above observations, temperature ranged between 24.2°C and 24.8°C, 24 and 48h LC50 values for the duck waste were found to be 0.06 and 0.04 per cent respectively, based on the regression equations, and the 'safe' concentration was calculated as 0.005 per cent. The heterogeneity between the observed and calculated survival values was non-significant. Based on the above experiments conducted in the laboratory, the observed data were further tested under semi-field and field conditions.

## POULTRY-CUM-FISH FARMING

This system utilises poultry droppings of fully built- up poultry litter for fish culture. The fish production obtained is about 5000 kg/ha/yr. with 1250 kg chicken meat and 70000 no. of eggs. Approximately 500-600 no. of birds is reared in a 1 ha pond. The Rhode Island or Leghorn variety birds are more preferred over others. They require 0.3-0.4 square meterspace/bird. Hoppers are used to feed them and to minimise feed wastage. The poultry birds (layers) are fed with starter, grower, and brooder feed according to their age. In India it is practised in Andhra Pradesh, Bihar, Haryana, Kerala, West Bengal, Uttar Pradesh, Maharashtra, Orissa, and Tamilnadu.

**Duck-Cum-Fish Culture**

The duck are commonly called as biologicals aerator. They are reared on the dyke of the pond in a low-cost house. This farming is practised in Tamilnadu, Assam, Bihar, Andhra Pradesh, Tripura, Orissa, Karnataka, Kerala and Uttar Pradesh. The 'Indian runner' and 'Khaki campbell' varieties are found more suitable in this culture. About 300 no. of ducklings (some spp. are reared 450-500 in no.) are reared to fertilize the 1 ha. pond. The duck not only act as live aerator by splashing water with their webbed feet but also control the aquatic weed (Lemna, Azolla, etc.), aquatic insects, molluscs, tadpoles, etc. Each duckling require about 0.3-0.5 square meter area as living space. The total production from such type of culture is about 3500-5000 kg fish, 18000-18500 eggs and 600 kg of duck meat. The duck droppings are used as manure for primary production.

**Pig-Cum-Fish Culture**

This system has certain advantages over others. The 30-35 pig's waste may produce 1 tonne of Ammonium Sulphate and 40-45 pigs are adequate to fertilize 1 ha water area under polyculture. Each pig requires about 3- 4 sq.m floor space. This system of integration is very common in China, Taiwan, Vietnam, Thailand, Malaysia, Hungary and some European countries. The White Yorkshire, Hampshire and Landrace are the popular breed of pig for integration with fish. Pigs need clean housing which should provide adequate protection from adverse climates. The pigs are fed on pig mash which is made up of rice bran, rice polish, wheat-bran, broken maize, ground-nut oil cake, fish-meal mineral mixture, salt, etc. The spoiled vegetables can also be mixed in it. This system provides about 3000-4000 kg/ha/yr fish, 4500 kg/yr pig meat and 800 no. of piglets every year.

**Cattle-Cum-Fish Culture**

It is a common practice all-over the world. The cow excreta is most abundant in terms of availability and a healthy cow may excrete over 4000-5000kg dung and 3500-4000 litre urine on an annual basis. The BOD of cow manure is lower than other livestock manure. About 5-6 cows can provide adequate manure for 1 ha pond in addition to 9000 kg milk and about 3000-4000 kg of fish annually. Cow-shed should be built close to fish pond to simplify handling of cow-manure.

**Goat-Cum-Fish Integration**

It is considered as poor man's cow and a goat's excreta is considered as a very good organic fertilizer. The goat excreta contains organic carbon-60 per cent, N-2.7 per cent, P-1.78 per cent, K-2.88 per cent and its urine is also equally rich in both N & P. At least 50-60 goats are essential to fertilize 1 ha pond. The goats should be provided with dry, safe, comfortable house protected from excessive heat. The goat breeds are Jamanapari, Beetal, Barbari for milk and Bengal, Sirihi, Deccani are used for meat purpose. Goats are selective feeders and consume Berseem, Napier grass, Cowpea Soybean, Mulberry, etc. This integration can provide 3500-4000 kg fish/ha/year without supplementary feeding and fertilizer.

**Rabbit-Fish Integration**

Rabbit meat is preferred by most of the health conscious consumers owing to its low fat in comparison to other meats. The important meat breeds are Soviet Chinchilla, Grey Giant, and White Giant, etc. Rabbits are reared in cage, hutch and floor system (floor should be cemented). Rabbit excreta contain organic carbon-50 per cent, N-2 per cent, P-1.33 per cent, and K-1.2 per cent. The rabbit excreta is high in nitrogen content and low in moisture, thus quality manure for sustained plankton production. It is estimated that excreta from 300 rabbits would be enough for 1 ha pond fertilization.

## FISH FEED

The abundance of feed grains in the U.S.A., often obscures the importance of industrial sources of raw materials for the domestic feed industry. Published data from research in poultry and swine nutrition show corn or wheat as the predominant dietary component and soybean meal or fish meal as the only dietary protein source in test diets. Often a test ration would consist of just a cereal grain and soybean meal plus mineral and vitamin supplements.

Increasing competition in the feed industry plus rising cost of traditional feed ingredients in recent years are forcing feed manufacturers to increase the use of less expensive feed ingredients such as by-products from the milling and food processing industries. Feed formulations have been aided by more complete and reliable information of the nutritive value of these products as well as by the development of linear programming techniques for least cost diet formulation based on a large selection of ingredients. Some of the more commonly used industrial by-products currently used for fish diet manufacture in the U.S.A., are listed below.

## MILL BY-PRODUCTS

### Wheat Germ Meal

Wheat germ meal consists chiefly of the germs of the wheat berry, with some bran and middlings. A rather wide variety of wheat germ grades are produced, depending on the area and regional demand. The quality of wheat germ meal is influenced by the presence of screenings and the level, of other wheat products, which can lower the fat or protein level. Excessive storage time may result in rancidity, due to the oxidation of the rather high level of fat. Generally, I wheat germ meal may have a crude protein level of 25-30 per cent; crude fat, 7-12 per cent; and crude fibre, 3-6 per cent.

### Wheat Red Dog

Wheat red dog consists of offal from the tail of the mill, together with some fine particles of wheat bran, wheat germ and wheat flour. Wheat red dog is a fine, floury, light-coloured feed ingredient. The colour may range from creamy white to light brown or light red, depending on the type of wheat being milled. Wheat red dog can act as a pellet binder, as well as contributor of protein, carbohydrates, minerals and vitamins to the feed. Wheat red dog may have a crude protein level of 15.5-17.5 per cent; crude fat, 3.5-4.5 per cent; and crude fibre, 2.8-4.0 per cent.

### Wheat Bran

Wheat bran is the coarse outer covering of the wheat berry. Sometimes screenings are ground and added to the bran. Wheat bran contributes bulk to ruminant feeds and is a source of carbohydrates, protein, minerals and vitamins. Generally, wheat bran will have a crude protein level of 14-17 percent; crude fat, 3-4.5 percent; and crude fibre, 10.5-12 percent.

**Wheat Middlings**

Wheat middlings consist of fine particles of wheat bran, wheat shorts, wheat germ, wheat flour and some of the offal from the tail of the mill. The quality of middlings may be influenced by the amount of screenings added and the fineness of grind. A moisture level over 14 percent may cause problems, especially in hot, humid climates. Wheat middlings have a crude protein, level of 15-17 percent; crude fat, 3-4 percent; and crude fibre, 8.5-9.5 percent.

**Wheat Mill Run**

Wheat mill run consists of wheat bran, fine particles of wheat bran, wheat shorts, wheat germ, wheat flour and the offal from the tail of the mill. Ground run of the mill screenings are normally added.

Wheat mill run is available in the west, but not normally found in other areas of the country where mill run is separated into bran, middlings and red dog. Wheat mill run may have a crude protein level of 14-17 percent; crude fat, 3-4 percent and crude fibre, 8.5-9.5 percent.

**Corn Gluten Feed**

Corn gluten feed is that part of commercial shelled corn that remains after the extraction of the larger portion of the starch, gluten and germ by the process employed in the wet milling manufacture of corn starch or syrup. Generally, corn gluten feed will contain a crude protein level of 21-22 percent; crude fat, 1-2.5 percent; and crude fibre, 8-10 percent.

**Corn Gluten Meal**

Corn gluten meal is the dried residue from corn after the larger part of the starch and germ have been removed and the bran separated by the process employed in the wet milling manufacture of corn starch or syrup, or by enzymatic treatment of the endosperm. Corn gluten meal may contain fermented corn extractives and/or corn germ meal. The crude protein level may range from 41-43 percent; crude fat, 1-3 percent; crude fibre, 4-6 percent; and xanthophyll, 140-220 mg/kg.

**Rice Groats**

Rice groats are the ground rice kernel, without the bran. Rice groats contain approximately a crude protein level of 8.6 percent; crude fat, 1.2 percent; and crude fibre, 1.0 percent.

**Rice Bran with Germ**

Rice bran with germ is primarily the pericarp or bran layer and the germ portions of the rice kernel. The crude protein level is approximately 13.3 percent; crude fat, 15.0 percent; and crude fibre, 11.0 percent.

**Rice Polishings**

Rice polishings are the outer portions of the rice kernel produced by the process used in producing polished white rice. Rice polishings have a crude protein level of 11.8 percent; crude fat, 13.2 percent; and crude fibre, 3.0 percent.

**Oat Groats**

Oat groats are the cleaned oats with their hulls removed. Generally, oat groats will contain a crude protein level of 16 percent; crude fat, 6 percent' and crude fibre, 2 percent.

## OIL EXTRACTIVES

### Soybean Meals

Soybean meal is produced in two major protein levels by different processes. Soybean meal must be heated (toasted) sufficiently to destroy, the trypsin inhibitor. Forty-four percent soybean meal is usually mechanically extracted to produce a meal of 44 percent crude protein; crude fat, 4.7 percent; and crude fibre, 6.0 percent. Forty-eight percent soybean meal is dehulled and solvent extracted to yield meal with a crude protein I level of 48 percent; crude fat, 0.9 percent; and crude fibre, 2.8 percent.

### Cottonsead Meals

Cottonseed meal is produced in three protein levels. Cottonseed meals are classified as low gossypol if they contain less than 0.04 percent free gossypol. Forty-one percent cottonseed meal has a crude protein. level of 41 percent; crude fat, 2 percent; and crude fibre, 12 percent. Forty-eight percent cottonseed meal has a crude protein level of 48 percent; crude fat, 1 percent; and crude fibre, 8 percent. Although all three cottonseed meals are solvent extracted, the lower protein meals may contain some hulls.

### Peanut Meal

Peanut meal is obtained by grinding the cake, chips or flakes obtained by removal of most of the oil from peanut kernels by a mechanical or solvent extraction process. Peanut meal will have a crude protein level of about 46 percent; crude fat, 1-7 percent; and crude fibre, 10-13 percent.

## ANIMAL BY-PRODUCTS

### Hydrolyzed Poultry Feathers

Feathers from poultry are collected, ground and hydrolyzed under pressure. During processing the cystine linkage is broken, increasing the value of the meal.

Not less than 75 percent of the crude protein must be pepsin digestible. Generally, hydrolyzed poultry feathers will range in crude protein from 80 to 85 percent; crude fat, 2.5 percent; crude fibre, 1.5 percent; phosphorus, 0.75 percent; and ash about 3 percent.

### Meat and Bone Meal

Meat and bone meal is the dry rendered product derived from mammalian tissue, exclusive of hair, hoof, horn, manure and paunch contents.

The relatively high fat content of meat and bone meal apparently helps protect the lysine content during rendering. Meat and bone meal generally contain a crude protein of 50 percent; fat, 8-11 percent; crude fibre, 3 percent phosphorus, 4.4-5 percent; calcium, 8.8-10 percent; and ash, about 30 percent.

### Fish Meals

Fish meals are manufactured by cooking fish, pressing to remove water and oil and then drying. Fish meals are often made from a single species of fish, e.g., herring meal, but meals containing more than one species, such as bottom fish meal, are also sold. Generally, the single species meals are more uniform in quality.

Some typical analyses follow: Blood meal is produced from clean fresh animal blood, exclusive of all extraneous material such as hair, stomach contents, etc., Blood meal may be dried by several processes, but most often by spray drying.

Spray dried blood meal has approximately a crude protein level of 85 percent; crude fat, 0.5-3 percent; crude fibre, 2.5 percent; ash, 6 percent; and lysine, 9-11 percent, with an availability of 80-90 percent.

| | Crude protein (%) | Crude fat (%) | Crude fibre (%) | Sodium (%) |
|---|---|---|---|---|
| Herring meal | 70 | 7.5 | 1 | 0.5 |
| Menhaden meal | 60 | 7.5 | - | 0.3 |
| Anchovy meal | 64 | 6 | 1 | 0.8 |
| Carp meal, whole | 75 | 9.5 | - | - |
| Shrimp meal | 36-48 | 3 | 11 | - |
| Crab meal | 30 | 1.7 | 11 | - |
| Bottom fish meal | 60 | - | - | - |
| Blood Meal | | | | |

## MISCELLANEOUS

### Corn Distillers Dried Grain with Solubles

This product is obtained by removal of ethyl alcohol by distillation from the yeast fermentation of corn or corn mixture by condensing and drying at least 75 percent of the solids of the resultant whole stillage. Corn distillers dried grain with solubles has a crude protein level of 26-27 percent; crude fat, 7-8 percent; and crude fibre, 8.5-9.5 percent.

### Brewers Yeast

Brewers dried yeast is the dried, sterilized, unextracted yeast (Saccharomyces) resulting as a by-product from the brewing of beer and ale. Brewers dried yeast has a crude protein level of 45 percent; crude fat, 1 percent; and crude fibre, 2.7 percent.

### Brewers Dried Grains

Brewers dried grain is the extracted dried residue of barley malt alone or in mixture with other cereal grain or grain products resulting from the manufacture of work or beer and may contain pulverized spent hops in an amount not to exceed 3 percent. Brewers dried grains may have a crude protein level of 24-30 percent; crude fat, 4.5-8.5 percent; and crude fibre, 10.5-16 percent.

### Dried Whey

Dried whey is the residue obtained by drying whey, a by-product of cheese manufacturing. It contains at least 65 percent lactose; crude protein, 13 percent; about 0.8 percent crude fat; and no crude fibre.

### Antioxidants in Compounded Feeds

Just as oxidation can cause rust and deterioration in metals, a similar type of oxidation occurs in feeds and feedstuffs, resulting in rancidity of fats, destruction of vitamins A, D and E, pigmenters (carotenoids) and amino acids with resultant lowered biological energy values for the diet. If this destruction is allowed to proceed unchecked in a feed, or even in a single ingredient, a lowered feed consumption may result in disastrous nutrient deficiencies. Researchers in a number of fields have been studying the various problems resulting from uncontrolled oxidation and have been developing ways of bringing these oxidation processes under control. It is noted that oxidative rancidity or lipid peroxidation, as contrasted with hydrolytic rancidity, results in a serious decrease in the energy value of a fat or oil.

Undesirable oxidation in feeds may be combatted in several ways. Care should be used to make certain that the ingredients included in the feeds provide adequate margins of safety of vitamins A, E and other natural antioxidants; e.g., lecithin. The use of unstable fats and oils or other pro-oxidants in the feed should be minimized whenever possible.

**Criteria for Selecting Feed Antioxidants**

Antioxidants have been used in commercial fish foods in the USA for over 20 years. Although hundreds of chemicals have been tested, only a few have shown the qualifications necessary to make them suitable for use in preventing undesirable oxidations in feedstuffs, in finished feeds and in the guts and carcasses of animals. In order for an antioxidant to be useful in animal feeding, it must have the following qualifications:

- It must be effective in preserving animal and vegetable fats, vitamins and other feed qualities subject to oxidative destruction;
- It must be non-toxic to man and to farm animals (i.e., chickens, swine, fish, etc.);
- It should be effective at very low concentrations; and
- It must be low enough in cost to be economically practical.

**Commonly Used Feed Antioxidants**

Of the chemical compounds that have been investigated thus far, three have been found to be outstandingly effective antioxidants for feeds and feed ingredients and can be used both efficiently and economically. They are:

- Ethoxyquin (generic term: 1,2-dihydro-6-ethoxy-2,2,4-trimethylquinoline)
- BHA (butylated hydroxyanisole);
- BHT (butylated hydroxytoluene)

Ethoxyquin, however, has been demonstrated to be the most efficaceous, followed closely by BHT and BHA.

With the advent of rations containing a high level of animal and vegetable fats, the requirement for antioxidant protection has become very apparent. The majority of studies over the last few years has focused on ethoxyquin as a preservative or antioxidant. Other chemical preservatives are: ascorbic acid, propionic acid, benzoic acid, citric acid and their various salts. There are technological problems (i.e., moisture level, etc.,) associated with the use of these preservatives. Economics, however, remain the most important consideration which limit their use in fish foods.

**Functional Effects of Antioxidants**

The functional effects of the antioxidants as they affect nutrients and the animals' utilization of them can be summarized as follows:

**Nutrient Deficiency Prevention**

Dietary deficiencies of vitamins A and E seem to be ameliorated in certain circumstances and ethoxyquin promotes higher levels of vitamin A storage in the liver. Repletion/deletion experiments show that in both monogastric and ruminant animals, a diet containing an anti-oxidant protects fat soluble vitamins throughout ingestion and metabolism. The important benefit of antioxidants most probably lies in their conservation of essential nutrients and their improved utilization by the animal.

Altogether too often, it is the practice to use levels of vitamin E far above the animals' nutrient requirement and the result is economically unfavourable. It has been shown in diets designed for chicken and turkey breeders that ethoxyquin has a vitamin E sparing effect.

**Prevention of Rancid Oxidation of Fats**

In lipid peroxidation, the unsaturated fatty acids undergo a loss of hydrogen, resulting in the formation of a free radical at the site of unsaturation. If the feed material in which this reaction is taking place does not contain vitamin E or some other effective antioxidant, the free radical is quickly converted to a fatty acid peroxide free radical and finally to a fatty acid hydroperoxide. An antioxidant can block this peroxidation by supplying a hydrogen in the first free radical formed, thereby reconverting it to the original fatty acid.

If the hydroperoxides are allowed to form, they continue to decompose by breaking down into a variety of aldehydes and ketones. Antioxidants prevent oxidative losses of vitamins A and E and pigmenters in stored mixed feeds. Antioxidants stabilize critical oxidation-susceptible nutrients that are naturally present in a fish feed composed of several feedstuffs so that losses are minimal from mixing and storing. If pigmenting substances are used, the anti-oxidants are definitely needed.

The benefits of adequate, consistent use span all facets of fish production which include the processing and handling of feedstuffs, formulation and fish cultural practices.

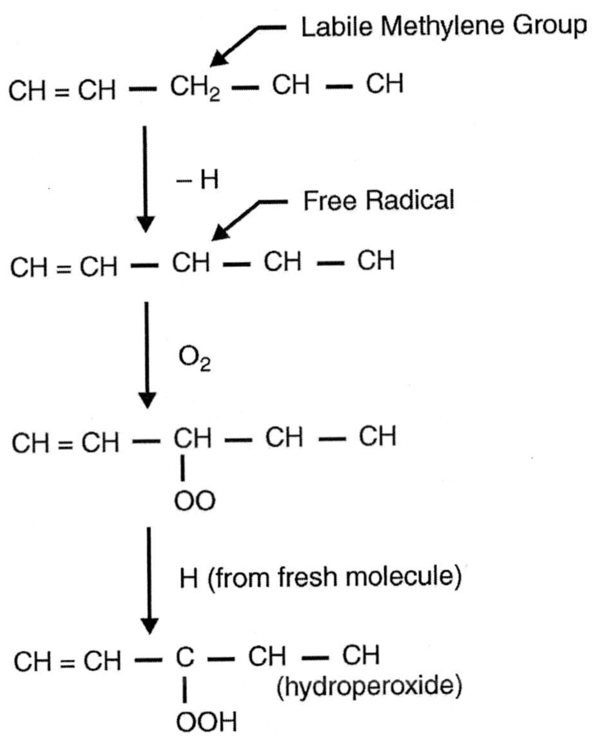


*Fig.2.1: Peroxidative Rancidity*

### Other Effects of Antioxidants in Feed

It was recently found that BHT, which is widely used as a poultry food additive, prevented mortality in chickens exposed to virulent Newcastle disease virus but prevented an antibody response when chickens were exposed to a virulent Newcastle disease virus.

This in vivo effect of BHT in rations containing 100-150 ppm suggests a possible explanation for vaccination failure sometimes encountered with live vaccines and possibly a new direction in the development of antiviral therapy.

Researchers are now trying to define the mechanism of the apparent antiviral action of BHT and extending their attention to other viruses using both BHT and other antioxidants.

### Adventitious Toxins in Feeds

Toxic materials affecting fish feed ingredients are my cotoxins, toxic products in plant materials, bacteria, residues of pesticides, drugs and agricultural chemicals.

### Chemical Contaminants

Work at the Columbia Pesticide Laboratory of the U.S., Fish and Wildlife Service shows that the most common dietary contaminants have been the organo-chlorine pesticides DDT, DDE, dieldrin, endrin and industrial chemicals such as polychlorinated biphenyls (PCB), phthalate esters and hexachlorobenzene (HCB). Most, but not all, residues are due to the presence of contaminated fish oils and/or meal in the finished diets.

### Pesticides and Chlorinated Hydrocarbons

The effects of the chlorinated hydrocarbons have been reasonably well documented in the published literature. Detrimental effects on egg hatchability and survival of young fish are quite striking.

Toxaphene has been shown to interfere with vitamin C metabolism which affects collagen synthesis and ultimately causes skeletal problems.

Dieldrin affects the phenylalanine hydroxylase enzyme which is involved in amino acid metabolism and glutamine synthetase which is involved in protein metabolism.

The inhibition of phenylalanine hydroxylase increased the level of blood phenylketo acids, a condition similar to the genetic metabolic disorder phenylketonuria (PKU) that is associated with mental retardation in humans; inhibition of glutamine synthetase might interfere with ammonia detoxification which would be physiologically deleterious.

A stimulation of thyroid activity has been associated with DDT and its analogues and endrin has been implicated in the inhibited mobilization of liver glycogen.

It would appear that serious attention should be focused on pesticides and other industrial contaminants in dietary feedstuffs and finished fish feeds. The Columbia National Fishery Laboratory has made recommendations that fish oils used at 3-5% of the diet should contain no more than 2 ppm and fish meals no more than 0.1 ppm of organochlorine contaminants, including PCBs.

In addition, the U.S., Food and Drug Administration (FDA) regulations state that the maximum amount of PCBs permitted in animal feed for food producing animals is 0.2 ppm and the amount permitted in animal feed components is 2.0 ppm.

### Seed Dressings

Another serious group of contaminants of the ration that may gain entry anywhere from the ingredient supplier to the fish feeder include the newer seed disinfectants and fungicides and certain drugs and chemicals added to feeds. Most seed treatments include organic mercury compounds which are very chemically reactive and readily absorbed. The compounds are highly toxic and the amounts absorbed in light, accidental, contacts accumulate and build up their effects on fish.

**Cross Contaminants**

Cross contamination occurs when trace amounts of a drug or chemical used as a feed additive are incorporated into a feed which is not supposed to contain the drug. The feed usually affected is the batch immediately following a medicated feed which legally contains the drug in question.

Measurable amounts of the drug-containing feed may remain in the production system and become intermingled with other feed being manufactured. It may occur in one piece of equipment or it may be a combination of residues throughout the entire system. To discover the source, all equipment from the point of addition of the drug to the point of shipping must be checked. Although there are some partial remedies that can be taken in scheduling feed production or with special procedures between feed mixings, experience has shown they are less than adequate answers to the problem. The safest procedures would involve having a completely separate production line or, better yet, a feed manufacturing facility devoted exclusively to fish feed.

**Other Sources of Chemical Contaminants**

Boiler water additives, hydraulic fluids, lubricants (on pellet mill rolls and other processing equipment), fumigants, defoaming agents and coating materials are examples of materials that could become feed additives during feed manufacture. Misuse of these materials could conceivably lead to human loss as well as fish mortality.

## BIOLOGICAL TOXINS

**Salmonella**

A very serious source of contamination usually overlooked is that of rodent contamination of stored ingredients. There are approximately 1200 serotypes of salmonella organisms that inhabit a great variety of warm and cold blooded animals, including fish. Of these, approximately 80 serotypes have been definitely associated with diseases. Animal by-product derivatives are the worst offenders and the primary source of salmonella contamination in mixed feeds. Fish meals represent the next highest source of salmonella contamination. Attention has thus far focused on feeds being the means of perpetuating the salmonella cycle (rat to faeces to by-products to feed to fish). Attention also should be given to the role of soil, water, contaminated feeding equipment and wild birds and terrestial animals as contributing to the presence of salmonella organisms in a given environment.

**Antinutritional Factors**

Adventitious toxins has to include the antinutritional factors in plant proteins. Nearly all sources of plant protein possess associated factors which must be eliminated by special processing techniques to make them of maximum nutritional value. For example, for over fifty years, soybeans have been known to be improved by heat treatment.

**Soybeans**

Factors present in raw soybeans can markedly affect the intestinal tract of animals and influence the digestion and utilization of many nutrients. Inclusion of small amounts of soybean meal will depress growth rate, increase pancreas size, decrease fat absorption and metabolizable energy of the diet of fish. In addition, it has also been found that the feeding of raw soybeans causes the gall-bladder to contract, increases excretion of bile acids, lowers intestinal proteolytic activity and affects methionine metabolism. Raw soybeans also contain protein which cause agglutination of red blood cells in vitro. It appears that the haemaglutinins (lectins) of raw soybeans are responsible for some of the decrease in efficiency of feed utilization. Apparently these lectins are all capable of causing release of intestinal membrane-bound lipases and amylases, causing these digestive enzymes to be eliminated in the faeces, thereby reducing their digestive capabilities. Fortunately, all of these factors can be destroyed or reduced to minimal levels by proper heat treatment.

**Other Vegetable Protein Sources**

Groundnuts contain trypsin inhibitor activity which is not destroyed by heat treatment. This is thought to be due to the fact that the inhibitor activity resides in the tannins which are a part of the groundnut skin. cottonseed contains gossypol and fatty acids with a cyclopropene ring which causes nutritional difficulties. Linseed meal contains an antipyridoxine factor and a cyanogenic glycoside. Rapeseed meal contains glucosides which when hydrolyzed yield a goitrogen. Most all plant protein sources contain phytic acid which can interfere with both mineral and protein availability.

Particular attention must be paid to mineral supplementation when formulating fish diets containing fairly high amounts of plant protein. Even though the temperature which destroys heat labile growth inhibitors is high, minimum protein damage is involved at these high temperatures provided the optimum peak of temperature is reached for a very brief period of time. The brevity of the period at peak temperature is more important than any other factor in obtaining! optimum protein quality.

**Unconventional Feed ingredients for Fish Feed**

The rapid world-wide expansion of aquaculture and livestock production strongly indicates that a crisis will be precipitated in the livestock and aquaculture feed industries in the near future. Food for humans is not included in this consideration because, generally speaking, livestock, fish and humans can all eat the same basic food commodities and, in emergencies or times of scarcity, feedstuffs are eaten first by humans. The consumption of cultured livestock, fish, etc., is linked to human affluence.

For example, per capita meat consumption in the United States before 1941 was about 50 lb; it is now over 150 lb. Similar percentage increases have occurred in Japan and the other industrialized countries of the world. Fish are probably the most efficient converters of feed to flesh, requiring from 2 to 4 lb of basic feedstuffs to produce 1 lb of fish. In contrast to land animals, however, fish are fastidious eaters in that they require higher levels of dietary protein. In addition, the amino acid requirements to promote rapid growth of fish appear to be more rigid than for land animals.

As an extreme example, the protein in the diets of fish such as eels and yellowtail need to be almost entirely of animal origin, while the protein requirements of ruminants can be partially satisfied from non-protein nitrogen sources such as urea and biuret.

## PROBLEMS ASSOCIATED WITH UNCONVENTIONAL FEEDSTUFFS

Faced with the food supply problem for cultured fish, nutritionists have done more work evaluating alternate protein sources in aquaculture diets during the last 7 years than during the previous 50 years. Feedstuffs of vegetable origin are as a whole lower in protein content when compared with those of animal origin. In addition, the presence of high amounts of carbohydrates, fibre and other organic molecules such as glucosides, phytates and cyclopropenes in these sources present the nutritionist with problems that are generally not encountered with sources of animal origin.

Despite these problems, practically all the commercialized feedstuffs are being used to some extent in commercial aquaculture diets. None, however, perform as well as fish meal on a protein equivalent basis. Of the non commercial items, only single cell protein (SCP), krill meal and possibly leaf protein concentrate have a chance of becoming commercial within three to five years. Because SCP are synthetic products and because the biomass of krill, the volume of either could dwarf everything except soyabean meal.

**Formulation Problems**

As previously mentioned, the nutritive requirements of fish are such that they probably offer less flexibility in diet formulation than do those of most land animals. First of all, several species of fish selected for culture are almost pure carnivores, requiring a diet of high protein content. These fish have very poor utilization of carbohydrate as an energy source and some evidence is developing that the inclusion of certain types of carbohydrates in the diet is, in fact, detrimental. Hence, it has been recently reported that soyabean meal extracted with alcohol performed better in rations than unextracted meal. This improvement has been attributed to the removal of low molecular weight carbohydrates by the alcohol.

## FISH FEED FORMULATION

Feed formulation is essentially applied nutrition. A number of terms and expressions are introduced that will be put to practical use as information is presented on the nature and qualities of various feedstuffs and the information presented on the nutrient requirements of fish.

Precise understanding of these terms is essential to their correct application. One must recognize that some of these terms have a built-in error that cannot be escaped. This does not eliminate their usefulness in feed formulation. However, one must appreciate the fact that some are useful approximations of the values and not true values.

The terms that one needs to understand to formulate practical fish diets are: crude protein level; energy level, either expressed as metabolizable energy (ME) or as digestible energy (DE); specific amino acid levels; crude fibre level; and ash level. Since, most complete practical fish diets are supplemented with a vitamin premix at levels in excess of the dietary requirement, this category of nutrients will be ignored temporarily.

The potential problems occur when one fails to recognize that all of the above mentioned terms, except ME and DE, represent the quantity or level of a nutrient in the feed as determined by chemical tests on a specific sample of a feedstuff. These chemical tests generally correlate well enough with biological methods of feed evaluation (growth studies, tissue, levels) to be very useful to feed formulators, but they are still chemical tests that are subject to experimental error during nutrient level determination. For example, the proximate composition of fish meals changes during the spawning season. Generally, the lipid levels increase before spawning and decrease after spawning. This will alter the percent of protein, ash and carbohydrates in fish meal as the seasons change. Similarly, many plant feedstuffs vary in proximate composition with their stage of maturity at harvest, location grown and other environmental conditions, such as the weather.

Tabled values represent an average value that is usually close enough to the actual value to allow accurate feed formulation. However, one must be aware that assumptions are being made in order to recognize the potential sources of error that may exist.

Metabolizable, energy and digestible energy values are obtained biologically and, thus, should accurately represent the true energy value of feedstuffs to fish.

However, ME values may be obtained in different ways (faeces collection methods) and thus may be subject to experimental error.

It has recently been reported that the digestibility of feed by rainbow trout was lower at 7°C than at 11°C or 15°C. At 11°C and 15°C body size (18.6 g, 207.1 g or 585.7 g) did not affect feed digestibility.

The digestibility of carbohydrate and energy was slightly reduced by meal size in rainbow trout fed at 1.6 percent body weight. Protein and lipid digestibility was not reduced by meal size. Obvious differences exist between fish species in nutrient digestibility, especially in the carbohydrate fraction of feed.

Herbivorous and, to a lesser extent, omnivorous fish have longer digestive tracts than do carnivorous fish and are able to obtain more digestible energy from carbohydrates. An awareness of these facts will prevent misuse of ME and DE values. Each feedstuff in any diet formulation should be present for a specific reason; i.e., it is a good energy source, it is rich in a limiting amino acid, etc.

In addition, each feedstuff in a particular diet formulation should be the least costly ingredient available for its particular function in the diet. This leads to another assumption in feed formulation; that is, any nutrient in a particular feedstuff, such as an amino acid, is just as valuable as the same nutrient in any other feedstuff. This allows feed formulators to interchange one feedstuff with another as cost and availability change. Thus, it is assumed that there is no "ideal formulation", but rather an almost infinite number of possible feed formulations that met the nutritional needs of the fish equally well. While this assumption may not be entirely valid and some nutritional judgement must be employed in any feed formulation, it does seem to be valid in most cases. As with the previously mentioned assumption, an awareness of the potential pitfalls involved is necessary for the fish feed formulation so that allowances can be made in diet formulation and problems can be anticipated and avoided.

**Balancing Crude Protein Level**

In most animal diets, protein is the most expensive portion and is usually the first nutrient that is computed in diet formulation. The energy level of the diet is then adjusted to the desired level by addition of high energy supplements) which are less expensive than protein supplements.

The square method is an easy way to determine the proper dietary proportions of high and low protein feedstuffs to add to a feed to meet the dietary requirement of the animal to be fed. For example, suppose rice bran and soybean meal were available as feedstuffs to prepare a diet for carp that was 25 percent crude protein.

A square is constructed and the two feedstuffs are put on the two left corners along with the protein content of each. The desired protein level of the feed is placed in the middle of the square. Next, the protein level of the feed is subtracted from that of the feedstuffs, placing the answer in the opposite corner from the feedstuff. Ignore positive or negative signs.

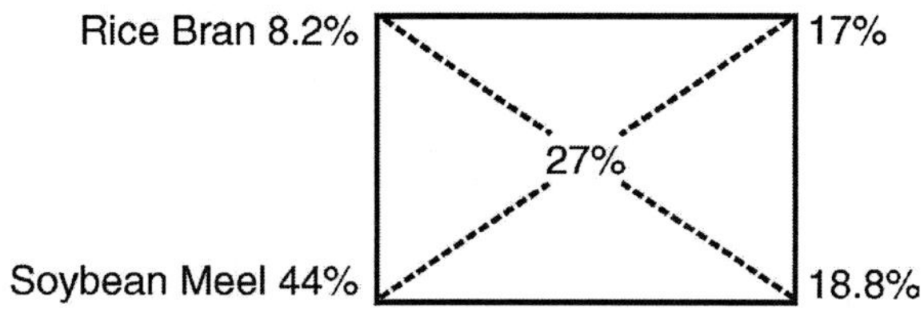


To make the 27 percent crude protein carp feed, we must mix 17/35.8 of rice bran with 18.8/35.8 soybean meal.

Rice Bran 17/35.8 = 47.5%

Soybean meal 18.8/35.8 = 52.5%

So to make 100 kg of this feed we must mix 47.5 kg of rich bran with 52.5 kg of soybean meal.

If more than two feedstuffs are used in a feed, they may be grouped into basal feeds (CP < 20 percent) and protein supplements (CP > 20 percent), averaged within each group and plugged into the square method. For example, suppose shrimp meal and corn were also available for the carp feed. The crude protein levels of the shrimp meal (52.7 percent) and of corn (10.2 percent) are averaged with soybean meal and rice bran, respectively.

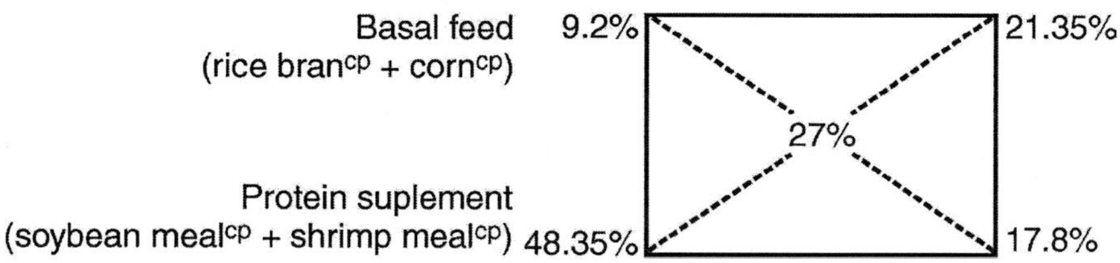


Basal feed = 21.35/39.15 = 54.53%

Protein supplement = 17.8/39.15 = 45.47%

Fish Farming 293

Thus, to make 100 kg of this feed one would mix the following:

| | |
|---|---|
| Rice bran | 27.265 kg |
| Corn | 27.265 kg |
| Soybean meal | 22.735 kg |
| Shrimp meal | 22.735 kg |

The square method is helpful to novice feed formulators because it can get them started in diet formulation without the need to resort to trial and error. The square method can also be used to calculate the proportion of feeds tuffs to mix together to achieve a desired dietary energy level as well as a crude protein level. If one wanted to make a feed containing 2 500 kcal ME/ kg using wheat middlings (1663 kcal ME/kg) and anchovy fish meal (4 371 kcal, ME/kg) a square could be constructed as follows: The square method cannot be used to simultaneously solve for both crude protein level and ME level.

**Steps in feed Formulation**

The first step in diet formulation is balancing the crude protein and energy levels. This can be accomplished by trial and error, by the square method for either crude protein level or energy level and then adjusting, or by solving simultaneous equations. At first, it is helpful to use at least three feeds tuffs during the initial balancing of protein and energy levels: one high in protein and high in ME, one low or intermediate in protein and high in ME and one low or intermediate in both protein and ME. Once practice makes one more proficient at diet formulation any number of feedstuffs can be used. One must remember to reserve room in the formulation for any feed additive, such as a vitamin or mineral pre-mix.

The second step in diet formulation is to check the levels of indispensable amino acids in the formulation to be sure the dietary levels meet the requirements of the animal to be fed. The requirements of fish for indispensable amino acids is expressed as the dietary level (as a percent of the diet) or as a percent of the dietary protein level. To convert an amino acid level from the percent of diet to percent of protein, divide the dietary level of each amino acid by the dietary protein level. It might be of interest to calculate the dietary levels of all of the indispensable amino acids, but it is not practical to do it all of the time. If the levels of arginine, lysine, methionine and tryptophan meet the dietary requirements of the fish to be fed, the levels of the other six indispensable amino acids will most likely be above required levels. When using unconventional protein supplements, the levels of all ten indispensable amino acids should be checked.

If the diet formulation is low in any amino acid, a feedstuff that contains high levels of that amino acid must be added to the diet at the expense of another ingredient. Once the amino acid requirements are met, the dietary protein and energy levels must be rechecked to, see if any substitution of ingredients has imbalanced the formulation.

A diet mixing sheet should be constructed to standardize diet formulation. The amino acids listed are for illustration purposes only and may be changed to suit different circumstances. In practical feed formulation, pellet quality and acceptability must be considered in addition to nutrient levels and cost. These considerations will vary from species to species and with the type of pellet being made and are dealt with in other sections of this manual.

**Best-Buy Techniques**

The price of the feedstuffs used in diet formulations must be considered to formulate a cost-efficient diet. Feedstuffs can be compared with one another on the basis cost per unit of protein, energy, or amino acid. For example, suppose one has wheat middlings and wheat millrun available for a fish diet, which feedstuff would be the least expensive source of energy?

Wheat millrun costs US $ 0.0858/kg and contains about 1200 kcal ME/kg.

$$\text{Cost/kcal} = \frac{.08758}{1200} = \text{US \$ 0.0000/15/kcal.}$$

Wheat middlings cost US $ 01883/kg and contain 1663 kcal ME/kg.

$$\text{Cost/kcal} = \frac{0.1883}{1663} = \text{US \$ 0.0001132/kcal.}$$

Thus, the wheat millrun which has a lower ME value for fish is the better buy because it costs less per kcal.

To compare oat groats and wheat middlings on a cost per unit ME basis one would do the following:

Wheat middlings = US$ 0.0001132/kcal and

Oat groats cost US $ 0.2652/kg and contain about 2450 kcal ME/kg.

$$\text{Cost/kcal} = \frac{0.2652}{2450} = \text{US \$ } 0.001082/\text{kcal.}$$

Oats groats, although costing more than wheat middlings, constitute a better buy on an energy basis.

The cost of protein is often the greatest part of the cost of a fish diet. Therefore, substantial savings can be made by using best-buy techniques to determinate least expensive protein supplement. To compare anchovy meal and herring meal, the following calculations are made:

Anchovy meal costs US $ 0.5357/kg and contains 70.9 percent protein.

$$\text{Cost per kg protein} = \frac{0.5357}{0.709} = \text{US \$ } 0.7556/\text{kg protein.}$$

Herring meal costs US $ 0.4709/kg and contains 76.7 percent protein.

$$\text{Cost per kg protein} = \frac{0.4709}{0.767} = \text{US \$ } 0.61395/\text{kg protein.}$$

On the basis of cost per unit protein, herring meal is less expensive as a dietary ingredient than is anchovy meal.

To compare feedstuffs on the basis of cost per unit of an amino acid, one can calculate the best buy in the same way as before. For example, sesame oil cake which has twice as much methionine content as does groundnut cake on a per unit protein basis would be a more attractive buy at comparable prices. These kinds of comparisons are only valid if the nutrient in one feedstuff is as valuable or available to the animal as the same nutrient in another feed. Such comparisons should be made whenever prices change.

❒

# 3

# Animal Husbandry

## UNDERSTANDING THE ANIMAL HUSBANDRY

The branch of science, which deals with the study of various breeds of domesticated animals and their management for obtaining better products and services from them is known as *Animal Husbandry.* The term husbandry derives from the word "husband" which means 'one who takes care'. When it incorporates the study of proper utilisation of economically important domestic animals, it is called *Livestock Management.*

### Different Categories of Animals

- **Wild :** Those that breed better where they are free than they do when they are captivated. They have no common use for humans. Example Lion, Tiger, Rhinoceres, Deer etc.
- **Tamed :** Those, which are caught from the wild and trained to be useful to humans in some way. Elephant, Chimpanzee, Gorilla, Yak etc.
- **Domesticated :** Those that are of use at home and are easily bred and looked after by humans. Common domesticated animals are dog, horse, cow, sheep, buffalo, fowl etc.

### Importance of Domestic Animals

*On the basis of utility, domestic animals are categorised into the following functional groups:*

- Milk giving animals:
  - Cattle,
  - Buffalo,
  - Goat,
  - Sheep etc.

- Draught (used for load bearing) animals:
  - Bullock,
  - Horse,
  - Donkey,
  - Mule,
  - Camel,
  - Elephant,
  - Yak etc.
- Fibre, hide and skin yielding:
  - Sheep,
  - Goat,
  - Cattle,
  - Buffalo,
  - Camel etc.
- Meat and egg yielding animals:
  - Fowl (hen) and duck,
  - Goat,
  - Buffalo,
  - Pig etc.

## SOCIAL ENVIRONMENT OF HUSBANDRY

Dairy cattle are social animals that exist within a herd structure and follow a leader. Cows exhibit wide differences in temperament, and their behaviour is determined by inheritance, physiology, prior experience, and training. Cattle under duress may bellow, butt, or kick; however, cows are normally quiet and thrive on gentle treatment by handlers. Cows learn to discriminate among people and react positively to pleasant handling.

Aversive handling leads to more incidents during handling and transport for calves than positive handling. Similarly, heifers and cows exposed to aversive handling took longer to traverse and more force to move than those handled more gently. Although the presence of an aversive handler reduced kicking during udder preparation, residual milk was 70 per cent greater than for the control milkings.

Cows have higher milk yields if handlers touch, talk to, and interact with them frequently. Cows should have visual contact with one another and with animal care personnel. Handling procedures are more stressful for isolated cattle; therefore, attempts should be made to have several cows together during medical treatment, artificial insemination, or when cows are being moved from one group to another.

This was verified by increased heart rate, hypothalamic-pituitaryadrenocortical axis activity, and vocalizations. Pain sensitivity is reduced during isolation, suggesting a stress-induced analgesia. Care should be taken to minimize the negative impact of moving cows to new groups by avoiding frequent regrouping and by always moving more than one animal at a time to a new group. The use of a trainer cow can have a positive impact on adjustment to feedlot environments where many heifers are raised. However, dairy calves had few indicators that repeated regrouping and relocations stressed calves. Aggression was rare and the calves seemed to habituate to the repeated mixing.

Calves from larger groups after weaning had fewer incidences of displacement of other calves from the feed barrier, were more active, and had more positive interactions with familiar calves. Calves, like cows, prefer familiar calves to unfamiliar calves during stressful situations, and a familiar companion calf improved cows' reaction to separation.

Social status can affect health issues such as lameness. Low-ranking cows spent more time standing and standing half in cubicles than did middleand high-ranking cows. Standing half in cubicles correlated positively with the number of soft tissue lesions related to lameness. Dairy cattle have traditionally been kept in groups of 40 to 100 cows, although specific research protocols may require smaller or larger group sizes.

Variation in group size—small, medium and large—does not cause a problem *per se*. Expansion to a larger herd size, however, can affect management decisions because overcrowding with an insufficient number of headlocks or inadequate manger space per cow, irregular or infrequent feeding, and excessive walking distance to and from the milking parlor have a greater impact on behaviour and well-being than does group size. Cattle of all ages are gregarious.

Socially isolated cattle show clear signs of stress: increased heart rate, vocalization, defecation/urination, and cortisol levels. In addition, there are benefits of housing cattle together. For example, pairs of calves are more likely to play than isolated calves, a behaviour thought to be associated with positive welfare. Young calves should be kept in groups from 2 to 7 animals in order for animals to benefit from social contact, but larger groupings are associated with health problems and morbidity.

Management of resources is an important part of reducing aggression and other problems, such as cross sucking, in groups of animals. Adult dairy cattle should have 1 freestall/cow to reduce competition. Similarly, dairy cattle with more space at the feedbunk engage in fewer aggressive interactions and the reduction of competitive behaviour associated with more feeder space is particularly marked in post-and-rail feeder design.

Cross sucking in calves is an undesirable behaviour performed in groups. Calves are typically fed 10 per cent body weight during the milk-fed period and there is clear evidence that this feeding level is insufficient. A combination of slower milk flow, hay feeding, and access to a nonnutritive artificial teat are also recommended to reduce cross sucking. Providing additional objects for oral manipulation, such as tires, has also been shown to reduce other problems such as stereotypic tongue rolling in calves.

**Restraint and Handling**

Vaccination schedules that are appropriate for the location and dynamics of the individual herd should be established with the advice of the attending veterinarian. Certain dairy cattle behaviours put at risk the health and wellbeing of herdmates as well as the humans handling the cattle. These behaviours can be reduced or modified by implementing principles of low-stress handling and restraint that include appropriate movement of people, well-designed facilities, optimal lighting, nonslip flooring, and smooth, quiet restraint devices.

Stanchions, head gates, and squeeze chutes can be modified to function optimally, but acclimation and positive reinforcement by individuals trained in low-stress handling can minimize the need for additional restraint by halters, rope, tail hold, and nose tongs. Hobbles and casting ropes should be used selectively and only when necessary. Chemical sedation is always preferable to excessive use of force or application of electrical prods. Information about calving management is given by Albright and Grandin.

First-calf heifers should be bred to calving-ease bulls and be of appropriate stature and body condition to minimize the chances of dystocia or the need for calving assistance. Optimal calving conditions in a clean, quiet environment with employees appropriately trained to follow calving protocols will result in more live calves and fewer calving injuries and illness.

Calving injuries should be assessed immediately so that appropriate footing is provided and proper treatment is implemented. Cows that are unable to stand should be moved to a soft-bedded pack and examined by a veterinarian within 2 to 4 h of calving. Calves require special handling and care from the time they are born. Colostrum should be fed or ingested within the first 5 h after birth always before milk is fed. Between 1.89 L and 3.79 L of colostrum are necessary to impart adequate immunity to the calf.

In the absence of colostrum, a colostrum replacement product that delivers at least 125 g of immunoglobulin should be given by bottle, bucket, or tube feeder. Colostrum is rich in nutrients and provides the calf with vital immunoglobulins and other important immune factors. Clean navels can be dipped in a dilute chlorhexidine solution as soon as possible after birth. Good nutrition as supplied by a combination of milk starter grain, and fresh water along with proper handling and close monitoring starts a calf on its way towards a healthy life.

**Standard Agricultural Practices**

All animals should be individually identified. Heifer calves should have supernumerary teats removed at an early age. Removal may be performed in the first 3 mo of life with a scalpel or sharp scissors. Older calves and heifers close to calving that have supernumerary teats should be examined by a qualified person. The removal of extra teats at this advanced age is necessary if they will later disrupt the milking process or be at risk of becoming infected. If so, they can be removed with proper restraint and use of appropriate anesthesia by a qualified and trained person. Milking procedures should follow National Mastitis Council guidelines. Routine breeding programmes should include housing and handling facilities that allow for effective implementation of artificial insemination programmes. Castration may be performed on male calves.

**Foot Care**

Lameness in dairy cattle is a major source of economic loss to the farmer and a serious cause of pain and discomfort to the cow. It is perhaps the most important condition affecting the welfare of cows on dairy farms. Lame cows suffer lowered milk production and reduced fertility, and are culled at 2 to 4 times the rate of healthy control cows.

*The pain associated with lameness results in changes in the animal's gait that include:*

- Arching of the back;
- Shortening of the stride length on the affected limb;
- Sinking of the dew claws on the unaffected contralateral limb;
- Head bob in a vertical plane;
- Reduction in walking speed, and frequent stops; and
- Swinging the affected limb in or out depending on the location of the painful lesion.

These alterations can be used to provide a locomotion score for each animal, and the most commonly used system in North America utilizes a 5-point system of scoring where 1 is nonlame and 5 is severely lame. Herd workers should be taught how to score locomotion so that they can identify cows with scores >2 for treatment by an attending veterinarian or hoof-trimmer. Around 85 per cent of lameness in dairy cattle is associated with lesions in the rear feet, particularly the outer claw, because of the overgrowth of horn resulting from the redistribution of weight as the cow walks on hard concrete surfaces, with a large udder occupying the space between her rear legs. This overgrowth of the outer claw may be removed and the weight transferred equally between the inner and outer claw by regular hoof-trimming.

Trimming to restore a normal toe length along the dorsal hoof wall of around 75 mm for mature Holstein cattle, combined with balancing weight between the inner and outer claw, lasts around 4 mo on average. Therefore, it is recommended that cattle be trimmed at 6-mo intervals, typically at the time of dry off and in mid-lactation around 90 to 150 d in milk. Some cows with pre-existing hoof disease may require attention more frequently.

*Hoof lesions causing lameness may be broadly classified into 2 groups:*

1. Infectious and
2. Claw horn.

Infectious lesions include digital dermatitis, interdigital phlegmon, and heel horn erosion. These lesions are associated with poor feet and leg hygiene and are a particular problem in free-stall environments, where the cow is exposed to alleyways contaminated with wet manure when she is not occupying a stall. Putative agents such as several species of *Treponema* and *Fusobacterium necrophorum* are involved in the pathogenesis of these conditions, but hydropic maceration of the skin of the interdigital space appears to be a prerequisite for the development of disease.

Infectious causes of lameness are controlled by improving leg hygiene by removing manure from the walkways and by the use of a topical antibacterial administered either directly to the lesion by a hand-held spray or via a footbath. The frequency of foot bathing is dependent on the degree of manure contamination of the cows, and a variety of chemicals are available for use, such as copper sulfate, zinc sulfate, and formalin.

Use of any of these chemicals should be done under veterinary direction. Claw horn lesions include sole hemorrhage, sole ulcer, toe and heel ulcer, and white line disease. These are clinical signs on the surface of the claw that represent the result of several possible causative pathways. Sinking of the third phalanx within the claw horn capsule, due to a breakdown in the connective tissue of the suspensory apparatus, may be caused by hormonal changes at calving time and nutritional events such as subacute ruminal acidosis. Sinking of the third phalanx compresses the corium below, interrupting the flow of blood and nutrients to the cells responsible for horn growth. As a result, a defect develops that becomes apparent several months later as the sole horn continues to grow.

Excessive removal of sole horn, either through poor hoof trimming or due to excessive wear from walking long distances on rough concrete will also contribute to lesion development. Flooring surfaces should be nonslip, avoid excessive trauma to the claw surface and be dry. Concrete should be grooved to improve traction; a pattern that utilizes parallel grooves 3/4 inch wide and deep, spaced 3 inches on center appears to provide a good compromise between sufficient traction to reduce injury while limiting the amount of wear.

For transfer lanes between milking centers and the living accommodation, a 1-m wide strip of rubber flooring has been used successfully to reduce trauma and wear, and rubber flooring has been used in parlor holding areas to provide cushion for cows that have to stand for long periods of time. The severity of the claw horn lesions that develop is influenced by the time spent standing each day, which results in increased loading of the claw and increased compression of the tissues below the third phalanx.

*Time spent standing may be increased by:*

- Poor stall designs that fail to provide surface cushion, room to lunge, and sufficient resting area;
- Overstocking: Providing fewer usable stalls than there are cows in a pen;
- Excessively prolonged milking times;
- Time spent locked up away from the stalls for management tasks; and
- Heat Stress: Cows may stand more in an attempt to cool off.

In addition, lame cows struggle to use stalls with hard surfaces because the act of rising and lying down becomes more challenging due to foot pain. These cows stand more in the stall and fail to gain adequate rest for lesion healing. For this reason, deep sand-bedded stalls provide the gold standard in cow comfort. If sand stalls are unavailable, lame cows should be treated and returned to a bedded pack area for rest and recuperation until normal ambulation returns.

Failure to identify a claw horn lesion early in its course may result in deep digital sepsis. This is a complication caused by infection of the deeper structures of the claw, including the distal interphalangeal joint and tendon sheaths. Such animals are usually severely lame and require euthanasia or extensive surgery. Seeking veterinary assistance is recommended for individual cows that show signs of lameness or if a significant lameness issue exists for the herd.

**Disbudding and Dehorning**

A review of horn anatomy and growth and dehorning and disbudding of cattle was provided by the AVMA. The AVMA also provides guidance on use of sedation, anesthesia, and analgesia and alternatives to horn removal. The AVMA policy on dehorning/ disbudding should be followed. Calves should be observed closely for 1 to 2 h following dehorning. No food or water should be offered until the sedation is completely worn off or reversed. Persistence of a depressed attitude, head-pressing, or an abnormal head tilt for more than 2 h should result in a complete examination.

**Tail Docking**

The bovine tail has several physiological and behavioural functions including dissipation of heat, and facilitation of visual communication among cattle and with human caretakers; the tail often serves as a primary mechanism of fly control. Removal of the lower portion of a cow's tail is commonly referred to as "tail docking" and the use of tail docking as a routine dairy farm management tool apparently originated in New Zealand.

New Zealand farmers responding to a 1999 survey believed removal of tails resulted in faster milking, reduced risks to the operator, and reduced rates of mastitis. Similar unsubstantiated claims have been made for the US dairy industry. Several European countries, some Australian states, and California have prohibited tail docking. Both the Canadian and American veterinary medical associations have policy statements that oppose the practice of tail docking for routine management of dairy cattle. The policy statement of the American Association of Bovine Practitioners (AABP) indicates that scientific evidence to support tail docking is lacking and recommends that "if it is deemed necessary for proper care and management of production animals in certain conditions, veterinarians should counsel clients on proper procedures, benefits, and risks.

Scientific studies have been performed to evaluate both the potentially negative and positive aspects of tail docking. Important welfare issues that have been evaluated have included pain caused by tail docking, changes in fly avoidance behaviour, immune responses, and changes in levels of circulating plasma cortisol. Experiments that have been performed on both calves and preparturient heifers have consistently concluded that the process of tail docking does not induce significant acute or chronic changes in plasma cortisol or other selected physiological measures. Modest changes in general behaviour of calves that have been docked using rubber rings or cautery irons have been reported but these changes have not been associated with significant differences in normal feeding, ruminating, or grooming behaviours. Likewise, few significant differences in general behaviour of docked preparturient heifers have been noted.

However, greater changes have been observed in tail surface temperatures of docked heifers compared with heifers with intact tails, indicating that heifers may experience chronic pain similar to the phantom pain reported by human amputees. Research has demonstrated that tail-docked heifers flick their tails more often and are forced to use alternative behaviours such as rear leg stomps, feed tossing, and head turning to try to rid themselves of flies. More flies settle on tail-docked cows than on intact cows, and the proportion of flies settling on the rear of the cow increases as tail length decreases. In another study, there were no significant differences in the numbers of stable flies found on the front legs of cows but docked cows had nearly twice as many flies on their rear legs compared with those with intact tails.

Fly avoidance behaviours were increased in the docked animals, whereas tail swinging was increased in the control animals. Foot stamping was identified only in docked animals and, overall, fly numbers and fly avoidance behaviours were increased in docked animals. Researchers have been unable to identify improvements in udder health or udder cleanliness for animals in commercial herds that have docked tails. In one study, the effect of tail docking on cow cleanliness and somatic cell counts (SCC) was evaluated over an 8-wk period for lactating cows that were housed in a free-stall facility. Standardized cleanliness scores obtained from the rump, midline of the back, or rear udder were not significantly different between docked and intact animals nor was there any significant difference in SCC or the number of teats containing obvious debris. In another study, SCC, occurrence of intramammary infections (IMI), and udder and leg hygiene scores were evaluated over an 8-mo period for lactating dairy cows that had been blocked by farm and randomly allocated to tail-docked or control groups.

No significant differences were found in SCC or udder and leg hygiene scores. The prevalence of contagious, environmental, and minor pathogens was not significantly different between cows with docked or intact tails. Although current studies do not indicate that the process of tail docking modifies physiological indicators of stress, several studies have documented changes in fly avoidance behaviour and recent research has suggested that docked tails have enhanced sensitivity to heat.

No benefits to cattle welfare have been associated with tail docking. The routine use of tail docking in research or teaching herds should be discouraged, and alternatives to tail docking are recommended when appropriate. Any use of tail docking, other than for medical reasons, should be reviewed and approved by the IACUC.

## EGG YIELDING ANIMALS

This category consists of egg producing animals whose eggs are used as food by mankind to provide proteins. Poultry farming is defined as a term for rearing and keeping of birds such as fowl, duck and hen for egg and meat. Poultry farming has become popular because it is comparatively easy to start and maintain. It gives quick return within one to six month of investments, is easily manageable and requires less space and labour. Poultry birds and their eggs are a rich source of nutrients. Figure gives a comparative account of the composition of fowl meat and that of eggs.

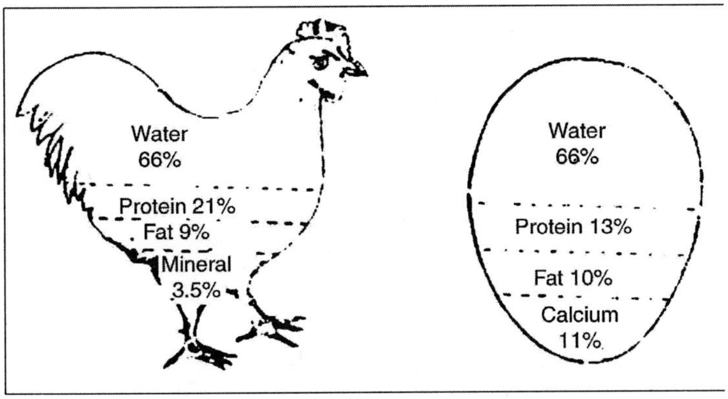


*Fig.3.1: Composition of Chicken and Egg*

**Common Breeds of Poultry Birds**

Indian poultry breeds provide good quality meat but produces small sized eggs. They have natural immunity against common diseases as compared to exotic varieties bred abroad which require greater protection and immunisation.

*The chicken is commonly classified on the basis of its origin:*

- American,
- Asiatic,
- Mediterranean and
- English
- Plymouth Rock, Rhode Island Red, New Hampshire-American
- Brahma, Cochin, Langshan-Asiatic
- Leg horn, Minoxa-Mediterranean
- Cornish, Australorp-English

**Indigenous Breeds**

- Aseel: Rajasthan, Andhra Pradesh, Uttar Pradesh
- Busra: Gujarat and Maharastra
- Chittagong: Eastern India
- Karaknath: Madhya Pradesh

**Indian Breeds**

The Indian breeds of hen include Aseel, Chittagaog, Ghagus and Basra. Their egg laying capacity is around 200 eggs per year.

### Exotic Breeds

These breeds are important from other countries and include White leghorn, Minorca, Rhode Island red. These birds have high egg laying capacity but carry less flesh as compared to Indian birds.

### Upgraded Variety

Some improved varieties have been developed in India by hybridisation such as B 77, ILS 82 etc., They grow fast and also have as high an egg laying capacity as the exotic varieties and are better suited to the Indian climate.

### Poultry Feed

Depending upon the requirement of meat or egg production, poultry feed mainly consists of maize, rice, wheat bran, ground nut cake, fish meal, lime stones, bone meal, common salt, vitamins and minerals.

## DRAUGHT ANIMALS

Draught animals are animals need for carrying load. From time immemorial a number of animal species have been used for special purposes by humans, utilising their mechanical strength, endurance and speed. These include horse for riding and swift running; elephant for riding, strength and heavy load lifting, camel for riding in sandy desert and ability to survive without water for long duration, donkey and mule (a hybrid of male donkey and female horse) for carrying load. Most of the draught animals are herbivorous and survive on leaves of trees, shrubs and bushes. While raising them, they are also fed on grains, beans, cottonseeds, maize and bran besides dry/green fodder. In Rajasthan, camel is used for yielding milk also.

### Horse

The horse has fast movement, great stamina and endurance. Its body is suited for ride, load pulling, mountain climbing and forest travelling. So the horse is an important draught or work animal. They learn fast and can be maintained easily in various climatic conditions. Due to their ability to move swiftly in rough areas, they are still useful in hills and in the deserts. Common Indian breeds and their distribution are as follows-

| Breed | Region |
|---|---|
| Kathiawari or kaunchi | Rajasthan and Gujarat |
| Marwari or malvi | Rajasthan |
| Bhutia | Tarai belt of Himalayan region (Punjab-Bhutan) |
| Manipuri Pony | Eastern hill region |
| Sipti Pony | Himachal Pradesh |

## FIBRE, HIDE AND SKIN YIELDING ANIMALS

Besides providing meat, milk and transport, livestock provide many commercially useful products such as fibre, skin and hide. Generally sheep and goat provide fibres for making of products like wollen strings, ropes, carpets, clothing and brushes etc.

## ANIMAL PROCUREMENT

When an institution acquires new animals, attention must be paid to applicable international, federal, and state regulations and institutional procedures, particularly those dealing with transportation and animal health. All animals must be obtained and transported legally. The attending veterinarian, in conjunction with the principal scientist, should formulate written procedures to assess the health status of a herd or flock obtained from a vendor before acquiring animals.

The institution should develop a mechanism and process of control for animal acquisition that ensures coordination of resources that will preclude the arrival of animals in advance of preparation of adequate housing and appropriate veterinary quarantine procedures. Quality control for vendors and knowledge of the history of purchased animals is part of an adequate institutional veterinary care programme.

Animals of unknown origin or from stockyards should only be used if necessary; such animals may pose significant unknown health risks compared with animals of known origin and therefore should be handled appropriately. Newly acquired animals should undergo a quarantine and acclimation period, including preventive and clinical treatments as appropriate for their health status.

### Acclimation and Stabilization

Newly arrived animals require a period of acclimation. Acclimation refers to a stabilization period, before animal use, which permits physiological and behavioural adaptation to the new environment. The attending veterinarian should establish general acclimation guidelines for each species. Any modifications to the general programme should be discussed with the attending veterinarian before animals are shipped. In some cases, animals may require an extended acclimation period because of their history or health status. On the other hand, some studies, such as comparisons of metaphylactic treatments for shipping fever, need to begin as soon as animals arrive. Such exemptions from the acclimation period must be scientifically justified and approved by the Institutional Animal Care and Use Committee (IACUC).

### Quarantine

Quarantine is the separation of newly received animals from those already in the facility or on the premises until the health of the new animals has been evaluated and found to be acceptable. The attending veterinarian should ensure that quarantine facilities or locations are appropriate and that quarantine procedures are consistent with current veterinary practices and applicable regulations. The quarantine period should be long enough to observe signs of infectious disease or obtain diagnostic evidence of infection status.

Quarantine and testing of animals before introduction is especially important for herds or flocks that have attained specific-pathogen-free status, but these additions should be discouraged. If the health history of newly received animals is unknown, the quarantine programme should be more comprehensive and sufficiently long to allow expression or detection of diseases present in the early incubation stage. Exceptions to quarantine practices should be approved by the attending veterinarian in advance of shipment of the animals.

The attending veterinarian, or skilled personnel under the direction of the attending veterinarian, should perform an initial examination and subsequent daily observations for newly arrived animals. Animals should be observed in quarantine until they are cleared for introduction into a herd or facility. During the quarantine period, animals should be vaccinated and treated for diseases and parasites as appropriate to protect their health and maintain the health of animals in the home facility. In addition to having adequate quarantine procedures, research facilities and animal use protocols should be designed to minimize the risk of introducing or transmitting disease agents.

## VENTILATION (ENVIRONMENTAL CONTROL) OF LIVESTOCK BARNS

Wide range of air temperatures if proper consideration is given to their surroundings. In cold weather, young calves and older cattle alike will be able to adapt to very low temperatures if a deep and dry litter is provided along with abundant fresh air without excessive draughts and high humidity. In hot weather, shade and fresh air help to avoid excessive temperatures that lead to heat stress. Rapidly moving fresh air (1-3 m/s) over the body of the animal increases the rate of convective heat transfer to the ambient air.

### Ventilation

Ventilation-directly and indirectly-impacts many aspects of animal health. Good ventilation assures that animals breathe quality air, important to respiratory health. Good ventilation helps to keep bedding dry, a factor in favour of good animal health. Good ventilation along alleys helps to keep walking surfaces dry, a condition that contributes to healthy feet.

Good ventilation may lead to greater productivity; e.g., maintaining air movement in the area of the feed manger makes the cattle more comfortable, especially important during hot weather as an aid to maintaining dry matter intake. A comfortable, well-ventilated stall area encourages animals to lie down, an important contribution to many aspects of animal health.

The ventilation process brings outside air into the barn where it collects moisture, heat and other contaminants. Air is then exhausted to the outside. Ventilation is an air exchange process-contaminated air inside the barn is exchanged for fresh outside air. To determine ventilation rates, we focus on the moisture content of the air, measured by relative humidity. But moisture is only one aspect. Ventilation removes other undesirable contaminants as well.

### Air Quality

Animal health and disease are influenced by air quality. Air quality, in turn, is related to ventilation and its impact on reducing concentrations of contaminants in the air. Empirical observations and field trials suggest that the aerosol spread of pathogens between animals and the influence of air pollutants on pulmonary defence mechanisms are important, especially to respiratory health. Excess moisture, gases and other contaminants in the air are considered to be problematic as well.

The term air quality itself is not easily defined. With respect to animal spaces, good air quality generally implies that the characteristics of ambient air bear no harmful effects on the animals in the space. Ambient air is a mixture of clean, dry air (a mixture of gases, chiefly nitrogen and oxygen) and varying amounts of water vapour. At high concentrations, even moisture in the air in an animal space is considered to be a problem and is then considered an air contaminant. Other contaminants may include pathogens, harmful gases, dust and undesirable odours. The contaminant itself does not give rise to concern.

Rather, it is the concentration of a contaminant above some predetermined level that causes concern and is considered when assessing air quality. In hot weather, ventilation improves the environment for animals by removing heat and other contaminants from the animal space. Higher air velocities (1-3 m/s) over the body of the animal increase the rate of convective heat transfer from the animal's body to the ambient air.

### The Dilution Effect of Ventilation

Ventilation is truly a process of dilution. Air moved through a barn serves to dilute the inside air and, very importantly, to dilute all of its components. Dilution reduces concentrations of moisture and heat. Dilution reduces concentrations of airborne disease organisms, harmful gases and dust, and undesirable odours as well. Reducing ventilation below recommended levelsusually in a misguided effort to warm the barn using animal heat-results in less moisture being removed.

If substantial quantities of heat are added to the air, relative humidity may remain in an acceptable range, as measured, and air quality may be deemed to be satisfactory. But even though excess moisture may not be apparent, the reduced dilution does indeed result in increased concentrations of airborne disease organisms, harmful gases and dust, and undesirable odours. If these increases are ignored, animal health problems are inevitable. Air quality is more than just measuring relative humidity. Through ventilation the air inside the barn is continually diluted, assuring that the air available to the animal has low concentrations of all contaminants that threaten the animal's health.

### Minimum Continuous Winter Ventilation

A minimum rate of ventilation is required in animal housing in the winter regardless of outside temperature, whether the barn is designed to be a warm barn or a cold barn. In addition, the minimum ventilation should be continuous. Continuous dilution of inside air acts to maintain concentrations of contaminants in the air at minimal levels. The minimum rate depends on outside weather design conditions, number and type of animals in the barn, age and size of animals, and whether the barn is intended to be cold or warm.

Deciding between warm and cold housing is critical to the design and subsequent management of the ventilation system. Understanding the differences between the two types of environments is especially important as related to the need for maintaining the minimum continuous ventilation for winter in either situation that is in the best interest of animal comfort and health. Cold housing with natural ventilation is preferred for beef animals. Natural ventilation depends upon thermal and wind forces to provide air exchange.

## VENTILATION DESIGN AND OPERATION FOR CATTLE BARNS

### Uninsolated Barns with Natural Vent

In a cold barn, indoor temperatures are allowed to fluctuate with outdoor temperatures. In winter, ventilation must be sufficient to maintain indoor temperatures within 3-5°C of outdoor temperatures. During summer, ventilation should be sufficient to maintain indoor temperature at or slightly below outdoor temperature. Moisture naturally present causes the barn itself to act as an evaporative cooler.

*A cold barn with natural ventilation has these general characteristics:*

- No insulation,
- Open ridge and eaves, and
- Sidewalls and endwalls that open.

Providing an open ridge and open eaves has long been recognized as a mean of creating a stack effect to cause air exchange, especially for controlling moisture in winter. Provide a ridge opening of 5 cm per 3 m of barn width and equivalent open area divided between the two eaves. Raised ridge caps are to be avoided. Spaced roof sheeting (gap between sheets 2cm) can also be effectively used to provide a uniform air escape pathway over the complete roof structure.

However, care must be taken with this form of construction in areas where snow may cause blockage of the ventilation openings. Summer ventilation mainly depends on the wind. Factors affecting ventilation rates due to wind include area of building openings, local obstructions (hills, vegetation, nearby buildings) and wind speed and direction. To obtain maximum air exchange rates due to wind forces, maximize inlet and outlet openings and site buildings for maximum exposure to existing winds. Orienting buildings perpendicular to prevailing warm weather wind is preferred.

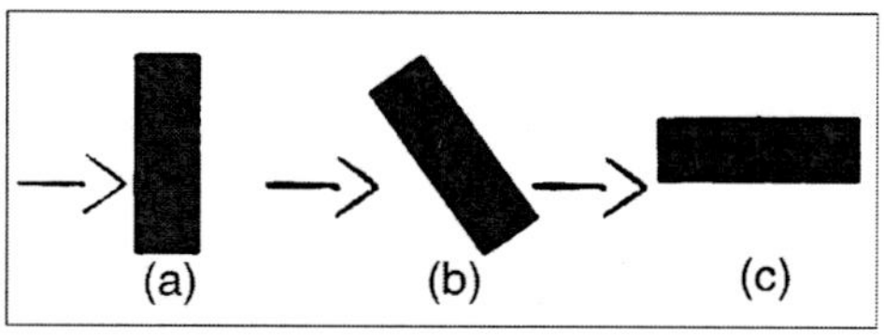


*Fig.3.2: Orientation of a Building According to Wind Direction (Perpendicular to the Wind, at an Angle to the Wind, Parallel with the Wind)*

Although, if sidewalls and endwalls are completely open and the barn is not long, say less than 30 m, orientation will be less critical. If a wind is blowing, a combination of thermal and wind forces will provide air exchange.

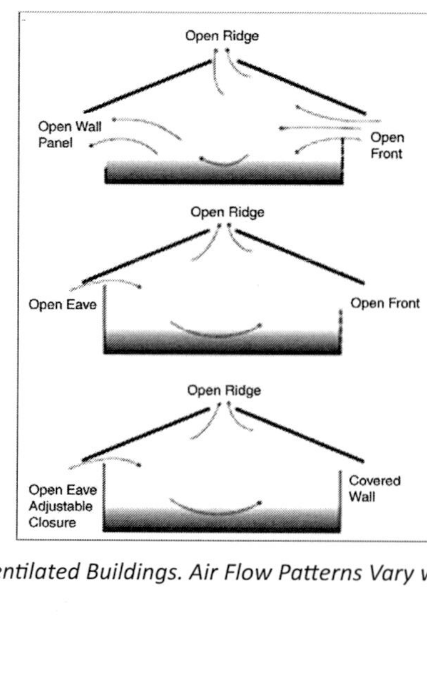


*Fig.3.3: Airflow in Naturally Ventilated Buildings. Air Flow Patterns Vary with Wind Direction and Velocity*

Fresh air enters through eave and sidewall openings, Figure. Air containing heat, moisture and other contaminants exists through the open ridge and downwind sidewall openings. Even with sidewalls closed on calm days, some air exchange occurs as a result of the chimney effect. Various materials and methods may be used to cover sidewalls for colder weather.

Automatic control or even frequent manual adjustment of air inlets is unnecessary. Cattle can tolerate usual diurnal fluctuations in environment and even fluctuations during the season, especially in summer. The simpliest and cheapest method of covering sidewalls uses a fabric covering over the full sidewall. For summer, the fabric is manually rolled up as a rug and tied.

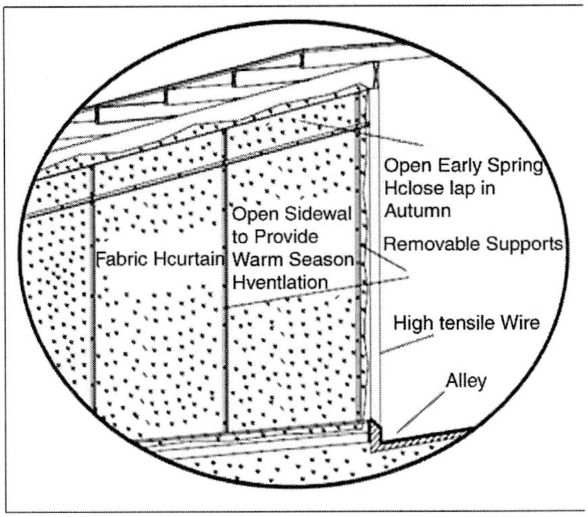


*Fig.3.4: Full-wall Ventilation Provided by Removing Fabric Curtain. Nailing Strips are Removed and Curtain is Rolled to the Horizontal Member Near the Top of the Wall and Tied in Place during Warm Weather*

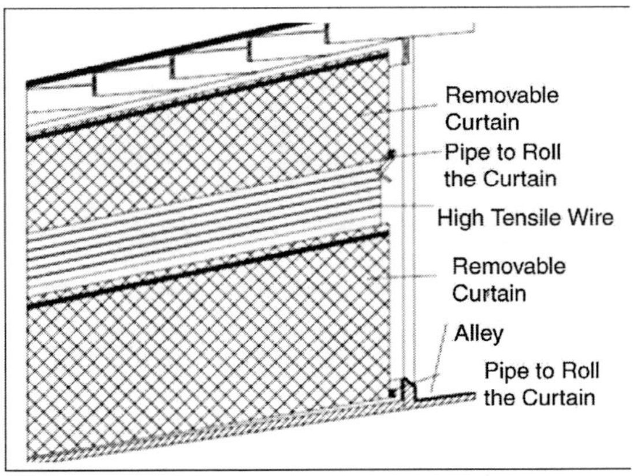


*Fig.3.5: Full-wall Ventilation with Curtains on the Upper Half and Lower Half of the Wall Operated Separately. Curtain Operation is Accomplished with a Small-diameter Metal Pipe Installed in the Hem at the Bottom Edge of the Curtain and a Simple Crank at the End for Turning the Pipe.*

To close the sidewall, ties are released and the hanging curtain is then fastened in place using a vertical nailing strip at each post and horizontal nailing strips all along the bottom. A variation on fabric covering is shown in *Figure.*

Fabric curtains to cover the top half and the bottom half of the sidewall are operated independently. A curtain is rolled up by fitting a crank to the small-diameter metal pipe installed in the hem at the bottom edge of each curtain. In regions that do not experience high temperatures or where animals will not occupy barns in summer, permanent "porous" sidewall construction is used. This can take the form of spaced boarding (e.g., 5-15 cm wide timber laths with 1.5-3.0 cm gaps) with height depending on the free area required.

Alternatively proprietary ventilated sheeting or flexible material can be used and manufacturer's data for free area of different types should be used for design purposes. The combination of the open ridge and eaves may be viewed as the sole source of ventilation only during the most severe winter weather-during periods when temperatures reach the lowest levels or times when especially windy, stormy conditions are present. During all other times in winter, additional ventilation must be provided.

Typically, doorways are left open for this purpose. Or, sidewalls away from prevailing winter winds may be left open. Then, as temperatures rise into spring and summer, sidewalls and endwalls are fully opened. As a general rule, too much ventilation is preferred over too little. In winter, suspend a thermometer inside a cold barn. If the temperature inside is more than 3-6° C above outside temperature, more ventilation will be necessary.

Also, persistent condensation on the underside of the roof is a further indication that additional ventilation openings must be provided. In summer, barns with open sidewalls and endwalls have improved ventilation resulting in lower average temperatures inside the barn. But, the real advantage to the cattle has to do with the extremes; specifically, during the heat of the day and the cool of the night. Cattle are not only exposed to lower temperature peaks during hot weather, they are exposed to these peaks for shorter periods of time. In addition, inside temperatures closely follow outside temperatures as they lower at night, allowing cattle to take advantage of whatever cooling effect may result from lower nighttime temperatures.

### Insolated Barns with Mechanical Ventilation

In an insolated barn, indoor temperature is maintained substantially higher than outdoor temperature during winter, at 5°C or higher to keep water lines from freezing or, as in the case of a calves nursery, at about 10-15°C with the addition of supplemental heat to meet the needs of the animals. These buildings are well insulated. Fans with thermostat controls automatically regulate the ventilation rate as outside conditions change, diurnally and seasonally.

Three levels of ventilation, using fans, must be provided if cattle occupy the barn year-round. Summer ventilation rates of 60 to 90 air changes per hour are not uncommon, requiring several fans. These levels are on the order of ten times the minimum continuous rate for winter.

### Warm Barns with Natural Ventilation

Well-regulated, naturally ventilated warm buildings, relying on stack and wind effects, have been successful. Natural ventilation for warm barns lowers investment and operating costs. Insulation and a warm environment in winter are the same as with mechanical ventilation.

Adjustable openings provide for modulating both the stack effect and the wind effect as necessary, depending upon outside conditions. Because frequent adjustments in ventilation openings, sometimes several times per day, are required to compensate for changes in outside conditions-wind velocity or direction, temperature, solar radiation, ventilation openings are usually opened and closed automatically by various types of actuators controlled by thermostats. Natural ventilation for warm housing has been described by Choiniere for buildings that are temperature-controlled in winter.

## ANIMALS, BUILDINGS AND EQUIPMENT DIMENSIONS

### BODY DIMENSIONS OF CATTLE

#### Basic Linear Dimensions

Space requirements for basic behaviours of young stock, e.g., lying, feed intake or walking depend on body dimensions of animals. Size of animals is defined by the basic measurements H = height at withers, L = diagonal body length and W = width of chest according to *Figure.*

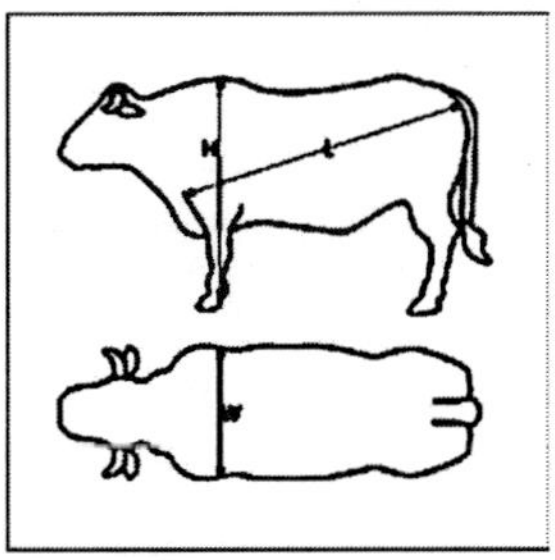

*Fig.3.6: Body Dimentions of Cattle*

#### Relationship between Body Weight, Age and Body Dimensions

When judging the space requirements of stock, the age of the animal is often used as the criteria for selecting dimensions. The animal's estimated or measured body weight can also be used. As animal's age is always known and their live weight is often known the relationship between age, body weight and body dimensions could be used to determine space requirements for the animals to be housed.

However, these relationships considerably can vary between different breeds, different production procedures and between individual animals of the same breed. Accurate data of the body dimensions of beef cattle from all breeds are not available. The results of measurements of the dimen-sions of Brown Swiss heifers of different ages showed a wide range of dimensions, e.g., 300 kg heifer had an average bodylength of 1.26 m and a variation from 1.17-1.34 m.

The differences between breeds of equal weight show a larger variation, e.g., a Simmental heifer shows a minimum length of 1.14 m and a Holstein Friesian heifer a maximum length of 1.40 m. While the best way to provide recommendations that can be used for practical design work is to find out the body dimensions by measuring some of the animals, agreed standards can be adopted for practical purposes. Table gives animal dimensions of beef cattle that can be adapted for practical design work, taking into account that designs should be based on the dimensions of the larger animals in the herd.

**Table. CIGR Standard Dimensions of Beef Cattle Related to Body Weight**

| Weight [kg] | H [m] | L [m] | W [m] |
|---|---|---|---|
| 200 | 1.09 | 1.17 | 0.34 |
| 300 | 1.19 | 1.31 | 0.40 |
| 400 | 1.27 | 1.42 | 0.46 |
| 500 | 1.33 | 1.51 | 0.51 |
| 600 | 1.38 | 1.59 | 0.55 |
| 700 | 1.42 | 1.65 | 0.60 |

In this section only loose housing is considered (because tied housing is not recommended). Loose housing systems provide more comfort for both stockmen and animals and thus improve productivity and welfare. In loose housing usually animals of equal line of production and similar age are kept in groups of at least four to five, usually up to twenty or, in large enterprises, even much more. Two major types of systems will be considered.

**Loose Housing**

Housing systems without cubicles provide an undivided lying area for all animals of a group. It is possible to design two-area or multiple area pens with littered lying areas or one area pens with deep bedding or without bedding. If no bedding is used, the pen floor will be designed as a fully perforated "slatted" floor or alternatively as a sloped area towards the dung removal system, so that faeces and urine of the animals are moved into or towards slurry tanks or channels by the walking activities of the animals.

**Cubicle Housing**

Male cattle deposit urine beneath their body thus wetting the bedding material of cubicles. This fact usually excludes male cattle from using cubicle housing systems. Thus cubicle systems are more suitable for female animals. It is important that each animal is provided with a reasonable clean, dry and resilient bed (upon which it can lie).

For female beef animals properly designed, constructed and maintained cubicles can satisfy these requirements. Since, cubicle houses can work with much or with very little bedding material, they can produce either solid manure or slurry. A disadvantage of the cubicle system is the inflexibility of the cubicles. Because of their fixed dimensions they can't take into account the changing body size of the animals.

**Loose Housing**

Beef cattle for practical reasons are usually kept at higher stocking density than cows. This can lead to reduced cleanliness, altered or aggressive behaviour and a higher risk of injury. Space available for bulls mostly is even more restricted especially in fully slatted floor pens. While the reduction of space for movement reduces fighting and mating behaviour, ethological sound systems avoid over crowded pens.

**Terminology**

One area systems are housing systems (pens) without division of the whole area into parts of different functions. All functions (lying, feeding, exercising, excreting) are carried out in one area. The floor can be fully slatted or solid with or without bedding.

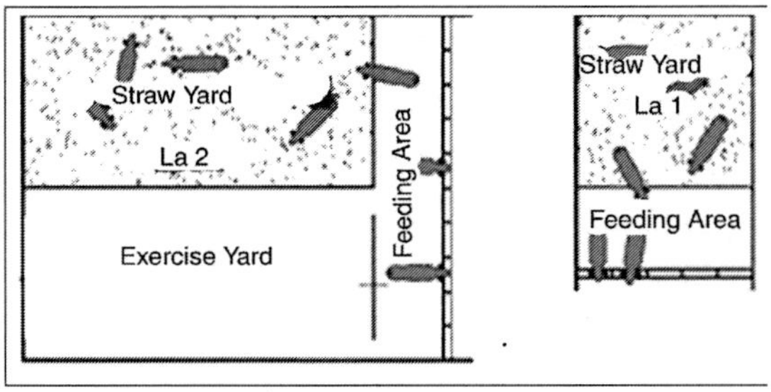


*Fig.3.7: Three (a) and Two (b) Area Straw Yard Systems*

Two area systems consist of the lying area and one other area, with unrestricted access, that provides sufficient space for feeding and exercise. Multiple area systems are those in which more than one area is provided for feeding and exercise. Any of the areas may be provided as uncovered outside yard. The lying area is separated from the other function areas.

Straw yards are unobstructed bedded lying areas for a group of cattle. Bedding is spread on top of the floor, with little (□ 2%) or no gradient, and soiled bedding accumulates in a deep layer, which is removed as necessary. To keep animal clean 1 to 1,2 kg straw/ $m^2$ day is required. Passages will be able to be slatted if the straw bedding is chopped or ground. The feeding area and the exercise yard could be divided or kept in one area.

Sloped floors are unobstructed lying areas for groups of cattle, that may be bedded or not. The floor has a gradient of 5 to 10% and the activity of the animals causes movement of bedding and/or manure down to the bottom of the slope, where it is collected. Straw should be added daily to the highest part of the sloped floor and the cattle will spread it themselves. The feeding area and the dunging alley could also be divided.

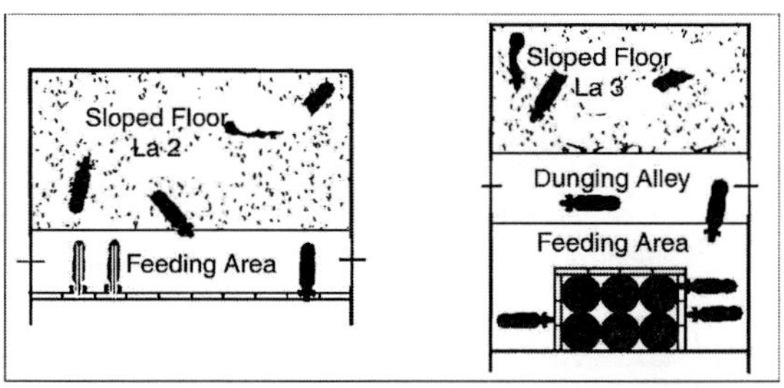


*Fig.3.8: Two (c) and Three (d) Area Sloped Floor Systems*

## SAFETY AND ANIMAL HANDLING

Stockmen working in animal housing and associated handling facilities are exposed to a number of potential risks and health hazards. Many stockmen work alone, handling big, sometimes dangerous animals as well as large groups of animals.

Several work tasks involve daily lifting, carrying of heavy loads and awkward working postures, which may cause overload injuries on the worker's musculo-skeletal system. Other potential risk factors contributing to accidents as well as to physical health problems and physiological stress for the worker is the fact that they operate in an environment where they are exposed to airborne particles, gases, noise.

The work environment is partly the same environment, which is provided for the animals, and it should be noted that there is a strong relationship between the animal welfare issues and the handling of the work environment problems in cattle houses.

## HEALTH AND INJURIES AMONG LIVESTOCK FARMERS

### Accident Agents

In an accident situation there is a complex interaction between man and injury agents. In animal husbandry the human is subjected to a high degree of exposure to a large number of factors that singly or in combination can be accident provoking, such as animals, equipment and building structures. Risky situations are often due to wet and slippery floors as well as systems for material and animal handling.

### Prevention of Accidents

*With reference to accident statistics some accident preventing facilities and measures can be listed:*

- Good cattle handling and handling facilities
- Pens from which the herdsman can easily escape if necessary in case of for instance frightened cattle and aggressive bulls
- Personnel passages through yard fences, properly placed
- Wide feeding passage or possibility to shut out the cattle from the feeding area
- Non-slip flooring
- Satisfactory lighting considering quality and quantity
- Well designed ladders and stairways
- Protective railings around the fodder hay-chute in two storey houses
- Handles and bolts that do not stand out in alleys and pathways
- Protectors for the knuckles on barrows
- Emergency stops on machinery

**Table. Recommended Illumination Level for Different Work Areas in Buildings used for Beef Production. Lux Values Refer to the Work Plane. In Addition to the Quantity, the Quality of Light must be Considered**

| Building or Work Area/Task | Intensity of Illumination, Lux |
|---|---|
| Animal housing area | 150 |
| Animal handling area | 250 |
| Veterinary treatment | 1,000 |
| Feed processing, feed alley | 250 |
| Silo, feed storage | 100 |
| Ladders and stairs | 250 |

### Ergonomics

Any normally fit adult person, regardless of sex, physical strength and body dimensions should be able to work comfortably in livestock buildings. Despite an increasing degree of mechanisation and automation many jobs in animal husbandry are still associated with lifting heavy loads, moving and carrying equipment, feed and other materials with manual methods. An important step towards improved human welfare within cattle housing is to eliminate unnecessary loads on the human musculoskeletal system.

**Health Aspects Related to Air Quality**

It has been known for decades that farm workers suffer health risks due to inhalation of gases and airborne particles commonly referred to as dust. The particles may be liquid droplets or solid. Several respiratory disorders have been reported, which are associated with dust and work in confined livestock buildings such as hypersensitivity, pneumonia, acute inflammation, chronic bronchitis, occupational asthma and toxin fever.

The respiratory problems connected to gases range from mild irritations of the respiratory tract to lethal effects. For the most frequent components in the air environment in livestock buildings there are statutory threshold limit values, which differ from country to country. It should be noted that threshold limit values in connection with animal welfare in many countries often are lower than the work environment legislation.

**Dust and Dust Reducing**

Dust in animal houses is generated inside the building and arises primarily from the animals and bedding and feed material. The airborne particles are often carriers of biologically active material like endotoxins, pathogens and allergens that can highly be disease provoking. Of special interest is the concentration (i.e., number of particles per air volume) of respirable particles with a diameter less than 5 µm that can be inhaled and deposited in the lung.

The smaller particle the higher possibility that the particle reaches the lower respiratory tract and the deeper the particle is deposited the higher is the risk for illness. Even if "common dust" can be seen by human eyes (larger diameter than 100 ìm), the very small respirable particles cannot be, so we are indeed dealing with a danger our senses are not able to detect.

*There are basically four approaches that can be used for airborne dust reducing:*

1. Prevent particle formation
2. Prevent particle release
3. Remove suspended particles from enclosed workspaces
4. Isolate workers from dust clouds in workspace.

Of course the best approach in this matter is to have the cattle and the working sites outdoors or in open barns. In the cattle barn the most effective way to obtain a low dust concentration level is to prevent formation by always using hygienically perfect forage and bedding material. Providing an effective ventilation system in a barn is a good practice to remove suspended respirable particles as well as gases.

**Gases and Reduction of Gas Levels**

In animal buildings over 150 different gases and volatile compounds have been identified. Most of the volatile compounds originate from biodegradation of animal excreta or are produced by the animals themselves such as carbon dioxide (by the respiration of the animal). The gases that are found in the highest elevated concen-trations are ammonia, carbon dioxide, hydrogen sulphide and methane.

*It must be emphasised that it is dangerous to enter any manure tank* without either using a self-contained air supply or combining several measures: testing the air, constant and adequate ventilation of fresh air and using an harness and lifeline on the person entering the tank. As well, human and animals positioned over a slatted floor with manure storage underneath are at risk during agitation, mixing or pumping of manure due to the gases, especially hydrogen sulphide. A good strategy is to evacuate dangerous zones during these manure-handling actions.

### Ammonia

Ammonia is the most common polluting gas in the atmosphere of the cattle barn. Animal manure is the main source of ammonia. The gas together with hydrogen sulphide a major component in what is termed odour, noticeable at ammonia concentrations of 5 ppm or more. Higher concentrations than that cause irritation to the respiratory organs and can aggravate the negative health effects of high dust concentrations.

Many factors affect the emission and concentration of ammonia such as air flow rate, manure and air temperature, manure surface area, density of animals, the degree of mixing of urine and faeces, time intervals between manuring, the pH-value, carbon/nitrogen ratio, mois-ture content and type of bedding. Consequently, many measures can be taken such as: proper ventilation and sufficient number of air changes, low air temperature in the barn and good urine drainage characteristics of the floor.

### Hydrogen Sulphide

Hydrogen sulphide is the most toxic gas in animal confinement houses and 200 ppm and more are lethal for humans. The presence of the gas is of concern in buildings with liquid manure systems particularly. During slurry clearing operations concentrations in the range of 1,500 to 2,000 ppm have been reported. Since, hydrogen sulphide is lethal the aim should be to keep it below detectable concentration at all working sites.

Special care has to be taken when pumping or agitating the manure. During emptying a slurry cellar the workers and the animal should be evacuated from the barn. In mechanical ventilated, closed animal houses continuously evacuation of the gases in an indoor slurry pit through a perforated duct under the floor and along the pit can reduce the gas concentrations above the slatted floor. By removing the slurry daily from the cattle barn to an outdoor storage it is possible to hold the concentration at an acceptable level.

### Methane

Methane is generated when manure is stored under anaerobic conditions. This occurs in all non-aerated manure storages. Primarily, methane is dangerous because of its flammability. If methane is mixed in a proper proportion with oxygen a spark will be able to set off an explosion.

### Carbon Dioxide

Carbon dioxide is present in all air, indoor as well as outdoors. Only extremely high concentrations (70,000 ppm or 7% and over) could have severe health effects. Mostly, incidents and accidents involving carbon dioxide are connected with asphyxiation due to oxygen deficiency rather than the direct effect of carbon dioxide itself. For instance, it is dangerous to enter a haylage silo during storing. In animal buildings the gas is more an indicator of ventilation efficiency than a health risk.

### Noise

Noise can be defined as "unwanted sound, rapid, annoying pressure vibration in the surrounding air". Ventilation fans, grinders, vacuum pumps and mechanical feeding and manure systems generate noise. High sound levels are a real stress factor. Exposure to noise will be able to cause temporary deafness and permanent hearing loss after a variable period if the level is over 85 dB(A). The unit, dB(A), is exponential and the human sense of hearing will perceive the sound level as halving if a reduction of 10 dB(A) occurs.

It is fairly easy to reduce the sound level of ventilation fans and other mechanical noise generators. Maximum noise level recommendations and regulations differ from country to country. Furthermore, it is important to reduce noise when handling cattle in order to improve animal movement and to make cattle handling safer. Cattle are more sensitive to high frequency noise than human. Animals will be calmer and easier to handle, if noise level is reduced. Clanging and banging metal parts should be silenced with rubber pads. Equipment operated with hydraulics should be engineered for quietness.

**Cattle Handling and Cattle Handling Facilities**

Handling facilities are an essential part of a safe, easy and rapid handling of cattle. Appropriate handling and handling facilities remove much of the stress and frustration of the workmen, which inevitably occurs with excited, stubborn or aggressive animals. Properly constructed facilities confine cattle safely and efficiently with minimal animal stress and risk of injury to both cattle and workers.

**Animal Behaviour and Improving Animal Handling**

Understanding cattle behaviour can help farm workers to avoid dangerous situations and minimise accidents to handlers, as well as to design the handling facilities appropriately. Animals have natural boundary called the Flight Zone.

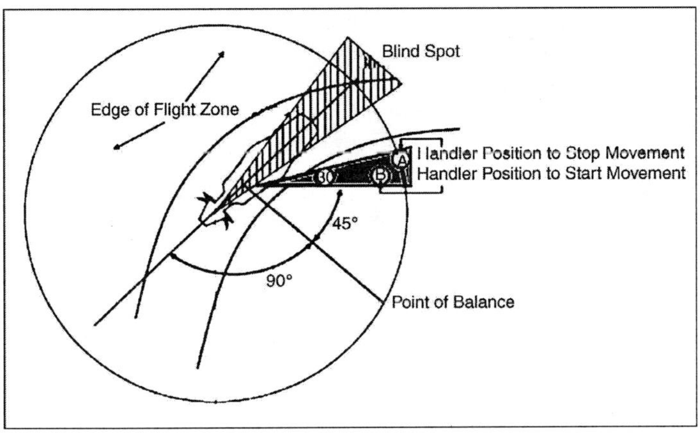


*Fig. The Flight Zone of Animals*

Deep penetration into the Flight Zone can cause panic and escape attempts. Handlers should have the possibility to remove, and should remove themselves from the Flight Zone, if the animal becomes aggressive. To move an animal forward: stand in the shaded area position B, behind the Point of Balance at the shoulder. Keep out of the Blind Spot at the rear of the animal. To stop movement: back off to position A. To make an animal back up: stand in front of the Point of Balance. To make an animal turn left or right: approach the animal head on. Factors reducing an animal's Flight Zone size: frequent contact with people; history of gentle handling; calm environment. Factors enlarging the Flight zone: infrequent contact with people; history of rough or abusive handling; excitement.

*To improve animal handling and animal movement, many technical measures can be taken such as:*

- Appropriate handling facility design.
- Animals tend to move from a dark to a more brightly lighted area. The light should illuminate the chute up ahead. Eliminate shadows and patches of light and dark, which may confuse animals. An approach is to illuminate the entire working area. Lamps should not shine into the eyes of approaching animals because glaring and blinding light impedes movement. Illumination should be uniform and diffuse.
- Prevent distractions, such as a chain hanging down in an entrance. Avoid sparkling reflection in a puddle, a moving reflection on a sheet of metal or bars of shadow across an otherwise sunlit alleyway. Dark colours can create shadow effects. Bright colours such as white and light yellow have been proven satisfactory.
- Reduce noise
- Animals might refuse to move, if they can see people ahead. Install shields to prevent animals from seeing farther ahead. Gates can be rigged with motor controls so a handler standing behind the cattle can open them.
- Solid sides that prevent the cattle from seeing outside the fences should be provided in the races and crowding pens. The crowding gate on the crowding pen should be solid as well, preventing animals from attempting to turn back to were they come from.
- Cattle are sensitive to changes in type and texture of floors and fences. Changes in type of flooring can cause balking. Use the same type of flooring throughout a facility, if possible. Use non-slip flooring. Drains should be located outside main drive alleys, chutes and crowd pens.

**Cattle Handling Systems**

A handling system has three main purposes: to sort, handle and treat cattle.

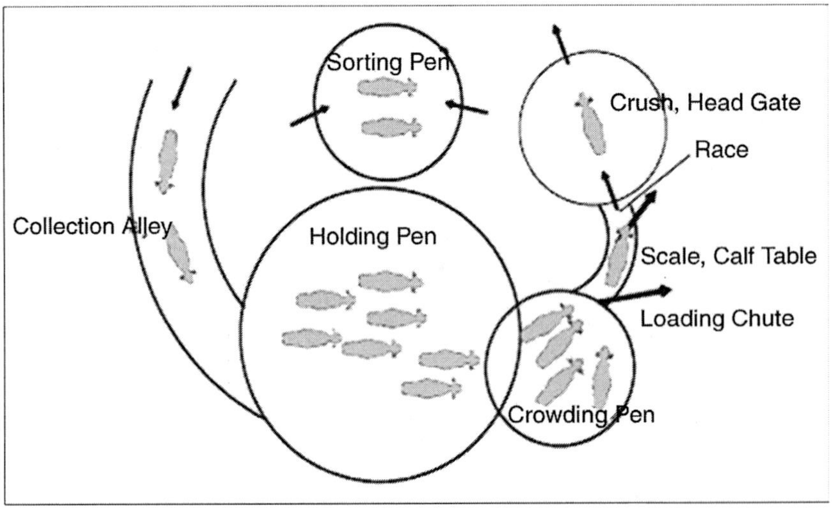


*Fig.3.10: Components of a Cattle-handling System*

*The parts and the requirements of a system are:*

- Collection alley to move cattle from the cattle house, pasture or feedlot to the holding pen
- Sorting Pens: Opening off the collection alley or holding pens, or after the working area
- Holding pens to hold either the whole herd or groups of 30-50 heads
- Crowding pen to move small groups of 8–10 cattle into the working area
- Single file race, at least 6 m long to hold 3–4 cattle at once
- Loading chute
- Crush, preferable type "walk-through" and with a self-locking headgate
- Options such as scales, calf crush or table, belly clipping crush, crush equipped for claw-trimming, access kiosk for artificial insemination and gynaecological examinations, shelf near the crush for veterinarian's equipment and materials, the availability of hot and warm water near the crush

The current trend in the design of cattle working facilities is to use circular crowding areas and working chutes.

If the single file race is bent too sharply where it joins the crowding pen, the cattle may refuse to enter, because it looks like a dead end. Cattle standing in the round crowding pen must be able to see a minimum of three body lengths up to the single file chute before the curve begins

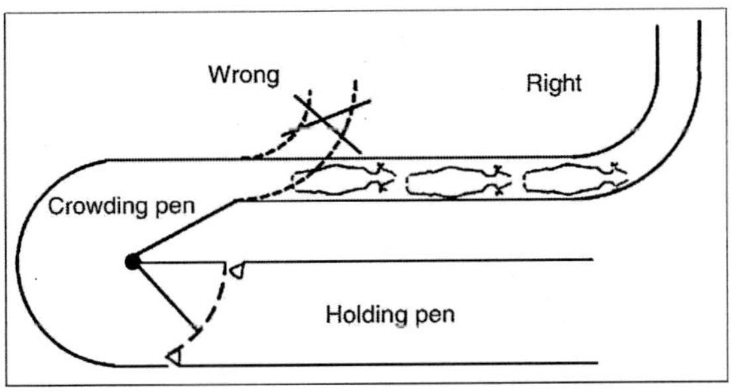


*Fig.3.11: Layout for a Curved Handling System*

The circular designs take advantages of cattle's tendency to circle and crowd towards the outside of a curved passage.

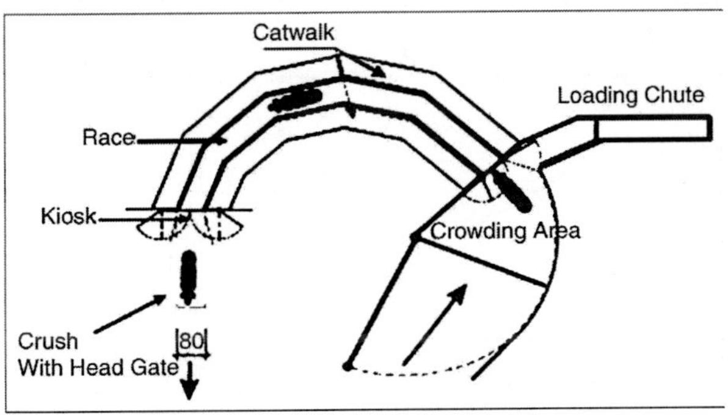


*Fig.3.12: Basic Layout for a Working Unit*

Cattle can normally be worked in less time with a round crowding pen and a curved race than a straight one. Round crowding pens should be laid out so the cattle make a 180° turn as they move though the crowding pen.

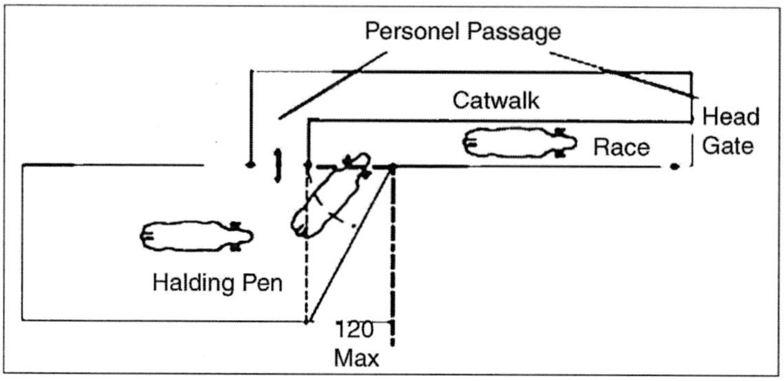


*Fig.3.13: A Straight-line Designed Working Unit*

However, a straight-line designed as well as a corner located working unit are area saving alternatives, especially valid for small herds of cattle and indoor, respectively.

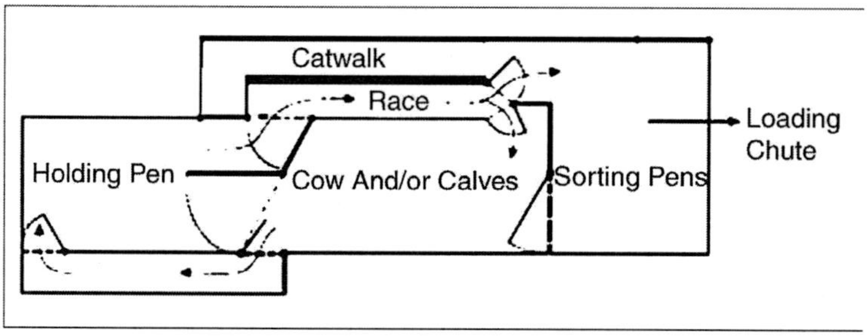


*Fig.3.14: A Sorting Unit, for Instance for a Suckler Herd*

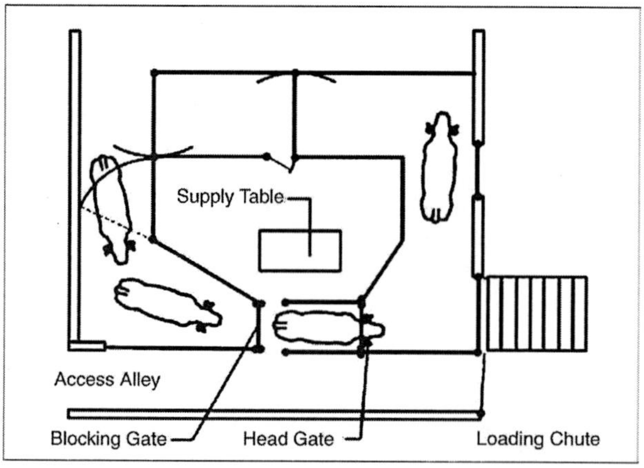


*Fig.3.15: A Corner Located Working Unit*

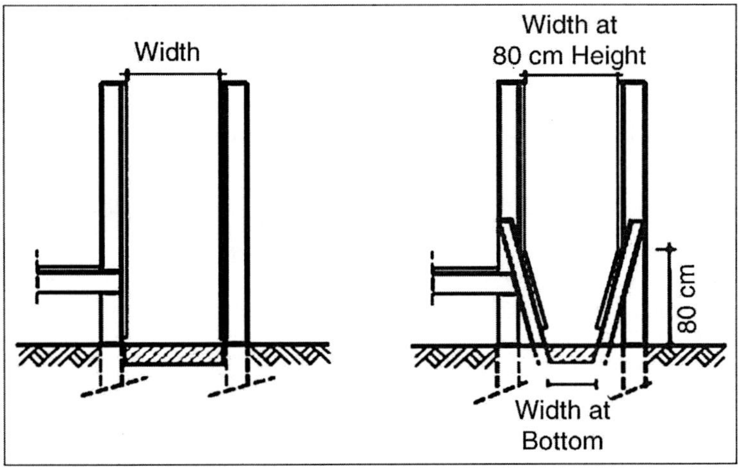


*Fig.3.16: Straight Sided (Left) and Half Tapered (Right) Race Design*

## THE ENVIRONMENTAL IMPACT OF INTENSIVE LIVESTOCK PRODUCTION

The intensification of livestock production has had not only a significant effect on animal welfare, but also a considerable impact on the environment. In this regard, the disposal of the enormous quantities of animal waste produced by animals confined in intensive livestock production units has created the greatest environmental problems. The reduction of manpower levels and the need for efficient animal management have meant that 'factory' farmers have often abandoned the use of straw as bedding in livestock houses; the animals instead stand on slatted or solid concrete floors. The faeces and urine which these animals produce must therefore be disposed of differently.

When straw bedding is used, manure is collected in dung heaps, exposed to air it gradually ferments, bacteria are thus to some extent destroyed and the excreta eventually becomes fertiliser to be spread on the land. Slurry, on the other hand, must be stored in tanks, where it may decompose and sometimes produce a variety of noxious smelling gases. This method does not kill pathogens quite as effectively as the traditional method.

While straw bedding most closely resembles the natural surface on which most animals lie—and is thus promoted as the ideal floor surface on which animals should be kept—it can provide the conditions under which disease organisms can flourish. If poorly maintained, such bedding when excessively dirty and wet not only causes distress to the animals, but can also lead to environmental mastitis in dairy cattle, 'farrowing fever' in pregnant sows and an increased exposure of poultry to the dangerous *E.coli* bacteria.

Slurry can be returned to the land as fertiliser, but its storage and application can be particularly problematic. It cannot be spread when the ground is too wet and must, therefore, be stored in huge tanks, sometimes for several months. The failure of these storage tanks would have a significant impact on the local environment, most particularly if pathogens, such as salmonella, E.coli and leptospira, which are dangerous to both human and animal health, were still present in the slurry. To reduce the risk of infection, farmers have been warned against spreading slurry on grazing land.

If they must do so, they are advised to allow the slurry to adequately ferment and to leave the land on which it has been spread unpastured for at least six weeks afterwards. The main problem with modern farms is that they do not always have enough land to absorb the waste that the animals produce. The waste must, therefore, often be transported elsewhere at considerable expense to the livestock holder. As Johnson suggests, waste disposal can be the main factor which determines how many animals can viably be kept in a livestock production unit, rather than animal welfare. To illustrate this problem, he describes the crisis faced in the Netherlands during the late 1980s.

The great concentration of factory farms had put so much pressure on land that by January 1987 the Dutch authorities placed a ban on the further expansion of livestock numbers. With farms producing around 100 million tonnes of effluent per annum, twice the amount of liquid waste accumulated than could safely be spread on the country's 2 million hectares of farmland. As a consequence, the transport of slurry to areas away from factory farms was encouraged and subsidised by the Dutch government and large-scale dumping of slurry was banned due to the potential pollution and health risks it presented. Dutch farmers are now required to pay the full costs of disposal through sewage plants if they are unable to find appropriate land to spread their farm waste on.

Like slurry, the production of silage—a grass crop harvested when green and then partially fermented to make animal fodder—can present serious environmental problems. The anaerobic fermentation which accompanies silage production can potentially produce a waste liquid which has been estimated to be 200 times more polluting than domestic sewage, particularly when the grass is wet. Such waste presents great pollution problems if it escapes the silos in which it is held and enters natural waterways. The aquatic life of rivers and streams can be either poisoned or starved of oxygen as a result of the introduction of this effluent.

The contamination of natural waterways is one of the most serious environmental consequences of modern agricultural practice. Aside from the problems posed by slurry and silage effluent, intensive livestock production contributes towards nitrate pollution. In addition to this, the additives used in animal feed and the antibiotics which the animals are routinely given are potential sources of environmental contamination. Although the blame for environmental pollution is often apportioned to industry, rather than agriculture, the intensification of farming methods—most particularly with respect to the waste it produces—presents a significant threat to the environment.

In addition to the phenomenal impact on animal welfare and the environment, the intensification of livestock production has created new opportunities for disease organisms to flourish and threaten the health of both animal and human populations. As this book has thus far clearly illustrated, our interactions with other animals have always brought with them the potential risk of infectious disease. However, the increasing exploitation of and dependency on animal resources, which has occurred through the intensification of livestock production, has meant that disease risks which did not exist, or were unthinkable, forty to fifty years ago are today commonplace. In short, the increase in stocking densities has led to the increase of opportunities for disease transmission.

The housing and living conditions of intensively farmed animals—most notably pigs and poultry—potentially provide significant exposure to bacteria and viruses, thereby enhancing the risk of disease. Disease risks can be greatly reduced with good stockmanship. On 'factory farms', however, animal management is primarily linked to maintaining or increasing productivity. In the past, stockmen could attend to animals more individually and were familiar with the small herds they tended.

Today, stockmen are not only fewer in number, but are also required to manage huge numbers of livestock as efficiently and cost effectively as possible. The reduction of manpower levels in livestock farming combined with the increasing numbers of animals kept on site can lead to inefficiency in disease control and hygiene which, in turn, may result in the outbreak of infectious disease amongst the animal stock and—depending on the nature of the disease in question—possibly even transmission to the humans who come into direct contact with them. This is, of course, not to mention the risk of contaminated animal protein entering into the food chain and putting human consumers at risk of infection.

One of the disease management techniques adopted in intensive livestock production is to accept the pervasiveness of infection. Antibiotic drugs and vaccinations are thus routinely administered in order to keep stock healthy and maintain productivity. When disease outbreaks occur, it may not be viable to cull stock given the size of the animal population housed. Similarly, farm buildings may have been too poorly constructed and cannot be properly disinfected or cleaned, the animal's excreta, as suggested above, creating potential hazards for both animal and public health.

Management of disease purely through drug intervention is far from ideal. Moreover, it arouses considerable consumer concern about the quality of the animal produce which ends up on our dinner plates. The use of growth hormones and the possibly harmful effects of veterinary drug residues in food have become an increasing source of consumer anxiety in recent years; as has the suggestion that the persistent administration of antibiotic drugs may ultimately lead to the evolution of pathogens resistant to such substances.

For fifty years, antibiotics have been added to animal feeds in order to improve feeding efficiency and growth rates. Since, the 1960s, scientists have looked into the possibilities of resistance risks and by 1970 the European community had made moves to prevent the antibiotics that are used in human medicine being used as animal growth promoters. Today, the issue of resistant risks has again become the topic of political and scientific debate, stimulated in part by the development of a veterinary antibiotic called avoparcin which is closely related to an important human medical antibiotic known as vancomycin. There is a concern that such veterinary antibiotics may promote the emergence of bacterial strains that have a genetic resistance to antibiotics.

Although there is currently little microbiological consensus on this topic, some scientists have gone so far as to suggest that the widespread use of antibiotics in livestock production, particularly those used to treat infections, may well be responsible for resistant strains of salmonella and campylobacter that are being found in increasing numbers of food poisoning cases in humans. In recent years, the problem of animal disease control has also been tackled from another angle, that rather than seeking to alter the living conditions of the animals, instead seeks to alter the animals themselves. In this context, attempts have been made to rear strains of 'minimal-disease' animals which are kept in highly controlled environments. Poultry flocks today can be bred to be 'specific-pathogen free', which essentially means that particular diseaseproducing agents have been eliminated by breeding and rearing birds in sterile conditions. Such isolation, however, can render such birds vulnerable to other microorganisms that might otherwise have been innocuous.

Modern intensive livestock production is a risky business and sometimes it is human health that is at stake. In spite of the industry's endeavours to produce animal products that are safe for human consumption, as indicated above, food-borne infections still pose a threat to public health. The intensification of poultry rearing is the main culprit for bacterial infections in humans. Salmonella infection is one of the ever-present hazards of broiler rearing. It is in fact widely accepted that salmonella will persist in poultry stocks, although it can be kept at bay by good feeding and housing practices.

The pervasiveness of this bacteria in poultry is largely due to contaminated feed, although people and wild animals or birds can also be the vectors of transmission. Intensively reared poultry, like other farm animals which can carry the salmonella bacteria, are generally fed on high-protein feeds which can contain slaughterhouse waste and other animal by-products such as dried poultry manure. If such feed is inadequately sterilised, disease organisms can persist and can be passed on to other animals. Sterilisation is a costly process which occurs through heat treatment. However, irradiation of animal feed is not always efficient because strains of salmonella have emerged which are heat-resistant and continue to contaminate feed.

The transmission of salmonella requires 'the transfer of faeces or intestinal contents from an infected individual to the digestive tract of a susceptible one'. Like animals, humans can become infected by salmonellosis through the ingestion of contaminated animal produce. The disease can cause gastroenteritis, septic shock syndrome and focal infection in humans, and can even be fatal to vulnerable individuals, such as infants or elderly people. It should be emphasised that good hygiene and effective cooking methods from the abattoir to the kitchen can reduce the risk of infection for the human consumer. The modern systems of livestock rearing, mass animal transportation and conveyor belt style slaughterhouses, however, increase the possibilities of cross-infection and the contamination of human food. Although the most common bacterial infection, salmonella is not the only disease which may be contracted from the ingestion of animal produce. Bovine tuberculosis, brucellosis, trichinosis, campylobacteriosis, listeriosis, staphylococcal enterotoxicosis, clostridial toxicosis and toxoplasmosis may be transmitted through tainted animal food and cause human illness.

Aside from food-borne infections and intoxications, consumer health is generally not affected by the diseases which farm animals carry. The people at greatest risk from agricultural animals and their products are in fact those who work with them; in other words, farm workers, veterinarians and individuals who handle animal carcasses occupationally. In Western Europe today, the major zoonoses, such as brucellosis (contagious abortion),

tuberculosis and anthrax, are uncommon. Other zoonotic diseases, however, present serious occupational hazards to those in the meat, dairy and animal product industry.

For example, leptospirosis—commonly known as Weil's disease—is a disease which can seriously affect dairy farmers, both economically and physically. It is a contagious bacterial disease which can produce a high abortion rate in cattle late in pregnancy; it can be responsible for high mortality in calves, reduced milk production and contaminated milk. The organisms that cause leptospirosis are transmitted through urine and live in water or moist soil. Cattle—and other livestock—become infected through being splashed with infected urine, grazing on contaminated pasture or by drinking infected water.

Other wild species, particularly rodents, are responsible for transmitting the disease to cattle, and humans can be infected by bathing in contaminated water or direct contact with infected urine. The effect of leptospirosis on humans varies from inapparent to acute febrile illness which can be accompanied by fever, hepatitis, jaundice and meningitis—amongst other maladies. Good animal management, vaccination and reduction of contacts between livestock and rodents reduce the risks of infection by leptospirosis. There are many more health hazards for those who come into routine contact with food-producing animals. Other occupational hazards for humans are presented by rickettsial diseases, fungal infections (e.g., ringworm), chlamydia infections and respiratory viral diseases, in addition to bacterial infections such as those described above.

The fact that intensive livestock production today happens within closed systems, away from public view, has much to do with the reduction of infection risks. Modern livestock housing is essentially designed to keep out diseasecausing organisms and their vectors of transmission and to keep disease-free animals in. Such systems are far from foolproof; infection may, for example, occur through the drinking water or animal feed. Furthermore, farmers, stockmen and veterinarians may introduce disease to livestock. It is commonplace when one enters a livestock production unit for one to have to don special overalls and boots in order to minimise the possibility of introducing new pathogens to the animals from outside. However, keeping all visitors out, apart from stock and veterinary personnel, not only aids disease prevention and control, but to some extent prevents consumers from gaining a first-hand glimpse of the conditions under which their food is produced.

Modern consumer society demands a continual, cheap and dependable supply of animal products which are pre-packaged and ready to enjoy: yet never before have the majority been so divorced from the production of the animal proteins which sustain them. The urban consumer is estranged from the origins of the food he eats and the leather he wears and has limited involvement in or knowledge of the circumstances of their production. The consumer is very much reliant on the producers and retailers to offer fresh and uncontaminated animal products—at a low price—on demand. The 'farm fresh' animal products which are nowadays found in urban supermarkets are however unlikely to have been produced locally, as was formerly the case. Animal produce may originate from farms and factories situated hundreds of kilometres from the consumer's domicile. The transport networks and storage capacities which today so efficiently ensure the swift despatch and delivery of farm-fresh animal produce to the consumer were not possible until recently.

Previously the movement of livestock and carcasses was fairly restricted, both within and across provincial or national borders, not only through lack of adequate transportation and refrigeration, but also due to the fear and possibility of the spread of contagious disease. Once a sufficient level of understanding and knowledge of transmission and control through governmental intervention had been reached, disease could be better contained, cross-infection prevented and animals could be more safely moved from one location to another.

Yet although governmental regulations pertaining to animal disease control have existed both nationally and internationally since, last century, it is still possible for contaminated animals to slip the net and infect others (be they animal or human). Given that infected livestock or tissue can easily and quickly be moved from one (international) location to another, new opportunities for disease-producing organisms can develop in areas and amongst animal-human groups previously unaffected. The risk of disease can be further exacerbated by the failure to properly disinfect vehicles used for animal transportation, and delays in the transfer of live animals or meat from one place to another facilitate contagion further. Since, on an international level, animal movements are more likely to increase than decrease as a result of political and economic accord, the potential problem of animal disease transmission could, in the future, be one of increasing significance.

**Veterinary Regime during the Twentieth Century**

As the above discussion suggests, the possibilities for the transmission of infectious diseases are very real, most particularly given the risks posed by intensive systems of agricultural animal management and animal transportation. It is largely for this reason that veterinary medicine has become so important during the twentieth century in maintaining and monitoring animal health, to keep the spread of infectious disease in check and to ensure that farmers adhere to and understand the guidelines and regulations concerning disease prevention and control. Yet while disease risks may today be far greater than ever before, the danger of humans actually contracting diseases from contact with animals or the consumption of animal produce is in fact relatively small.

Throughout the course of the twentieth century, the veterinary regime has continued to move from strength to strength. The state veterinary services that were instituted in the industrialised nations of Europe during the late nineteenth century have played an increasingly important role in the control and prevention of animal disease. Legislative measures to combat the effects, spread and introduction of contagious disease have been enforced with increasing vigour.

The successes of earlier campaigns and stringent legal controls to stamp out the animal plagues that devastated European livestock populations provided the basis for future legislation. For example, as we saw in the previous chapter, veterinary inspection and the rigorous enforcement of all regulations pertaining to the importation, transport, sale, slaughter and destruction of livestock successfully led to the eradication of contagious bovine pleuropneumonia in the Netherlands by 1887 and Britain in 1898.

The introduction of measures to financially compensate farmers for their losses through compulsory slaughter policies undoubtedly provided an incentive to abide by governmental regulations and allowed veterinary officials to perform their duties without hindrance. Eventual success in eradicating disease helped to persuade livestock producers to accept the ruthless and restrictive regulations that the state sought to enforce. As a consequence, state veterinary intervention has become institutionalised within modern livestock production. Moreover, during the twentieth century, the appreciation of the need for animal disease control and prevention has more or less been incorporated into the habitus of livestock producers.

Scientific developments have, of course, played a crucial role in the prevention and control of animal disease. The development of the science of bacteriology, advances in pathology, parasitology, immunology and microbiology and so forth have provided important contributions to advances in animal and public health. By the turn of the century, European governments had become increasingly aware of the need for better scientific understanding of animal disease if they were to reduce the risks that it posed. In the Netherlands, for example, the State Serum Institute was founded in 1904-by the pioneering veterinarian and bacteriologist Jan Poels—with a view to steering the work of the established Dutch Veterinary Service towards more scientific means of preventing and curing livestock disease.

The Serum Institute experimented with the production of a serum against foot-and-mouth disease and an anthrax vaccine. Moreover, it conducted bacteriological and chemical investigations into milk and dairy produce. Interestingly, this new institute operated specifically outside the dominion of the veterinary school, being instead an organ of the state. In 1933, nearly three decades later, the State Veterinary Research Institute was established, primarily to study and develop a vaccine against foot-and-mouth disease—a highly infectious disease that has perhaps wreaked the greatest havoc on European livestock and the livestock industry during the twentieth century. By 1946, the Institute's director, H.S. Frenkel, had succeeded in developing a method by which a vaccine against foot-and-mouth disease could be produced in large quantities. This method, however, only proved effective until 1951, when a more virulent strain of the disease struck Dutch livestock.

From 1945 onwards, the structure of the state veterinary machine became increasingly more complex, as government-subsidised Animal Health Services were established in each province within the Netherlands. The earliest regional animal health service had in fact already been established in Friesland in 1919. Its early work led to significant progress in the battle against bovine tuberculosis. The new regional services were modelled on their Friesian predecessor and strove for the coordinated control of animal disease, involving not only scientific and governmental veterinary advisors, but also representatives of local farmers and dairy organisations and practising veterinarians.

The eleven regional Animal Health Services were in turn coordinated by the Industrial Board for Agriculture, who established an Animal Health Committee to deal with the allocation of funds and organisation of schemes for disease control. After the Second World War, the regeneration of the meat and dairy export industry became an important part of Dutch economic recovery. A key aspect of this was a national plan to rid Dutch cattle herds of tuberculosis, thereby ensuring the safety and quality of the national product. A considerable portion of the Marshall Plan funds that were made available to the Netherlands to assist post-war economic reconstruction was devoted to achieve this end. By 1956, the disease had been conquered due to the efforts and cooperation of the Animal Health Services, practising veterinarians and the meat inspection service.

On the basis of this national plan's success, similarly successful attempts were made to control and eradicate brucellosis from the Dutch livestock population. By 1957, the Serum Institute and the State Veterinary Institute amalgamated to form the Central Veterinary Institute, which functioned under the auspices of the Dutch Ministry of Agriculture and Fisheries. The Veterinary Service was effectively given the governmental mandate, through the establishment of legislation such as the Livestock Act and the Veterinary Medicines Act, to prevent animal disease and preserve public health.

The work of the Central Veterinary Institute continued to grow and diversify throughout the 1960s and 1970s. In 1986, it consolidated and moved to new premises in Lelystad. By 1994, the CVI amalgamated with a number of other agricultural animal research institutes to create the Institute for Animal Science and Health. Today, this institute employs over 600 people and conducts research into animal health, breeding and reproduction, animal welfare, stress and management, animal nutrition, and so forth. Moreover, it is responsible for diagnostic work, the production of vaccines, specific-pathogen free animals, diagnostic preparations, etc., and the control and standardisation of veterinary medicines.

The developments in state-directed animal disease control in the Netherlands can be mirrored in the rise of the State Veterinary Service in Great Britain. There too was an understanding for the necessity of improved scientific knowledge and diagnosis of animal disease. The first governmental diagnostic laboratory was set up in 1894 in response to an outbreak of swine fever. This was followed by the establishment of the Central Veterinary Laboratory at Weybridge, Surrey, in 1913. Initial research was conducted into spontaneous abortion, swine fever, scrapie, foot-and-mouth disease and diseases of poultry.

As farmers began to increase the size of their flocks, as the process of intensification of production began to take off, the laboratory found itself increasingly dealing with the effects and greater incidence of poultry disease. During the 1930s, the laboratory began to research and produce tuberculin, in addition to an anti-abortion vaccine. The Agricultural Act of 1937 facilitated further expansion of the laboratory. New research departments of bacteriology, biochemistry, parasitology, pathology and poultry disease were established and a further laboratory was set up in Scotland.

By 1960, the Animal Health Division successfully completed its programme to eradicate tuberculosis from the British cattle population. During the 1960s, the new challenges to animal health presented by the changing methods in livestock production gave extra impetus to the fight against animal disease. The intensive rearing of calves, for example, led to an increasing incidence of respiratory disease. This unforeseen consequence of new methods of animal husbandry required urgent bacteriological and virological investigation.

Similarly, the development of artificial insemination and its widespread use in cattle presented new problems for animal disease control. The movement of inseminators between farms and the importation of and trade in semen presented new hazards for the transmission of infectious animal disease. In 1955, legislative measures were taken to prohibit importation of foreign animal semen without a licence and the Animal Health Division took steps to screen the health of bulls.

In addition to the Central Veterinary Laboratory, the Veterinary Investigation Service was established in 1922, with regional centres throughout Britain. This service essentially provided local laboratory facilities on which practising veterinarians could rely to help diagnose and investigate animal health problems in the herds that they attended. Initially, the Veterinary Investigation Centres were attached to agricultural colleges, but in 1946 they were incorporated into the Ministry of Agriculture, Fisheries and Food. The interaction between local veterinarians, veterinary investigation officers, the researchers of the Central Veterinary Laboratory and legislators in fact provides a good illustration of the increasing complexity of animal disease control during the twentieth century. At the grassroots level, practising veterinary surgeons observe and report the local incidence of animal disease.

This in turn is investigated by veterinary investigation officers who conduct field investigations and epidemiological studies to gauge the extent of animal health problems. In the meantime, the Central Veterinary Laboratory attempts to understand the aetiology of the disease and explores how it may effectively be controlled. These combined investigations may in turn lead to the inception of statutory control measures, vaccination, test and slaughter programmes to contain and eradicate animal disease. In Britain, this kind of cooperation eventually led to the eradication of brucellosis and is today responsible for the investigation and extensive monitoring of new pathogens and diseases, e.g., bovine spongiform encephalopathy. In October 1995, the Central Veterinary Laboratory and the Veterinary Investigation Service merged to form the Veterinary Laboratories Agency in a further bid to improve the collaboration necessary to ensure animal disease control and the provision of advice to the Ministry of Agriculture, Fisheries and Food and other veterinary health workers.

Throughout the twentieth century, the necessity for collaboration and cooperation has extended far beyond the activities of local and nationally organised veterinary organisations. As illustrated in the previous chapter, international cooperation on matters of veterinary public health first began during the nineteenth century as a result of the devastation caused by the cattle plague. In 1924, the Office International des Epizooties was established in Paris. This intergovernmental organisation initially sought to promote and coordinate research into the control and surveillance of animal disease, and has remained active on this front to this day; its original membership of 28 having gradually been expanded to some 144 member states.

During the post-war period, additional international fora for dealing with the economic and health problems associated with animal disease were institutionalised. In Europe, the European Union—and its former incarnations, i.e., the EEC and EC—have provided the main political arena within which European governments can jointly discuss and legislate on matters pertaining to veterinary public health and animal welfare. The European Economic Community (EEC) was originally established in 1958- following the signing of the Treaties of Rome -with a view to achieving economic and political union amongst its member states, namely Belgium, Germany, France, Italy, Luxembourg and the Netherlands. In 1973, Denmark, Great Britain and Ireland became members of the EEC. In later years, Austria, Greece, Finland, Spain, Sweden and Portugal joined the ranks of states seeking European economic union; the organisation is set to expand yet further in future as former Eastern Bloc countries vie for membership.

Since, its inception, the European Union has had a critical impact on agricultural practice and the trade in live animals and animal produce within Europe. The Common Agricultural Policy was instituted during the early 1960s with a view to increasing agricultural productivity, ensuring a fair standard of living for the agricultural community, stabilising markets, ensuring food supplies and providing consumers with food at reasonable prices. It has been perhaps the most important Common Policy that operates within the Union and has served as an important precursor to the 'single market' that is today intended to guarantee the free movement of goods, services, capital and people between the fifteen member states. The Common Agricultural Policy greatly influenced the economics of livestock farming within Europe and initially encouraged farmers to intensify production. Ultimately this led to massive overproduction and the creation of huge surpluses, which in turn depressed market prices. 'Butter and beef mountains' came to symbolise the crisis in European agriculture; livestock numbers needed to be reduced and milk quotas were introduced. The Common Agricultural Policy has consequently undergone significant reforms and today it even encourages the extensification of production methods, particularly in the beef sector.

Free trade between member states remains at the top of the European Union's agenda, and trade naturally includes the trade in livestock and animal produce. As the epizootics of the past clearly evidenced, the movement of animals across national borders presents potentially great hazards to both public and animal health. Each member state has its own internal legislation and procedures regarding the control and prevention of livestock disease; the efficacy of which is entirely dependent on the efficiency of and cooperation between livestock producers, veterinarians and governmental agencies. However, membership of the European Union has required that each country's system of animal disease control be brought in line with those of other member states, in order to ensure a harmonisation and uniformity of disease prevention. Moreover, a system of veterinary inspection and veterinary and live-stock regulations have necessarily been introduced in an attempt to ensure the health of animals and the safety of meat that are crossing national borders.

With regard to livestock, each animal that is traded between member states, or enters the Union from a non-member state, must be accompanied by a veterinary health certificate that has been signed by an official veterinarian. Two types of certificates exist: one for animals intended for breeding and production; and another for animals intended for slaughter. The health requirements for breeding animals are much more stringent than for those destined for slaughter. These certificates detail the animal's origins, destination, means of transport, age, breed, type, means of identification and whether they passed through a market or assembly point. Such certificates are valid for ten days after the animal has been loaded for transport. In this way, diseased animals can be traced along with those that they came into contact with during transport.

The health certificate states that the animal has been examined and has been passed as healthy by an official veterinarian and that it originates from a herd or region free from specified diseases. Animals may have to undergo further tests depending on their origin, type and destination. Traded livestock must meet a number of welfare considerations determined on a Union-wide basis. Likewise, the rules for the trade in meat have been harmonised throughout the European Union, in order that animal flesh is produced, preserved and transported according to rules of hygiene identical to every member state. Certificates issued by official veterinarians at the place of meat production provide a guarantee that the meat is fit for consumption and serve as a valid transport document which testifies to the safety of the product. Produce from outside the European Union is subject to similar checks at border inspection posts and is required to meet the standards deemed acceptable within the Union.

The veterinary regime has thus been further consolidated on an international level and has led—at least in principle—to the standardisation of the control of animal disease, welfare and health care and the quality of meat and other foods of animal origin within Europe. The legislators in Brussels have ensured that member states adopt uniform policies with regard to livestock production. European legislation, therefore, has increasingly come to determine the nature of national legislation. For example, since, 1988, EU countries have maintained a ban on all growth-stimulating hormones, although such products are still widely employed in the USA. Attempts to eliminate the illegal trade in such hormone products even led to the murder of a Belgian veterinary inspector in 1995. An illustration of the impact of the EU's veterinary regulations on member states can also be provided by events surrounding the bovine spongiform encephalopathy (BSE) crisis. The severity of the legislation has greatly disabled the British livestock and meat trade and has also had significant repercussions for other countries.

It seems likely that the public health issues and trade problems surrounding BSE will continue to feature prominently on the European economic, agricultural and veterinary agenda in Brussels in the future. Similarly, the way the 1997 outbreak of classical swine fever in the Netherlands has been dealt with has to a great extent been affected by EU regulations. While vaccination may provide the key to ending the crisis, the EU has committed itself to a policy of eradication of classical swine fever and, at present, forbids the use of a vaccine which may be effective against the disease. The Dutch pig industry has been crippled by this outbreak, export embargoes have been instituted and over three million pigs have been destroyed, not necessarily because they had contracted the disease, but to prevent overcrowding of pig stalls.

While animal disease control and prevention measures have become increasingly stringent throughout Europe during the twentieth century, leading to the virtual eradication of the majority of animal plagues that decimated livestock and played havoc with the European economy in centuries past, we cannot forget that the modern global economy and the routine movement of individuals—both human and animal—across and between continents also have a bearing on veterinary public health within the bounds of Europe. Diseases such as tuberculosis and classical swine fever, for example, are known to have been transmitted to western European livestock from live animal imports or animal produce from Eastern Europe.

Similarly, imports from countries where animal disease control is not so advanced or strict may still pose a threat to public health since, spores of diseases such as anthrax, which have more or less been eradicated in advanced Western societies, can still be introduced through the import of hides, animal foods etc. from regions where the disease still persists. It must also be noted that while a highly effective veterinary regime exists within Europe, veterinary policing is not always as efficient as it should be and regulations are not always well enforced.

Essentially, it only takes one weak link in the chain of interdependencies involved in the process of transforming animals into safe food to lead to inefficiencies and failures in animal disease control. Again, the recent BSE crisis provides a clear example of this. Inadequate compliance with and policing of the meat and bone meal bans, first introduced by the British government in 1988 to prevent the feeding of mammalian protein to ruminants, appear to have allowed the epidemic to continue, when it might otherwise have been curtailed. One may thus conclude that any animal disease control measures that the legislators introduce can only be as good as their policing.

The control of animal disease today is far from simply a local or regional problem, it has instead become a global one. The involvement of veterinary experts in the policy making and execution of the World Health Organisation (WHO) and the Food and Agriculture Organisation (FAO) certainly attests to this. However, although advanced industrialised societies have the animal disease problem more or less under control—producing significant animal protein surpluses in spite of continuing population growth—the (rural) populations of developing nations across the globe continue to suffer both the economic and health effects of animal disease. Furthermore, animal diseases can affect livestock populations and food production to such an extent that they do not even return a profit. Livestock disease therefore not only generates economic problems, but also wastes resources which could help to solve the problem of world food shortages.

While the focus of this chapter is far from global, it is still important to be aware of the fact that the relationship between humans, animals and the environment in which they all live is a continually changing one which is not confined within national borders. The complexity and scale of interdependencies between humans and other animals is such today that failure to keep disease-causing microorganisms adequately in check could be potentially devastating for both the physical and economic health of world populations. The necessity of an effective and globally-oriented veterinary regime in present-day society is, therefore, manifest.

❐

# 4

# Dairy Cattle

Dairy cattle (dairy cows) are cattle cows (adult females) bred for the ability to produce large quantities of milk, from which dairy products are made. Dairy cows generally are of the species Bos taurus.

Historically, there was little distinction between dairy cattle and beef cattle, with the same stock often being used for both meat and milk production. Today, dairy cows are specialized and most have been bred to produce large volumes of milk, with little or no regard for their production of meat. Between 1959 and 1990, US milk production doubled while the number of dairy cows declined 40 per cent.

## COW

Dairy cows may be found either in herds on dairy farms where dairy farmers own, manage, care for, and collect milk from them, or on commercial farms. Dairy cow herds range in size from small farms of fewer than five cows to large herds of about 20,000.

The average dairy farmer in the United States manages about one hundred cows but this varies from an average of 800 cows in California to under 80 in the North East states. Herd sizes vary around the world depending on landholding culture and social structure. In many European countries the average herd size is well below 50. In the UK it is over 100 in New Zealand 350 and Australia 280.

To maintain high milk production, a dairy cow must be bred and produce calves. Depending on market conditions, the cow may be bred with a "dairy bull" or a "beef bull." Female calves (heifers) with dairy breeding may be kept as replacement cows for the dairy herd. If a replacement cow turns out to be a substandard producer of milk, she then goes to market and can be killed for beef.

Male calves can either be used later as a breeding bull or sold and used for veal or beef. Most dairy farmers begin breeding heifers at fifteen months of age. A cow's gestation period is approximately nine months, so most heifers give birth at around two years of age.

A Californian industry report, the natural lifespan of a dairy cow is approximately 15–25 years, however dairy cows are rarely kept longer than five years prior to slaughter. Herd life is strongly correlated with production levels. Approximately 17 per cent of the US beef supply comes from cull dairy cows: cows that can no longer be seen as a economic asset to the dairy farm. These animals may be sold due to common diseases of milk cows including mastitis, lameness, or other diseases.

In India, the Hindu majority holds the cow as sacred and a motherly figure due to her capacity to give milk. Cow slaughter is legally banned in India (except in the state of Kerala, West Bengal and the seven north eastern states). Thus, spent dairy cows don't go to slaughter, but are often seen as roaming on the city streets and die of old age or disease. Some pious Hindu organizations manage "old age homes" for old dairy cows.

**Cows Used for their Milk**

Cows produce milk for the same reason that humans do: to nourish their young. In order to force the animals to continue giving milk, factory farm operators typically impregnate them using artificial insemination every year. Calves are generally taken from their mothers within a day of being born—males are destined for veal crates or barren lots where they will be fattened for beef, and females are sentenced to the same fate as their mothers.

After their calves are taken away from them, mother cows are hooked up, several times a day, to milking machines. These cows are genetically manipulated, artificially inseminated, and often drugged to force them to produce about four and a half times as much milk as they naturally would to feed their calves.

Animals are often dosed with bovine growth hormone (BGH), which contributes to a painful inflammation of the udder known as "mastitis." (BGH is used widely in the U.S., but has been banned in Europe and Canada because of concerns over human health and animal welfare.) According to the industry's own figures, between 30 and 50 per cent of dairy cows suffer from mastitis, an extremely painful condition.

A cow's natural lifespan is about 25 years, but cows used by the dairy industry are killed after only four or five years. An industry study reports that by the time they are killed, nearly 40 per cent of dairy cows are lame because of the intensive confinement, the filth, and the strain of being almost constantly pregnant and giving milk. Dairy cows' bodies are turned into soup, companion animal food, or low-grade hamburger meat because their bodies are too "spent" to be used for anything else.

## CALF

Market calves are generally sold at two weeks of age and bull calves may fetch a premium over heifers due to their size, either current or potential. Calves may be sold for veal, or for one of several types of beef production, depending on available local crops and markets. Such bull calves may be castrated if turnout onto pastures is envisaged, in order to render the animals less aggressive. Purebred bulls from elite cows may be put into progeny testing schemes to find out whether they might become superior sires for breeding. Such animals may become extremely valuable.

Most dairy farms separate calves from their mothers within a day of birth to reduce transmission of disease and simplify management of milking cows. Studies have been done allowing calves to remain with their mothers for 1, 4, 7 or 14 days after birth. Cows whose calves were removed longer than one day after birth showed increased searching, sniffing and vocalizations. However, calves allowed to remain with their mothers for longer periods showed weight gains at three times the rate of early removals as well as more searching behaviour and better social relationships with other calves.

After separation, most young dairy calves subsist on commercial milk replacer, a feed based on dried milk powder. Milk replacer is an economical alternative to feeding whole milk because it is cheaper, can be bought at varying fat and protein percentages. A day old calf consumes around 5 liters of milk per day.

## BULL

A bull calf with high genetic potential may be reared for breeding purposes. It may be kept by a dairy farm as a herd bull, to provide natural breeding for the herd cows. A bull may service up to 50 or 60 cows during a breeding season. Any more and the sperm count will decline, leading to cows "returning to service" (to be bred again). A herd bull may only stay for one season since, over two years old their temperament becomes too unpredictable. Bull calves intended for breeding commonly are bred on specialized dairy breeding farms, not production farms. These farms are the major source of stocks for artificial insemination (AI).

## HORSES

### Social Enrichment

As prey species, horses are highly motivated to interact with individuals of their own species for comfort, play, access to food and shelter resources, and as an antipredator strategy. During fearful situations and when separated from closely bonded companions, restlessness, pacing, and vocalizations occur and suggest experiences of acute anxiety and distress. Horses housed singly display greater activity and reduced foraging compared with horses kept in pairs or groups. Horses housed singly also display more aggression towards human handlers and learn new tasks more slowly than horses housed in groups.

Confining horses for long periods may produce behavioural problems that sometimes progress to the exhibition of stereotypies, commonly referred to as vices. Examples include stall weaving, cribbing, or wind sucking. Management efforts to minimize stereotypies include companionship, exercise, environmental enrichment objects, or increasing dietary fibre by pasture grazing, availability of hay, or providing multiple forage types. In feral and wild situations, horses maintain longterm relationships.

Stallions and mares stay together year-round over multiple breeding seasons, whereas colts and fillies emigrate from the natal herd when they are juveniles. Mare–mare bonds are very stable and persist for years, although social interactions decrease markedly during the postparturient period when mares direct social behaviour towards their foals. For mares and fillies, social bonds are likely to develop between individuals that are familiar, closely related, and similar in social rank.

Social relationships between females are characterized by mutual grooming and maintaining close proximity. In the absence of these factors, social bonds are directed towards unfamiliar individuals that have the same coat colour as the filly's dam. Mutual grooming is directed towards the withers and neck region and is associated with reduced heart rate suggesting a role in reducing anxiety. Mutual grooming is rarely performed by stallions, except following periods of social deprivation.

In contrast, colts and gelding are highly motivated to play with each other. When housed in extensive conditions, colts perform hourly play bouts, such as mock fighting, whereas mares do not typically engage in this behaviour. Because aggression and play can result in injuries, stallions are typically housed singly. Aggression is influenced by reproductive status, with greater aggression in established groups occurring in the breeding and foaling season.

In mixed groups, mares display more aggression in the postparturient period, primarily in the form of interventions to protect foals from barren mares and geldings. Similarly during feeding trials, yearling females perform significantly more agonistic interactions than geldings of the same age, likely because of circulating steroid levels at estrus. When horses are housed singly or in isolation facilities, distress associated with social deprivation can be alleviated by providing visual contact with other equids.

Weaving and head-nodding stereotypies, which are associated with frustration are significantly reduced when horses can see other equids through grilled side windows or when mirrors or life-sized poster images of a horse's face are placed in the stalls. Lateral visual contact appears to be important, because weaving is significantly more likely to occur when stalls are arranged face-to-face than side-by-side. In the absence of equids, horses readily form social relationships with other species, such as goats, dogs, and humans.

Intensively managed horses detect and respond to subtle indicators of emotional state and confidence in their human handlers, eliciting both fearfulness and calmness. Horses accept being groomed by humans; reductions in heart rate that occur when horses perform mutual grooming are also observed when humans brush or scratch the withers and neck regions. However, this positive association with tactile stimulation by humans appears to be learned rather than innate and in the absence of positive interactions, foals begin to avoid humans at 3 wk of age.

**Physical Enrichment**

Horses provided access to paddocks or pasture can alleviate foraging motivation through grazing, but horses also benefit from opportunities to exercise, with activity positively associated with paddock size. Horses appear to be motivated to perform exercise in its own right, with motivation building up and compensatory activity performed after periods of deprivation.

Furthermore, horses provided with turn-out display more varied rolling behaviour, which is believed to be associated with comfort. In a study of racing horses, benefits of regular turn-out also included less aggression directed towards handlers and superior race and career performance.

**Occupational Enrichment**

In the absence of turning out in paddocks or pastures, horses can direct play behaviour towards "toys" placed in the stall. Several commercially available products such as the large durable balls designed to be used with stabled horses can be provided, as well as home-made devices such as plastic jugs hanging on ropes. Scientific evidence regarding the efficacy of these products is lacking.

### Sensory Enrichment

In many stables, it is common for background noise to be provided by a radio, with the assumption that this provides a calming effect on the horses and alleviates boredom. However, the presence or type of music was not found to significantly affect the behaviour of ponies subjected to short-term isolation distress. These authors speculate that background music may indirectly affect equine behaviour through the attitudes of their human caretakers. Conversely, a synthetic Equine Appeasement Pheromone product is commercially available, and there is minimal evidence that this product effectively reduces behavioural and physiologic fear responses of horses subjected to a stressful situation.

### Nutritional Enrichment

Opportunities to forage provide significant enrichment for stabled horses. Horses typically spend 10 to 12 h grazing per day and lactating mares spend 70% of their time grazing on pasture. In the absence of foraging material, horses frequently may direct foraging towards the stall bedding or stall surfaces or may display oral stereotypies such as crib-biting, wind-sucking, sham chewing, hair eating, and wood chewing/licking. Undesirable oral behaviour can be addressed by providing at least 6.8 kg of hay per day, providing multiple forages, and dividing concentrate feed into smaller and more frequent meals throughout the day.

Horses provided with straw bedding perform less stereotypic behaviour than those bedded on paper or shavings. Several food toys are commercially available, which horses manipulate to obtain high-fibre food pellets. These food-balls result in increased foraging time and reduced stereotypic behaviour. Toys with round or polyhedral designs are most effective. These toys can be provided in the manger to prevent horses from ingesting pathogens and nonnutritive materials from the stall bedding.

## SHEEP AND GOATS

### Social Enrichment

Validation of enrichment devices and procedures for sheep is extremely limited. However, sheep are highly social animals, and if social contact must be limited it may be beneficial to provide the sheep with visual contact with other sheep through fencing or other transparent materials. It has also been suggested that a mirror or an inanimate object covered with animal skin could serve as a social surrogate. Mirrors can reduce but do not abolish the physiological stress response to social isolation in sheep. However, because sheep appear to treat their own reflection as a strange individual it is also possible that a mirror image could cause social stress.

### Nutritional Enrichment

Devices that provide feed supplements when manipulated by licking or pushing with the head may occupy the animals' attention. However, care must be taken to keep these objects clean, as they quickly become contaminated with manure.

### Occupational and Physical Enrichment

An undesirable behaviour called wool biting may develop in confined sheep. Wool-biting sheep take bites of and eat wool from other sheep. This may compromise the health and well-being of the sheep that are "victimized," and may alter the nutritional status of the sheep performing the wool biting. Wool biting seems to be a redirected behaviour of confined sheep, and lack of environmental stimulation and diet may contribute to the onset of wool biting.

Strategies that have been used to prevent or stop wool biting include hanging chains above the surface of the pen, adding objects to the pen playing music, and altering the diet. Increasing the roughage content of the diet may reduce the incidence of wool biting, although definitive methods for preventing or reducing this behaviour have not been reported.

Goats will climb a variety of objects such as tables, empty cable spools, or even elaborate jungle gyms. These structures will be used throughout the day. An enriched environment has been shown to increase feed consumption and reduce aggression in goats in feedlots. Care must be taken to provide appropriate climbing space that is ample for the number of animals in the group, as dominant animals will displace subordinates. Also, climbing devices should be placed in such a manner as to prevent the goats from vaulting out of the enclosure.

## SWINE

An enriched environment contributes to pig wellbeing in numerous ways, as indicated by increased behavioural diversity, adaptability to novelty, and learning ability, coupled with reduced aggression, fearfulness, stereotyped behaviour, belly nosing, and tail and ear biting. An extensive enrichment programme would provide sufficient environmental complexity to enable pigs to express a wide range of normal behaviour and to exercise a degree of control and choice in their environment, but also needs to promote pig health and be practical to employ.

### Social Enrichment

Housing pigs in stable social groups with ample space and environmental complexity enables them to adjust their proximity to different individuals according to their social relationships and current state. Alternative housing systems that minimize regrouping and social stress are available and may be of use for certain research and teaching protocols or in certain herds.

When pigs must be isolated from conspecifics for experimental purposes, friendly social contact with familiar caretakers could be especially important. Pigs recognize familiar caretakers using visual as well as vocal and olfactory cues. Caretakers can develop positive social contact with pigs by moving slowly and calmly, crouching to reduce apparent body size, avoiding aversive or inconsistent handling, and stroking or scratching pigs that approach.

When pigs have a positive attitude towards caretakers, they will approach confidently and seek interaction, which may have positive implications for handling strategies. Providing companionship from familiar pen-mates and a warm, artificial udder with flexible nipples can decrease distress in piglets that must be weaned at an early age for experimental reasons.

### Occupational Enrichment

Occupational enrichment is achieved by allowing and promoting physical exercise, foraging, exploration, nest-building, playing, and manipulative and cognitive activities. Access to pasture, soil, straw, peat, mushroom compost, hay, bark, branches, logs, and other malleable materials helps to satisfy these urges. These materials provide an outlet for exploration, sniffing, biting, rooting, and chewing activities, reducing the likelihood that these behaviours will be redirected towards the bodies of pen-mates or pen fixtures.

Such enrichment materials can lower the risk of injuries and harassment from tail biting, ear chewing, and belly nosing, as well as reducing aggressive behaviour and wear and tear on housing fixtures. Pigs are initially attracted to materials that are odorous, deformable, and chewable, but for sustained occupational enrichment, the best materials are complex, changeable, manipulatable, destructible, and are ingestible or contain sparsely distributed edible parts. Thus, pigs prefer to root in and manipulate materials such as corn silage mixed with straw, compost, turf, peat, forest soil, beets, spruce chips, and fir branches.

Although somewhat less preferred than these materials, long straw is a useful enrichment material, being more effective than chopped straw, sand, or ropes, and much more effective than indestructible objects such as hoses, chains, and tires. Unattached objects presented at floor level may be more attractive to pigs than hanging objects but lose their attractiveness when soiled with excreta. Most research on enrichment materials has focused on straw. The amount of behaviour directed towards long straw rather than towards pen-mates is proportional to the amount of straw provided.

Although providing straw only after tail biting has started can reduce the behaviour, it does not act as a complete curative. Providing straw from an early age helps to prevent tail biting, lowers aggression, and maintains normal activity. However, the risk of tail biting is elevated, and activity is depressed, if pigs initially reared with straw are subsequently housed without straw. These findings highlight the importance of continuing an enrichment programme once it has started.

Slatted floors and liquid-manure systems usually preclude the provision of ample amounts of long straw and other particulate foraging materials. In this situation, offering small amounts of such materials in racks or troughs, and replenishing the supply frequently, stimulates sniffing, rooting, and chewing while maintaining a degree of novelty that is important for sustaining the interest of curious pigs. When particulate materials cannot be used, hanging ropes with unraveled ends that can be pulled, shaken, chewed, and torn apart are the next best option.

Less-destructible novel hanging objects can offer short-term enrichment by attracting exploration and stimulating play but they need to be changed frequently because pigs rapidly lose interest in such objects when they are no longer novel. Enrichment materials and objects should be monitored to ensure that they do not cause health problems or compromise food safety.

Supplying ample free access to preferred enrichment materials and objects will minimize aggressive competition for these resources. Offering opportunities for pigs to respond to environmental cues to find occasional food rewards and to work for access to foraging materials and hidden food treats can be rewarding. This form of enrichment has been found to speed wound healing.

At least 24 h before farrowing, provision of an earth or sand substrate along with straw, branches, or other nesting materials enables sows to address their strong motivation to engage in nest-building behaviour, which, under natural conditions, involves digging a shallow depression with the snout and then gathering nesting materials such as long grass, twigs, and branches, carrying them to the nest site in the mouth, and arranging them into a nest.

Providing nest materials can contribute to early piglet survival although results are variable. Long straw is preferred over cloth tassels as a nesting material although the latter may have some benefit in liquid-manure systems that preclude the use of straw.

**Physical Enrichment**

Pigs show spatial separation of different behaviours such as lying, feeding, and excretion. Providing ample space or appropriate subdivision of the enclosure area enables the establishment of separate functional areas. For example, Simonsen subdivided pens into areas with straw bedding, a pigoperated shower, straw racks, and logs hung on chains, and Stolba and Wood-Gush subdivided enclosures into areas for nesting, feeding, rooting, and excretion.

Two-level pens also subdivide the pen space, thereby encouraging exercise, making handling and herding of pigs easier, and allowing pigs to exercise choice of thermal environment. Habituation to ramps and alleys in the housing environment reduces novelty-induced fear when pigs are subsequently handled. Allowing pigs daily access to enriched areas that are not accessible full time can stimulate anticipation and play.

To avoid overcrowding and competition in one area of a subdivided or multi-level pen, calculation of stocking density and feeder space should take into account variations in the distribution of pigs across different areas of the pen. Providing visual barriers helps pigs to avoid aggressive pen-mates. This can be achieved by installing solid partitions between feeding spaces, boxes, or holes in the wall where pigs can hide their heads, straw bales, dividers between different functional areas, or an upper pen level accessed by a ramp.

In outdoor pens, bushes, trees, and varied terrain can serve to create visually discrete areas. Loose housing of sows allows freedom of movement leading to a shorter farrowing duration and lower stress at parturition relative to confinement in crates, and the risk of injuries can be reduced by secure footing and well-managed bedding. Pens with stalls along with communal activity and resting areas allow gestating sows in groups to move freely and rest together while enabling temporary separation in stalls for feeding or experimental purposes.

In addition to providing occupational enrichment, bedding gives thermal comfort in cool weather as well as cushioning the body against hard surfaces. Only good-quality bedding should be used to avoid introduction of mycotoxin molds, and bedding must be managed to avoid wet litter and high ammonia emissions. Certain types of artificial lying mats may also contribute to lying comfort.

In outdoor pens, huts or kennels supplied with straw create suitable lying areas in cold weather. In hot weather, wallows, snout coolers, or snout-operated showers aid thermoregulation. An earth substrate allows pigs to dig a simple depression in the ground for nesting. Shade may be needed to protect outdoor pigs from heat stress and sunburn.

**Sensory Enrichment**

Pigs can learn to associate olfactory, vocal, and colour cues with a food reward. For example, pigs use the odour of dimethyl sulfide to locate buried truffles, a highly desired food item that has a musky garlic/mushroom flavour and contains the boar sex pheromone 5-□-androstenol. Pigs also seek opportunities to interact with materials that provide tactile stimulation of different areas of their snout and mouth. Sensory cues paired with rewards, including access to enrichment materials, can be used to stimulate anticipatory excitement and play.

Habituation to a wide array of nonharmful sensory stimuli when young may reduce fear in novel situations when older, and exposure to sensory stimuli that evoke comforting associations may be helpful at times of unavoidable stress. Decisions about cleaning regimens should take into account that pigs communicate through odours. It is important to avoid disruptive cleaning routines during the first week after farrowing, which is an important time for social attachment between the sow and her piglets and the establishment of the teat order.

Although moderate levels of ammonia do not appear to be highly aversive and do not disrupt social recognition, keeping ammonia to a minimum should facilitate exploration of diverse environmental odours. Enrichment materials with noticeable odours attract exploration, and pigs show preferences for foods with certain odours or flavours, whereas materials soiled by excreta are aversive.

Providing chewable tubes offering flavoured water may not be sufficient to prevent tail biting. To facilitate vocal communication between pigs, continuous loud noise should be avoided. This is especially important in the farrowing area because vocalizations between sows and piglets are important for social bonding and effective nursing, and masking these vocalizations with high levels of ambient sound can disrupt suckling behaviour.

Piglets should be handled in a manner that minimizes loud vocalizations that signal piglet distress and disturb the sows. Consideration should be given to handling piglets outside the hearing range of sows if loud calling by piglets is unavoidable. Silence is more effective in quieting piglets separated from the sow than playback of meditation music, white noise, or vocalizations of unfamiliar piglets.

Furthermore, pigs are not especially attracted to enrichment materials that produce sound when manipulated. On the other hand, habituation to a variety of environmental sounds should help to reduce fear when pigs are moved to new environments, and playing a radio may be useful for masking sounds on occasions when sudden, unpredictable, loud noises are anticipated, such as those generated during construction.

**Nutritional Enrichment**

When feeding concentrated diets, feed restriction is usually needed during pregnancy to prevent excessive weight gain, which may result in later difficulties during farrowing and lactation. Although the ration fulfills their nutrient requirements, the sows eat it quickly and are hungry for much of the day. The sows' normal response is to forage for additional food. When sows are housed in an environment with no outlet for diverse foraging behaviours, aggression may increase, foraging behaviour may be channeled into a few elements performed repetitively in stereotyped sequences or abnormal amounts of water may be consumed.

These behaviours are reduced by providing straw and other ingestible foraging substrates that occupy the sows in diverse foraging activities and by feeding a diet high in fermentable nonstarch polysaccharides to increase satiety. Although increasing the fibre content of the diet does not always influence stereotyped oral-nasal-facial behaviours, the incidence of gastric lesions may be reduced in pigs given straw compared with those lacking access to roughage.

Chewable and destructible but inedible substrates and objects such as ropes and cloth tassels are less satisfying to sows than straw or other fibrous materials but are better than hard, indestructible objects such as chains and stones towards which sows direct stereotypic behaviour. Incorporating a nutritional reward in a rootable or chewable object increases its attractiveness over objects that do not provide food reinforcement.

Although stereotyped behaviour peaks in the period immediately following a meal suggesting that limit-fed sows should be given concentrated feed in a single daily meal rather than multiple smaller meals, provision of small food rewards does not appear to cause stereotypic behaviour when combined with loose housing in straw-bedded pens.

Under these conditions, limit-fed sows can be extensively occupied by provision of food in devices that require work to extract it. It is important to make sure that there are sufficient nutritional enrichment devices to avoid aggressive competition. In general, the benefits of environmental enrichment for pigs are likely to be greatest when multiple forms of enrichment are supplied.

## CATTLE OF BEEF

Beef cattle includes all animals of the genus Bos and their close relatives that are raised primarily for meat production. As ruminants, beef cattle are capable of utilizing a wide range of feedstuffs and consequently are maintained in an array of situations ranging from extensive grazing to confined feedlot pens and intensive laboratory environments. Regardless of the housing system, basic needs for food, water, shelter, and comfort should be met.

## FACILITIES AND ENVIRONMENT

### Ideal Thermal Conditions

Under most environmental conditions, temperature represents a major portion of the driving force for heat exchange between the environment and an animal. However, moisture and heat content of the air, thermal radiation, and airflow also affect total heat exchange. Thus, a combination of environmental variables contributes to the conditions to which an animal responds. Under conditions in which relative measures and comparisons of the effect of different environmental variables could be determined, the apparent ambient temperature at which animals can cope has been defined with a reasonable degree of accuracy; however, variation does exist among animals. Environmental conditions that provide maximum comfort and require little or no energy expenditure for maintenance depend on cattle age, metabolic size, and/or body mass and surface area. The TCZ generally ranges between 15 to 25°C for most cattle less than 1 mo old; between 5 and 20°C for a mature beef cow consuming a maintenance diet; and between–10 and 20°C for yearlings with ad libitum access to energy-dense feedlot diets.

Based on physiological responses and heat load thresholds, Bos indicus and some heat-tolerant Bos taurus cattle breeds have a TCZ at least 5°C greater than typical Bos taurus cattle. Encompassing the TCZ is the thermoneutral zone (TNZ). Within the TNZ, an animal can maintain homeostasis through normal physiological and metabolic processes, which may require minimal expenditure of energy when the animal is exposed to conditions outside the TCZ. The TNZ generally ranges between 10 and 30°C for most cattle less than 1 mo old; between–15 and 28°C for a mature beef cow consuming a maintenance diet; and between–35 and 25°C for yearlings with ad libitum access to energy-dense feedlot diets. Even though the upper end of the TNZ for most Bos taurus cattle is between 25 and 30°C, for high-producing cattle with high intakes of metabolizable energy the upper limit may be closer to 20°C on sunny days when little or no wind is present.

When given sufficient time, cattle acclimate and adapt to colder or hotter conditions. It should be noted that cattle that are adapted to–35°C may be uncomfortable at 10°C. Thus, the TCZ and TNZ serve only as guidelines to describe the limits within which cattle are comfortable and can adapt to, respectively. Independent of these guidelines, performance standards that indicate a problem with the thermal environment include, in cold weather, shivering, huddling, and loss of body condition/weight; and in hot weather, panting, sweating, and a reduction in feed intake. Primary factors that affect thermal comfort include feed/energy intake and body condition/fat cover.

## Thermal Indices

At the present time, the temperature-humidity index {THI; THI = 0.8 × ambient temperature + [( per cent relative humidity/100) × (ambient temperature–14.4)] + 46.4} has become the de facto standard for classifying thermal environments in many animal studies and selection of management practices during seasons other than winter. The THI, first proposed by Thom has been extensively applied for moderate to hot conditions, even with recognized limitations related to airspeed and radiation heat loads. A THI between 70 and 74 is an indication to producers that the potential for heat stress in livestock exists. In particular, when THI values are above 70 by 0800h, it is recommended that managers of confined cattle that have high metabolic heat loads initiate or prepare to initiate heat-stress management strategies before cattle become exposed to the excessive heat load.

A THI of 84 or above can cause death, especially in feedlot cattle that are within 45 d of slaughter and consuming high-energy finishing diets. Modifications to the THI have been developed to overcome the shortcomings related to the lack of airflow and radiation heat load in the index. Eigenberg also developed similar adjustments based on predictions of respiration rates using ambient and dew point temperature, windspeed, and solar radiation. These models have merit in that the combined effects of multiple environmental factors can be taken into account when determining animal comfort.

Gaughan developed a more extensive index as a guide to the management of feedlot cattle during hot weather. The heat load index (HLI) incorporates black globe temperature, relative humidity, and windspeed. A threshold above which cattle are less efficient at dissipating heat was developed for a reference animal. The threshold for a full-blood Brahman steer is 96. Also, adjustments to the threshold are possible for use of shade, clean dry pens, cattle coat colour, and days on feed. The thresholds are lowered if cattle are sick or not acclimated to summer conditions. Very limited data exist for assessing environmental effects on reproduction.

However, Amundson found THI and daily minimum temperature to be equally good predictors of pregnancy rate at 42 d into the breeding season. However, the combination of wind speed and THI had the greatest correlation to pregnancy rate. Indices for cold stress are not as well defined as for heat stress. The wind chill index (WCI) has traditionally been used to derive an apparent temperature for humans. In 2001, the National Weather Service released a new WCI that may have merit for assessing effects of wind on domestic livestock.

## Range and Pasture Systems

Acceptable systems for grazing beef cattle on pasture and rangeland vary widely. Cow body condition is an excellent performance standard for monitoring the well-being and nutritional status of range cattle. Special consideration needs to be given to environmental factors that affect grazing beef cattle. In areas where heat stress is common, provision of shade to decrease the solar heat load is the most practical intervention in pasture and range systems.

The need for artificial shade should be assessed after careful consideration of the adequacy of naturally occurring sources. Heat stress is evidenced when respiration rates begin to increase. Prolonged increases in body temperatures will result in decreased feed intake, body condition, and weight. In areas where exposure to extreme cold is likely, provision of shelter for grazing beef cattle may be desirable. Grazing beef cows decrease grazing time and forage intake as ambient temperature decreases below 0°C, although such changes are small in adapted beef cows. Cattle use windbreaks to decrease wind chill and prevent exposure to blowing snow, although it has not been clearly established that windbreaks improve animal performance.

Supplementary feed should be provided during periods of heavy snow cover that preclude grazing. An adequate supply of forage should be available to grazing cattle. Intake and performance may be decreased when the amount of standing forage is lacking but the appropriate quantity of forage dry matter per hectare varies with the pasture or range type and the stocking rate. Guidelines for acceptable amounts of standing forage per unit of body weight at given stocking rates are available but additional research is needed with a variety of pasture and range types. Grazing beef cattle should be provided with supplements for nutrients that are known to be deficient in pasture and range forage in particular localities. In almost all grazing environments, range cattle require free-choice access to supplemental salt as a source of supplemental sodium.

Typically, these salt-based, free-choice mineral supplements will also be fortified with trace minerals. Observation and monitoring of range cattle often occur less regularly than for other livestock. When supplemental feed is provided, cattle are usually observed at least 2 or 3 times weekly. Unsupplemented cattle on open range may be observed less frequently. However, it is recommended that range cattle be observed at least once per week. In certain areas, grazing beef cattle may be affected by predators and poisonous plants. Careful attention should be given to such problems, and efforts should be made to decrease or eliminate these adverse conditions. Availability of fresh, unfrozen water is critical for grazing beef cattle, and distance to water should be given consideration in pasture and range systems.

If cattle are required to travel long distances to water in hot, dry climates, animal performance and utilization of pasture forage can be affected. Holechek recommended that distance to water be no greater than 1.6 km in rolling, hilly country and in undulating, sandy terrain. This recommendation was decreased to 0.8 km in rough country, increased to 2.4 km in smooth, sandy terrain, and increased to 3.2 km in areas with flat terrain. Thus, the distance to water for grazing cattle should not exceed 3.2 km, and every animal should have the opportunity to drink ad libitum at least once per day.

**Feed and Water**

Diets for beef cattle should be formulated according to the recommendations of the NRC. Formulation of diets should consider factors such as environmental conditions, breed or biological type, sex, and production demands for growth, gestation, or lactation. Feed and water should be offered to cattle in ways that minimize contamination by urine, feces, and other materials. Feed bunks should be monitored daily and contaminants or spoiled feed should be removed. In most situations, feed should be available at all times.

However, restricted feeding of high-energy diets may be practiced to meet maintenance requirements or targeted levels of production. When restricted feeding is practiced, feed must be uniformly distributed in the bunk to allow all cattle to have simultaneous access to the diet. When high-energy diets are fed, increased attentiveness should be given to possible occurrence of dietrelated health problems such as grain overload, lactic acidosis, and bloat. Abrupt changes in diets should be avoided. Feed deprivation for more than 24 h should be avoided, and feed deprivation for any length of time must be justified in the animal use protocol. Cattle can vary considerably in body weight and condition during the course of grazing and reproductive cycles. Feeding programmes should allow animals to regain the body weight that is lost during the normal periods of negative energy balance.

Confined cattle should have continuous free access to a source of water, except before surgery or weighing if the research or animal care protocol requires such restriction. When continuous access to water is not possible, water should be available ad libitum at least once daily and more often if hot weather conditions exist or cattle have high levels of metabolizable energy intake for purposes of achieving high output. Under winter range conditions, Degen and Young found that snow can be used as a water source for beef cows and growing calves. However, there was evidence that the snow resulted in reduced water intakes as evidenced by compensatory water intake when water was reintroduced following 84 d of consuming water in the form of snow. When snow was the only source of water, total water intake reductions averaged approximately 10 per cent among the cattle groups.

The quantity and, possibly, quality of water available will influence animal comfort, especially under hot conditions. Evaporation of moisture from the skin surface or respiratory tract is the primary mechanism used by the animals to lose excess body heat in a hot environment. Estimates of daily water requirements for beef cattle are reported in NRC.

During summer months, in particular, waterer space available and water intake per animal becomes extremely important. Under these conditions, Mader found that as much as 3 times the normal waterer space may be needed to allow for sufficient room for all animals to access and benefit from available water. Additional waterer space recommendations are provided by MWPS.

**Feedlot and Housing Systems**

Beef cattle used in research or teaching may be housed in intensive management systems, either indoors or in open lots, with or without shelter. Facilities for beef cattle should provide cattle with opportunities for behavioural thermoregulation. Management of dairy beef is similar to other cattle, although, some feeding, housing, and marketing regimens are unique to Holsteins. Proper airflow and ventilation are essential in intensive facilities. In feedlots, cable or wire fencing has minimal effect on natural airflow in summer. However, high airflow rates are undesirable during periods of low temperature, and tree shelterbelts and other types of windbreak can decrease the rate of airflow past the cattle. An 80 per cent solid windbreak 3 m high decreases wind speed by half for about 45 m downwind and controls snow for about 8 m; a similar windbreak 4 m high decreases wind speed by half for about 65 m downwind and controls snow for about 10 m.

A windbreak is recommended in mounded, south-sloping feedlots in the northern United States to provide dry resting areas with low air velocities. Caution should be exercised when placing cattle in sheltered areas in the summer because of the adverse effects of restricted airflow on cattle reared in hot environments. During potentially stressful heat episodes, panting scores (1 = elevated respiration rate, 2 = drool or saliva present on side of mouth, 3 = open mouth breathing observed, and 4 = tongue and neck extended with open mouth breathing) can be utilized as an excellent indicator of stress levels experienced.

When cattle are beginning to experience panting scores of 2 or greater some means of cooling may be needed. Cattle learn to take evasive action to alleviate heat stress and such competition for cooler areas in a pen or around the water trough increases even during cooler days in which heat alleviation methods are not utilized. When this occurs evidence of crowding is observed, which exacerbates the heat stress problems.

Wetting the ground or floor of holding facilities can be an effective method of cooling cattle managed in unshaded, outdoor units where surface vegetation is sparse or nonexistent. Direct wetting of cattle during extreme heat is also an effective practice and is often used as an emergency measure. Benefits of sprinkling are enhanced if sprinkling is started in the morning, before cattle experience high heat loads. Generally, a daily application of 0.5 to 1.0 cm of water is sufficient to cool pen surfaces. However, applying 1.25 to 1.50 cm every other day is acceptable and will not sufficiently contribute to mud buildup in normally dry pens.

In areas with high evaporation rates additional water may be needed, which can serve to cool pen surfaces as well as eliminate potential dust problems. The size of the area needed to be sprinkled would be similar to the shade area recommendations. As a routine protective practice, wetting can be efficiently accomplished by utilizing a timer to provide 5 to 10 min of spray during each 20-to 30-min period.

Fogger nozzles are often mistakenly recommended for wetting animals. Fogger nozzles are less effective than sprinkler nozzles because of the barrier formed by the fine droplets. These droplets adhere to the outer hair coat of the animal, causing the heat for evaporation to come from the air rather than from the body. Mitlöhner et al. reported that misting cattle was not as effective as shade in decreasing heat stress, and in some cases, caused respiration rate to increase compared with nonmisted cattle.

Shade for cattle can provide the margin of survival for animals that are unconditioned to a sudden heat wave with high solar radiant loads in central and southern regions of the United States. Mader found limited performance benefits of utilizing shade in the north-central region of the United States, in contrast to the findings of Mitlöhner where shade was effective in southern regions.

Also, use of shade in northern climates may be costly and logistically prohibitive because of snow load requirements, potential mud problems under shade and the low percentage of time that cattle may actually benefit from using the shade. However, benefits of using shade for maintaining animal comfort will almost always be found in any area or location in which abnormally hot or hot and humid conditions arise or persist, including northern climates, and when cattle have not had the opportunity to acclimate. Mitlöhner et al. found excellent results when shades were provided for feedlot cattle reared in the south-central region of the United States, an area where more consistent benefits of shade would be expected to be realised. For optimum benefits shades should be 3.6 to 4.2 m high in areas with clear, sunny afternoons to permit maximum exposure to the relatively cool northern sky, which acts as a radiation sink.

In areas with cloudy afternoons, shades 2.1 to 2.7 m in height are more effective, as they limit the diffuse sky radiation received by animals beneath the shades. The amount of shade required for young cattle is 0.7 to 1.2 m2 per animal, whereas larger cattle need 1.8 to 2.5 m2 per animal. Shades are strongly recommended for sick cattle or for animals in hospital pens. Cold housing can be provided for beef cattle. Open sides of any cattle building need to face away from prevailing winds. Such structures are ventilated by natural airflow, and the resultant winter temperatures are typically 2 to 5°C above outdoor conditions as a result of body heat. Totally enclosed housing requires ventilation to maintain the air temperature at acceptable levels and to minimize the accumulation in the air of water vapour, noxious gases, other odourous compounds, and dust. Ventilation systems may be either natural or mechanical.

Type of pen surface affects dustiness during hot dry weather and mud or manure build-up during wet periods. Good drainage of outside pens is imperative. Dirt pens should be regularly cleaned of animal waste residues and maintained to minimize accumulation of water. A hard surface apron in front of the feed bunks and around water troughs and shelters should be considered in dirt pens. Mounds should be provided in dirt pens for cattle to lie on during inclement weather. Accumulation of mud in a pen or on the cattle can influence maintenance requirements and thermal balance. Properly designed pens with adequate slope are extremely important for minimizing mud and related health and behaviour problems. In areas where slope or drying conditions are limited, adding mounds is very useful for keeping cattle clean and dry. Under hot-humid conditions, mounds aid in preventing animal crowding and improve exposure to airflow for the animals that utilize them. Additional information on feedlot/drylot pen design and layout has been published by Pohl and Henry. For hard-surfaced pens, materials should be durable, slip-resistant, and impervious to water and urine; easily cleaned; and resistant to chemicals and corrosion from animal feed and waste. Concrete floors should be scored or grooved during construction to improve animal footing.

Properly designed slotted floors are self-cleaning. Fences, pen dividers, walls, gates, and other surfaces must be strong enough to withstand the impact of direct animal contact. Configuration and treatment of contact surfaces must minimize or eliminate protrusions, changes in elevation, and sharp corners to minimize bruising and injuries and to improve the efficiency of cattle handling. Proper lighting permits inspection of animals in feedlots and other cattle housing systems and provides safer working conditions for animal care personnel. Maintenance of facilities should be timely and ongoing.

**Husbandry**

Adequate care of cattle and calves is especially important for establishing and maintaining optimal immune system function. Good husbandry can minimize health problems and infectious diseases. The risk of disease and mortality in young calves is related to immune status. It is critical that newborn calves nurse or ingest colostrum soon after birth. The health of young growing cattle should be assessed regularly pre-and postweaning. Animal care personnel should be taught to recognize signs of illness and external parasites.

Alert caretakers should have the ability to perceive appropriate behaviour and posture. A system of monitoring calves through critical stress periods such as weaning should be established. Any sick or injured calves should be treated promptly. Daily records should be kept. For cattle reared in close confinement assessments should be done at least once daily and more often if cattle have been stressed or potentially exposed to conditions in which their health could be compromised.

In general, confined feedlot cattle, especially new incoming cattle, require more frequent observations than nonconfined cattle because of the greater probability of animal health being compromised due to comingling, dehydration, digestive problems, respiratory problems, and interaction of any of these factors with environmental stress. Signs of healthy calves are alert ears and clear eyes, no signs of diarrhea, and, upon arising, resumption of a normal standing posture after stretching.

For feedlot cattle provided energy-dense diets, caretaker knowledge of acidosis and management regimens necessary to minimize digestive problems are essential. Appropriate medication and vaccination programmes should be used to reduce the incidence of disease and mortality, improve cattle health and performance, and ensure that no illegal residues occur in the carcass. Treatment and vaccination schemes should be based on veterinary advice and experience.

### Weaning

In typical beef cow/calf production systems, calves are artificially weaned from their dams by physical separation. This process, albeit important to the efficiency of the cowherd, can be stressful to both the cow and calf. The most common weaning procedure involves an abrupt separation of cows and calves resulting in increased walking and vocalization and decreased eating and resting. An alternative to abrupt weaning and permanent separation is a period of fenceline contact between cows and calves in adjacent but separate pastures.

This weaning management alternative has been shown to decrease vocalization and walking and increase the time spent resting and grazing. This fenceline weaning procedure may also decrease the incidence of calf illness. Within the weaning pasture or pen, a mature cow can be included in the group of freshly weaned calves. This "trainer" cow can assist in introducing the weaned calves to the location and facilitating consumption of feed and water.

Despite the weaning process selected, it is important that weaned calves be provided access to clean water and a source of feed and/or forage. To encourage intake, highly palatable forage and feed sources are recommended until calves become accustomed to the separation from their dams. Additionally, feed and water sources should be placed close to the perimeter of the fenceline, because calves will typically spend a majority of their time in these areas as they seek to reunite with their dams.

### Social Environment

Cattle are social animals. Each individual in the group should have sufficient access to the resources necessary for comfort, adequate well-being, and optimal performance. Mixing, crowding, group composition, and competition for limited resources are part of the social environment and in some circumstances, may be social stressors for certain cattle.

Generally, cows from similar environments but from different social groups can be mixed with little or no long-term adverse effect on performance; however, because introduced cows may be the recipients of aggression, the number of mixing episodes should be minimized. Mixing of older cattle, especially bulls, results in more fighting than occurs when younger cattle are mixed.

Fighting and mounting can be a problem associated with keeping bulls in social groups and can present a significant welfare problem if not managed carefully. Attempts should be made to keep bulls in stable social groups and to minimize mixing. When feed, water, or other resources critical for comfort or survival are limited, or when large differences exist among cattle in size or other traits related to position in the social order, some animals may be able to prevent others from gaining access to resources.

In properly designed facilities, all individuals should have sufficient access to feed, water, and resting sites to minimize the correlation between position in the social order and productive performance. Proper animal care includes observation of groups and of individuals within groups to ensure that each individual has adequate access to the resources necessary for optimal comfort, welfare, and performance.

### Floor or Ground Area

Area recommendations for open lots and barns are listed in Table. Every animal should have sufficient space to move about at will, adequate access to feed and water, a comfortable resting site, and the opportunity to remain reasonably dry and clean. These suggested recommendations alone do not ensure that an ideal environment exists; however, in some cases these conditions can be met with less than the recommended area.

The area required is affected by type and slope of floor or soil surface, amount of rainfall, amount of sunshine, season, group size, and method of feeding. Open feedlot pens need to be sloped to promote drainage away from feed bunks, waterers, pen dividers, and resting areas. Space allocations are related directly to slope. In temperate Midwestern climates, the following relationships have been found to be workable: 2% slope or less: 37 to 74 $m^2$ per animal; 2 to 4% slope: 23 to 37 $m^2$; and 4% or greater slope: 14 to 23 $m^2$.

Space allocations can be less in drier regions of the country. In the Southwest, at 0% slope, typical allocations are 14 to 23 $m^2$ per animal. In other regions, space allocations may need to be increased above Midwestern norms in consideration of such factors as soil type and rainfall distribution. The area requirements for cattle are greatly influenced by group size. One animal housed separately in a pen requires the greatest amount of floor area on a per-animal basis. As group size increases, the amount of area required per individual decreases.

When an animal is housed individually, the minimum pen width and length should be at least equal to the length of the animal from nose tip to tail head when the animal is standing in a normal erect posture. Acceptable indoor pen floor surfaces for beef cattle include unfinished concrete, grooved concrete, concrete slats, expanded metal, plastic-covered metal flooring, and rubberized mat. The floor surface in stanchions and metabolism stalls may be concrete, expanded metal, wood, rubberized mat, or a combination of materials that provides support for the animals' bodies; does not damage hooves, feet, legs, and tails; and can be cleaned.

**Standard Agricultural Practices**

For beef cattle, management procedures may be performed by properly trained, nonprofessional personnel. These include, but are not limited to, vaccinating, dehorning and castrating young cattle, horn-tipping, ear-tagging, branding, weighing, implanting, use of hydraulic and manual chutes for restraint, roping, hooftrimming, routine calving assistance, ultrasound pregnancy checking, feeding, and watering.

Other husbandry and health practices used in beef cattle research and teaching that similarly may be performed by properly trained, nonprofessional personnel, but that require special technical training and advanced skill levels, include artificial insemination, electroejaculation, pregnancy palpation, embryo flushing and transfer, nonroutine calving assistance and dystocia treatment, emergency cesarean section, retained placenta treatment, and dehorning and castration of older cattle.

One of the main animal husbandry concerns is that of pain and distress, especially pain inflicted from standard husbandry procedures. Dehorning, castration, and branding are husbandry procedures that can cause pain and discomfort; nevertheless, these procedures are justified as a management tool to minimize injuries or other problems associated with confining horned cattle and commingling bulls.

**Dystocia Management**

Matings should be planned to lessen the genetic probability of dystocia. When dystocia does occur, proper care and assistance at calving can decrease injury or death of both calves and heifers/cows. Parturition without complication is common in beef cows. Therefore, before administering assistance to a cow experiencing difficulty with calving, personnel should be familiar with the stages associated with approaching parturition and the signs of normal delivery.

As a general rule, females should be examined within 30 to 60 min following presentation of feet, nose, or fetal membranes if delivery of the calf does not appear imminent. However, heifers or cows exhibiting signs of a malpresentation, oversized fetus, fetal anomaly, or other obvious complication must be assisted immediately. Facilities should be provided that are designed for restraint of cows and heifers experiencing dystocia.

Because many animals, especially heifers, lie down during the obstetrical procedure, sufficient space should be provided to permit adequate freedom of movement. It is important that the obstetrical restraint facility be fitted with side gates, both of which are hinged at the head end, so that the animal can become fully recumbent and the obstetrical procedure can be performed with safety and efficiency.

In dystocia cases where fetal presentation appears to be compromised or there appears to be a disparity between the size of the fetus and the diameter of the birth canal, assistance of the delivery by personnel appropriately trained in the judicious use of a fetal extractor may be attempted. In general, if more than slight traction is required on the fetal extractor, the procedure should be stopped and a veterinarian called immediately to perform a caesarean section or fetotomy. Use of excessive force can damage the calf and/or dam and lead to suffering and/or death. Strict sanitation should be used with all obstetrical procedures.

**Vaccinations and Drug Administration**

Vaccinations are a key component to any herd health programme. Care should be taken to ensure the proper use, handling, and storage of vaccines and approved or investigational drugs. The preferred site of injection is the neck for either intramuscular or subcutaneous injections; however, for investigational drugs used in research, alternate sites of administration may be required or preferred as dictated by the research protocol. Investigators and animal care staff should utilize best management practices associated with the use of syringes and handling needles. Use and regular replacement of disposable syringes and needles is highly recommended to avoid excessive trauma and disease transmission.

**Castration**

Castration of male beef cattle is performed to reduce aggressiveness, prevent physical danger to other animals in the herd and to handlers, enhance reproductive control, manage genetic selection, and satisfy consumer preferences regarding taste and tenderness of meat. Castration of young bulls is a necessary management practice in beef production.

Several methods for castrating cattle are acceptable, including surgical removal of the testicles using a knife or scalpel to open the scrotum and cutting or crushing the spermatic cords with an emasculatome or emasculator. Bloodless procedures utilizing specialized rubber rings or surgical tubing bands are available to create devitalization and eventual sloughing of the tissues below the ring or band.

High-tension banding systems may be used with appropriate veterinary supervision and/or training in those situations where surgical castration may predispose to postsurgical complications or when surgical castration is not appropriate because of its effect on research protocol. The castration method used should take into account the animal's age and weight, the skill level of the technician, environmental conditions, and facilities available as well as human and animal safety.

Whatever the method of castration, the procedures should be conducted by, or under the supervision of, a qualified, experienced person and carried out according to castration equipment manufacturer recommendations and accepted husbandry practices.

Surgical castration is normally a short-term event with short-term duration of pain-associated responses. Bloodless castration has been associated with lower short-term pain indicators but longer chronic pain indicators. Bloodless castration should be used when surgical castration may predispose to postsurgical complications or when surgical castration is not appropriate because of its effect on the research protocol.

Castration is least stressful when performed at or shortly after birth, but lower stress is reported if performed before 2 or 3 months of age or before animals reach a body weight of 230 kg. It is strongly recommended that calves be castrated at the earliest age possible. It may be desirable to inject local anesthetic in the scrotum of calves heavier than 230 kg when surgical methods of castration are used or when the spermatic cords are crushed.

Topical local anesthetics may also be used on open wounds. Improved animal performance, as one potential indicator of improved animal welfare, has not been observed in animals locally anesthetized at the time of castration. It should be recognized that the effect of anesthetic agents is short-lived. Nevertheless, procedures should be implemented to minimize pain and discomfort, especially in older cattle.

Castration of older, heavier bulls should be performed only by skilled individuals. When it is necessary to castrate these heavier bulls, techniques and procedures to control bleeding must also be used. No advantage to use of anesthesia is apparent when bloodless castration is practiced. The possibility of infection should be given additional consideration after castration. Equipment should be sterilized, and facilities should be clean and sanitized.

Infection following castration can be minimized by keeping the animals in a clean area and away from excessive mud or contaminants following the procedure until the wound is healed. If tetanus is a common disease associated with the premises, or if a bloodless castration method is utilized, the herd health veterinarian should schedule a prophylactic tetanus immunization programme.

**Dehorning**

Horns on cattle can cause bruises and other injury to other animals, especially during transport and handling. Horns on adult cattle also can be a hazard to humans. Hornless cattle require less space in the feedlot and at the feed bunk. Polled breeds should be used whenever possible. Disbudding and dehorning of cattle in the United States is not currently regulated.

The Canadian Veterinary Medical Association recommends that disbudding be performed within the first week of life. In the United Kingdom, disbudding with a hot iron is preferred to dehorning and it is advised that this should be performed before cattle reach the age of 2 mo. In Australia, dehorning without local anesthesia or analgesia is restricted to animals less than 6 mo old.

Calves suffer less pain and stress, have less risk of infection, and have better growth rates when dehorning is performed at a very young age. Stafford and Mellor found that the use of local anesthetics virtually eliminated the escape behaviour of calves associated with the dehorning process and that a 2-h delay was observed in the cortisol response to horn amputation. Whenever possible, the use of a local anesthetic is encouraged when dehorning.

When horned breeds of cattle are selected, dehorning should be performed under the supervision of experienced persons using proper techniques. The horn buds should be removed at birth or within the first month after birth by several means, including hot cauterizing irons, cauterizing chemicals, a sharp knife, or commercially available mechanical devices. It is strongly recommended that calves be dehorned at the earliest age possible. When it is necessary to remove horns from older cattle, methods that minimize pain and bleeding and prevent infection should be employed.

Dehorning should be performed by a person knowledgeable and experienced in the appropriate procedures. Appropriate restraint and local anesthesia to control pain should be used when cattle older than 1 mo of age are dehorned. Cattle should be monitored for hemorrhage and infection following dehorning.

Adult cattle should be dehorned if aggressive behaviour is displayed towards herd mates or humans. Dehorning may temporarily depress the growth of cattle. In the event that bunk and pen space are ample, then tipping the horn may be considered as an alternative to minimize potential bruising or injury of pen mates. However, Ramsay reported that, after transport, carcass bruises were as common among tipped cattle as among horned ones.

**Identification Methods**

Proper animal identification is essential to research, facilitates record keeping, and aids in the routine observation and repeat identification of cattle. Methods of identification include skin colour markings, ear tagging, tattooing, hot branding, freeze branding, and electronic identification. Ear tags are best used in conjunction with a more permanent form of identification such as a tattoo or brand, as ear tags are sometimes lost.

Hot branding the hide is utilized as a means of identification; however, loss in hide value and studies indicating that freeze branding is less painful than hot branding have begun to minimize the use of hot branding. Alternatives to hot branding should be considered. However, skin and hair colour in addition to a limited access to liquid nitrogen or dry ice in extensive range operations may affect the ability to achieve a quality freeze brand.

At some locations, branding is required by law. Both hot branding and freeze branding should be performed by trained personnel to minimize skin contact with the branding device to only that required to achieve a useful brand. Advent of a national animal identification system (NAIS) in the form of visual or *radio frequency identification* (RFID) ear tags serve as an additional means of identification. As this system will become standard for all cattle as part of a national programme, managers of beef cattle as part of resident herds used in research should comply with the established guidelines.

**Implanting**

Implanting of cattle is a management practice for the administration of growth promotants and potentially as a means of delivery of investigational compounds used in research. For proper absorption and maximum response, implants should be placed correctly and in the correct location. Traditionally, implants are placed beneath the skin on the back side of the middle third of the ear; however, alternate implantation sites may be required as designated by the research protocol.

Proper disinfection of the implant site is required to prevent infection. Care should be taken not to injure major blood vessels or the cartilage of the ear when implanting in the ear location. Utilization of best management practices associated with the use of the implant device and correct needlehandling procedures are required by suitably trained personnel.

**Intensive Laboratory Facilities**

Some research and teaching situations require that beef cattle be housed under intensive laboratory conditions. Cattle may be kept in metabolism stalls, stanchions, respiration chambers, or environmental chambers. Housing cattle in such facilities should be avoided unless required by the experimental protocol and then should be for the minimum amount of time necessary to accomplish the teaching or research objective.

Cattle that are held or penned temporarily in crowded areas, frequently disturbed, or come into close contact with humans, or exposed to unfamiliar conditions or laboratory/ teaching settings should have calm dispositions and be adapted to frequent contact with animal care personnel and to those conditions that could result in the animal having an adverse reaction.

In some cases, it may be advantageous to train such animals to a halter. Time spent preparing cattle for use in a laboratory improves the quality of research and the safety of both the animals and the humans. Cattle should not be housed in isolation unless approved by the Animal Care and Use Committee for specific experimental requirements. Whenever possible, cattle should be able to maintain visual contact with others.

Unless the experimental protocol has special requirements for lighting, all animal rooms should be designed to minimize variation in light intensity. During light periods, the minimum light intensity for intensively housed cattle is 70 lx. If possible, a diurnal light-dark cycle should be used and a standard daily schedule established. Excreta should be removed from enclosed laboratories at least once daily. Pens or stalls should be washed thoroughly at the beginning of every trial.

If excreta or other foreign materials such as wasted feed cannot be adequately removed through daily cleaning, additional washing may be needed during a trial. The method of collection of feces and urine from cattle in metabolism stalls, stanchions, and chambers depends on the design and construction of the unit. Additional management may be needed to keep animals clean when they are housed in stalls or stanchions.

Cattle may need to be washed and curried regularly to maintain cleanliness and to avoid fly infestations. Pens, stalls, and stanchions should be large enough to allow cattle to stand up or lie down without difficulty and should be long enough to allow cattle to maintain a normal standing position. Because of the operating costs associated with singlepass ventilation systems in controlled environmental facilities, partial recirculation of exhaust air from animal rooms is common and acceptable in many studies.

In facilities designed to recirculate even a small part of the exhausted air, treatment is necessary to remove odorous compounds, gases, and particulate matter. Cattle maintained in some laboratory environments have their activity restricted more than cattle in production settings. The length of time that cattle may remain in stanchions, metabolism stalls, or environmental chambers before removal to a pen or outside lot for additional exercise should be no longer than that necessary for conducting the study.

Opportunities for regular exercise should be considered if they do not disrupt the experimental protocol; care must be taken in moving animals from the laboratory to the outside environment for exercise when a large temperature differential exists. If cattle are to be housed in such laboratory environments for more than 3 wk then particular attention should be given to alertness of the animal; appetite; fecal and urinary outputs; and condition of the feet, legs, and hock joints. Rubber mats or suitable alternatives should be used to increase the comfort of cattle maintained for lengthy periods on hard surfaces.

**Care of Genetically Engineered and Cloned Beef Cattle and Use of Beef Cattle in Biomedical Research**

Relative size, cost of maintaining beef cattle, and the use of alternate animal models in biomedical research have largely minimized the use of beef cattle in this regard. Nevertheless, beef cattle have played a role in understanding such maladies as lysosomal storage diseases and hemochromatosis, among others, which have similarities to diseases, often genetically based, found in humans; therefore beef cattle may serve as highly valuable biomedical models in some cases.

In addition, the potential use of cattle as bioreactors for the production of human gene products or pharmaceuticals in milk, blood, urine, or tissues may further extend the use of beef cattle for biomedical applications. Standards for the care and welfare of beef cattle used in biomedical research should be the same as that applied to all beef cattle.

However, institutional or biomedical funding agencies may require more specific disease entry testing requirements for cattle used in biomedical research, in addition to having more stringent procedures with respect to adherence to alternate oversight committee guidelines for reporting, housing, observation and care procedures than might be utilized or generally accepted under typical agricultural research and production systems.

In some cases, in which in vitro reproductive technologies are used for the production of beef cattle in research, maturation, fertilization, manipulation, and/or culture, differences can exist in fetal morphology, physiology, and in the expression of developmentally important genes that may require alteration in management strategy. For example, cattle produced in this manner may exhibit "large calf syndrome" and therefore may require extra assistance at calving.

The animal biotechnology sector continues to grow, with significant advancements being made that may directly and indirectly affect beef cattle research, and it is important to recognize that alterations through the genetic engineering of beef cattle may similarly require alterations in beefcattle care practices. With respect to genetic engineering, unanticipated results from genetic modifications have been observed in several genetically engineered species that require diligence on the part of the researcher and animal care staff in assessing animal welfare.

However, the general standards of care associated with genetically engineered and cloned beef cattle should be the same as that applied to all beef cattle unless the specific genetic modification requires an alteration in management within the research environment to specifically facilitate animal welfare.

**Euthanasia**

The USDA and Food Safety and Inspection Service (FSIS) Humane Slaughter of Livestock regulations, floors of livestock pens, ramps, and driveways of harvest facilities shall be constructed and maintained so as to provide good footing for livestock. Animals shall have access to water in all holding pens and, if held longer than 24 h, access to feed. Also, for animals held overnight there shall be sufficient room in the holding pens for the animals to lie down.

The AVMA *Guidelines on Euthanasia* lists several methods of euthanasia that are appropriate for ruminants. Intravenous administration of barbiturates, potassium chloride used in conjunction with general anesthesia, and penetrating captive bolt are acceptable means of euthanasia in all cases. Other conditionally acceptable methods include intravenous administration of chloral hydrate, gunshot to the head, and electrocution.

In all cases, euthanasia should only be performed by trained individuals. Agents that result in tissue residues cannot be used for the euthanasia of ruminants intended for human or animal food, unless those agents are approved by the Food and Drug Administration. Carbon dioxide is the only chemical currently used in euthanasia of food animals that does not lead to tissue residues.

Use of carbon dioxide is generally not recommended for euthanasia of larger animals. The carcasses of animals euthanized by barbiturates may contain potentially harmful residues, and such carcasses should be disposed of in a manner that prevents them from being consumed by humans or animals.

Dying, diseased, and disabled livestock shall be provided with a covered pen sufficient to protect them from adverse climatic conditions. Incurably ill or injured animals in chronic pain or distress should be humanely euthanized as soon as they are diagnosed as such and according to AVMA recommended procedures. Their disposal should be accomplished promptly by a commercial rendering service or other means according to applicable ordinances and regulations.

**Cattle and Buffalo Development**

The broad frame-work of the cattle and buffalo breeding policy being followed since, the mid-sixties envisaged selective breeding of indigenous breeds in their breeding tracts and use of such improved breeds for upgrading of the nondescript stock. While the States accepted the framework, appropriate implementation through field level programmes could not be done.

Lack of interest in promoting Breed Organisation/Societies and related farmers' bodies contributed to the gradual deterioration of indigenous breeds. Government intervention for breed improvement is not available to majority of owners of indigenous breeds of cattle. Eventually, the availability of good quality bulls needed for natural mating in breeding tracts became scarce, leading to further deterioration of indigenous breeds in these tracts.

Production of quality indigenous bulls has been a long-neglected area and would require a major thrust in order to harvest the best male germplasm available in the country. The present production capacity of frozen semen doses is about 30 million against the estimated requirement of 65 million doses annually.

Except for a few pockets in important breeding tracts and in sperm stations, indigenous bulls of unknown pedigree and with poor quality semen are generally used. Crossbreeding, which was to be taken up in a restricted manner and in areas of low producing cattle, has now spread indiscriminately all over the country. Continuous emphasis on cross breeding with exotic breeds even in the tracts of indigenous breeds led to the near extinction of some of the known breeds. Further, the indiscriminate use of contaminated semen or infected bulls results in the spread of sexually transmitted diseases like Infectious Bovine Rhinotracheitis (IBR) at an alarming rate.

## GOAT DEVELOPMENT

Despite the least attention from the planners, goat population in India has increased at the fastest rate among all major livestock species during last two decades. However, instead of increasing the goat population, emphasis should be laid on productivity per animal, organised marketing and prevention of emergence of new diseases like Peste des petits ruminants (PPR) which has led to higher mortality and abortion in goats. The goat improvement programme is to be given a push through extending credit to the poor landless farmers.

## ANIMAL HEALTH

Since, the Second Plan, efforts have been made to control diseases namely, Rinderpest, Foot and Mouth Disease, Haemorrhagic Septicemia, Black Quarter and Anthrax. Although Rinderpest has been eradicated from the country, the prevalence of the other diseases continues to be one of the major problems in the animal production programme.

Some of the emerging diseases like PPR, Bluetongue, Sheep Pox and Goat Pox, Classical Swine Fever, Contagious Bovine Pleuropneumonia, New Castle Disease (Ranikhet Disease) are causing substantial economic losses.

The programme for creation of diseasefree zones was sanctioned in the Ninth Plan but was not implemented. The Department of Animal Husbandry and Dairying is also not well equipped with the necessary infrastructure and qualified technical manpower to execute the programmes and perform its mandatory duties and responsibilities like disease diagnosis and accreditation as per the international standards, development of an effective surveillance and monitoring system for diseases, mass immunisation against the most prevalent diseases etc.

Dovetailing the Animal Research Institutes of the Indian Council of Agricultural Research (ICAR) with the Department would not only improve its efficiency but also provide it with an effective delivery machinery to carry out its regulatory and certification authority functions, including the conservation of endangered breeds of livestock.

The suggestion for the establishment of an Indian Council for Veterinary and Fisheries (ICVFR) by carving out the animal science and fishery institutes from ICAR has not yet materialised.

## TRANSFER OF TECHNOLOGY

Use of technological and marketing interventions in the production, processing and distribution of livestock products will be the central theme of any future programme for livestock development. The generation and dissemination of appropriate technologies in the field of animal production as also health care to enhance production and productivity levels will be given greater attention.

Integration of Animal Research Institutes with the Department of Animal Husbandry and Dairying is essential to facilitate transfer of technology as well as to undertake sanitary and phyto-sanitary measures. This would provide an effective delivery machinery to the Department enabling it to work primarily as a regulatory body in the liberalised era.

## POULTRY

### Social Enrichment

Socialization of poultry with humans can be carried out with relative ease by frequent exposure to kind, gentle care. Even brief periods of handling, beginning at the youngest possible age, confer advantages for ease of later handling of birds and increase feed efficiency, body weights, and antibody responses. In addition, Gross and Siegel found that positively socialized chickens had reduced responses to stressors and that resistance to most diseases tested was better than that of birds that had not been socialized.

### Occupational Enrichment

A primary method for promoting exercise in poultry is the provision of perches or other elevated areas that encourage the use of vertical space in the enclosure. Egg-laying strains of chickens are highly motivated to use perches at night and the entire flock will utilize perches at night if sufficient perch space is provided. When hens are housed in floor pens, perches allow them to roost comfortably with a minimum of disturbance and provide them with an opportunity to seek refuge from other birds to avoid cannibalistic pecking.

Perches can also minimize bird flightiness and fearfulness and the exercise facilitated by vertical movement can improve bone strength. Early exposure to perches during rearing facilitates perching behaviour in adult birds. Poults and young broiler chickens also use perches but use tends to decrease when the birds are older. At later stages of the production cycle, perches are used much less frequently by broilers and turkeys than by laying hens.

Because of their body size and conformation, older turkeys and broiler chickens need to be provided with lower perches of a shape and size that allow them to easily access the perches and to balance properly when perching. For older turkeys it advisable to locate the perches high enough that turkeys on the ground cannot peck and pull the feathers of perching birds; ramps can be installed in front of these higher perches to facilitate access.

Straw bales can also be added to pens to provide an elevated surface for broilers and turkeys but again ramps may need to be installed so that older birds can easily access these. Because straw is also used as a foraging substrate, however, the bales may be rapidly pecked apart and scattered.

In general, perches should be free of sharp edges, of a size that can be readily gripped by the claws but large enough in diameter that the bird's toenails do not damage its footpad, and made of a material that is nonslip but that can be cleaned.

Perches soiled with feces are a major contributing factor to the development of a painful foot condition, bumblefoot, in floor-housed poultry, so it is important that perches be properly designed to minimize this problem. In addition, hens may develop deviated keel bones from resting on perches, although it is unknown if this condition is painful. Laying hens prefer high perches.

However, hens tend to develop osteoporosis and this makes perch placement critical to ensure that the hens can navigate the perches without breaking bones during landings. Ducks will swim if water of sufficient depth is provided. If swimming water is made available to ducklings, the water should be very shallow so that the ducklings do not drown, and care must be taken until their waterproof feathers emerge to ensure that they do not become soaked and chilled.

## LEVELS OF MILK PRODUCTION

A cow will produce large amounts of milk over her lifetime. Certain breeds produce more milk than others; however, different breeds produce within a range of around 15,000 to 25,000 lbs of milk per lactation. The average for dairy cows in the US in 2005 was 19,576 pounds.

Production levels peak at around 40 to 60 days after calving. The cow is then bred. Production declines steadily afterwards, until, at about 305 days after calving, the cow is 'dried off', and milking ceases.

About sixty days later, one year after the birth of her previous calf, a cow will calve again. High production cows are more difficult to breed at a one year interval. Many farms take the view that 13 or even 14 month cycles are more appropriate for this type of cow.

Dairy cows may continue to be economically productive for many lactations. Ten or more lactations are possible. The chances of problems arising which may lead to a cow being culled are however, high; the average herd life of US Holsteins is today fewer than 3 lactations. This requires more herd replacements to be reared or purchased.

*Over 90% of all cows are culled for 4 main reasons:*

1. Infertility: Failure to conceive and reduced milk production. Cows are at their most fertile between 60 and 80 days after calving. Cows remaining "open" (not with calf) after this period become increasingly difficult to breed, which may be due to poor health. Failure to expel the afterbirth from a previous pregnancy, luteal cysts, or metritis, an infection of the uterus, are common causes of infertility.
2. Mastitis: Persistent and potentially fatal mammary gland infection, leading to high somatic cell counts and loss of production. Mastitis is recognized by a reddening and swelling of the infected quarter of the udder and the presence of whitish clots or pus in the milk. Treatment is possible with long-acting antibiotics but milk from such cows is not marketable until drug residues have left the cow's system.
3. Lameness: Persistent foot infection or leg problems causing infertility and loss of production. High feed levels of highly digestible carbohydrate cause acidic conditions in the cow's rumen. This leads to laminitis and subsequent lameness, leaving the cow vulnerable to other foot infections and problems which may be exacerbated by standing in feces or water soaked areas.
4. Production: Some animals fail to produce economic levels of milk to justify their feed costs. Production below 12 to 15 liters of milk per day are not economically viable.

Herd life is strongly correlated with production levels. Lower production cows live longer than high production cows, but may be less profitable. Cows no longer wanted for milk production are sent to slaughter. Their meat is of relatively low value and is generally used for processed meat.

**Reproduction**

Since, the 1950s, artificial insemination (AI) is used at most dairy farms; these farms may keep no bull. Advantages of using AI include its low cost and ease compared to maintaining a bull, ability to select from a large number of bulls to match the anticipated market for the resulting calves, and predictable results.

More recently, embryo transfer has been used to enable the multiplication of progeny from elite cows. Such cows are given hormone treatments to produce multiple embryos. These are then 'flushed' from the cow's uterus. 7- 12 embryos are consequently removed from these donor cows and transferred into other cows who serve as surrogate mothers. The result will be between 3 and 6 calves instead of the normal single, or rarely, twins.

**Hormone Use**

Hormone treatments are given to dairy cows to increase reproduction and to increase milk production. The hormones are used to produce multiple embryos have to be administered at specific times to dairy cattle to induce ovulation. Frequently, for economic considerations, these drugs are also used to synchronize a group of cows to ovulate simultaneously. The hormones Prostaglandin, Gonadotropin Releasing Hormone, and Progesterone are used for this purpose and sold under the brand names Lutalyse, Cystorelin, Estrumate, Factrel, Prostamate, Fertagyl. Insynch, and Ovacyst. They may be administered by injection, insertion or mixed with feed.

About 17% of dairy cows in the United States are injected with Bovine somatotropin, also called recombinant bovine somatotropin (rBST), recombinant bovine growth hormone (rBGH), or artificial growth hormone. The use of this hormone increases milk production from 11%-25%, but also increases the likelihood of cattle developing mastitis, reduction in fertility and lameness. The U.S., Food and Drug Administration (FDA) has ruled that rBST is harmless to people, although critics point out increased levels of insulinlike growth factor 1 (IGF-1) in milk produced using this hormone. The use of rBST is banned in Canada, parts of the European Union, Australia and New Zealand.

**Nutrition**

Nutrition plays an important role in keeping cattle healthy and strong. Implementing an adequate nutrition programme can also improve milk production and reproductive performance. Nutrient requirements may not be the same depending on the animal's age and stage of production.

Forages, which refer especially to hay or straw, are the most common type of feed used. Cereal grains, as the main contributors of starch to diets, are important in meeting the energy needs of dairy cattle. Barley is one example of grain that is extensively used around the world. Barley is grown in temperate to sub-artic climates, and it transported to those areas lacking the necessary amounts of grain. Although variations may occur, in general, barley is an excellent source of balanced amounts of protein, energy, and fibre.

Ensuring adequate body fat reserves is essential for cattle to produce milk and also to keep reproductive efficiency. However, if cattle get excessively fat or too thin, they run the risk of developing metabolic problems. Scientists have found that a variety of fat supplements can benefit conception rates of lactating dairy cows. Some of these different fats include oleic acids, found in canola oil, animal tallow, and yellow grease; palmitic acid found in granular fats and dry fats; and linolenic acids which are found in cottonseed, safflower, sunflower, and soybean. It is also important to note that proper levels of fat also improve cattle longevity.

Using by-products is one way of reducing the normally high feed costs. However, lack of knowledge of their nutritional and economic value limits their use. Although the reduction of costs may be significant, they have to be used carefully because animal may have negative reactions to radical changes in feeds. Such a change must then be made slowly and with the proper follow up.

**Pesticide Use**

A survey of the primary dairy producing areas in the US indicated that 13 per cent of lactating animals were treated with insecticides permethrin, pyrethrin, coumaphos, and dichlorvos primarily by daily or every-other-day coat sprays. Workers, particularly in stanchion barns, may be exposed to higher than recommended amounts of these pesticides.

**Breeds**

In the United States, dairy cattle are divided into six major breeds. These are the: Holstein-Friesian, Brown Swiss, Guernsey, Ayrshire, Jersey, and Milking Shorthorn. In Rajasthan, an indigenous breed called Tharparkar exists, named from the Tharparkar District, now in Sindh Pakistan. Another type of dairy cow known as Nagauri from Nagaur District, the bull of which is renowned for its ability to plow fields and run. Traditionally, they used to pull covered wagons, known as rath, and in marriages to transport the newlywed couple. They are now a crutch for thriving agricultural and livestock rearing societies of the Thar Desert. Many other breeds are used nearly exclusively for beef, or for both dairy and beef purposes.

## MILK PRODUCTION

Milk production in India remained more or less stagnant from 1950 to 1970. Thereafter, it increased rapidly, reaching 84.6 million tonnes (mt) in 2001-02 (anticipated). But the Ninth Plan target of milk production (96.49 mt) was not achieved. The per capita availability of milk increased from 112 gm per day in 1973-74 to about 226 gm per day in 2001-02. However, it is still below the world average of 285 gm per day. Investment in the dairy sector in the Ninth Plan decreased significantly compared to the Eighth Plan. Out of 168 Milk Unions, 58 Milk Unions (34.5 per cent) were running in loss as of March 2000.

So far, the Government policy in the dairy sector has been to give preference to the establishment of milk processing plants linking rural milk producers to urban consumers through a network of cooperatives.

Restrictions on establishing new milk processing capacity under Milk and Milk Products Order (MMPO) has now been removed. No policy measures have been undertaken so far to give a fillip to the unorganised sector involved in the production of Indian dairy products (like ghee, paneer, chhena, khoa etc.), which have tremendous potential in the export market in Asian and African countries.

## MILK QUALITY AND MARKETING

Milk is sold as sour milk, butter or ghee and some cheese. Very little milk is sold per household due to low productivity or lack of markets. The little milk sold directly to consumers and some to milk vendors who sell to consumers but such milk is very much prone to milk adulturation by water, cow's urine, coconut milk or cassava milk. There is a lot of milk wastage especially during the rainy season when the supply is high and marketing conditions are poor.

In recent years there has emerged a strong argument advocating the use of decentralised rural based milk processing as an appropriate system of milk marketing in a situation where smallholder milk production is thinly scattered and situated far away from urban markets.

### Liquid Milk

Apart from boiling of milk before consumption there are no known traditional technologies for preservation of liquid milk through heat processing in Tanzania. Indeed is has been reported that in some pastoral communities it is a taboo to heat milk (Shallo, 1987). Table gives the technical possibilities of applying conventional milk technology processing in rural milk processing.

It is obvious that for technical and economic reasons, technologies involved in liquid milk processing (refrigeration, steam generation, pasteurization, sterilization/aseptic packing) are not immediately accessible to the small scale milk processor. It follows then that the small scale manufacturer must undertake the processing of preserved dairy products with long shelf life at ambient temperatures such that marketing is done only once or twice a week.

Some simple equipment could be used in decentralized rural dairies in developing countries (Bachmann, 1979; Kurwijila, 1986; Schulthess, 1990). The setting up of such rural industries would create employment in the rural areas, promote local skills, as some of the equipment could be made locally, and stimulate growth of production of milk by providing an assured market for local milk.

**Fermented Milk**

Production of fermented milk is widely spread in Tanzania. In most tribes, milk is allowed to ferment naturally without addition of starter culture. Milk is accumulated over a number of days in a clay pot vessel of 2 - 4 litres volumetric capacity or a bottle gourd (O'Mahony and Bekele, 1985) and allowed to develop acidity up to 1% lactic acid. In cold weather, the container is kept near the fire to keep it warm. Soured milk is consumed as a side dish. If not consumed, sour milk is churned into butter. The shelf life of naturally fermented or sour milk is only 72 hours at ambient temperature (Ali, 1990 and Ryoba and Kurwijila, 1992). The disadvantage of this type of milk is that since, it is not boiled there is always a danger of people getting TB or Brucellosis.

Among the pastoralists like the Maasai and others, milk vessels are smoked using specific wood which produce embers in the fire (Shallo, 1987; Kurwijila, 1988b). Smoke application appears to improve the colour, flavour and extend the shelf life up to 20 days to 3 months (Bekele and Kasaye, 1987 and Ryoba and Kurwijila, 1992). Preparation of fermented milk and smoking of milk vessel have been discussed in details by Shallo and Hansen, (1987). Fidder (1966) and Knowles (1975) reports that the smoke contains primarly phenols of about 21 components as identified by the gas chromatography which have the ant bacterial effect in smoked milk thus prologing the shelf life of milk (Ryoba and Kurwijila, 1992).

Apparently no research has been done in identifying, characterizing and classifying the plants and no analysis of the smoke components and its effects on the milk components has been done. Fidder (1966) reports that methods of generating the smoke, collecting the phenolic fractions and identifying the components have not been uniform or reproducible. The correlation of results from the investigations to obtain a meaningful information about the desirable phenol composition of smoke and the best parameters for its production is difficult. It is therefore a big challenge to the African researchers.

Natural fermentation of milk exploits lactic acid producing Streptococci and Lactobacilli which are present in any milk and which generally suppress spoilage and pathogenic organisms. The processing steps of heating milk followed by cooling and inoculation of starter culture to achieve a controlled fermentation is not done traditionaly in Tanzania. Heating kills undesirable organisms and also concentrates the milk" giving the fermented milk a heavier body (Fox, 1967). The use of pure cultures enables different acid flavours to be developed leading to a range of fermented (cultured) products. Since, cultured milk has better keeping quality than fresh milk and better product consistency than naturally soured milk, their introduction to smallholder processing systems should be considered.

Standard technology of fermented milk manufacture is first to boil at 80 - 90°C for 5-30 minutes to reduce the microbial population. It is then cooled, inoculated with starter culture or previously fermented milk and incubated at 30°C to 38°C for 4-16 hours. Higher temperatures cause wheying off while lower temperatures result in slow fermentation and may lead to the establishment of undesirable micro-organisms. Fermented milk can be made in simple containers of any size.

**Marketing**

The development of a marketing network and remunerative price support to the producers are great incentives for higher animal productivity and these will be encouraged for all types of livestock products. Even the advanced countries are giving direct and indirect price support to livestock farmers. Priority attention should also be given to improve processing, marketing and transport facilities for livestock products and value addition thereon.

External markets are an extremely important source of demand and these will be tapped much more aggressively. In order to encourage exports, licensing control for processing of livestock products/by-products will be repealed and restrictions on the export of livestock and its products will be removed.

The immediate focus will be on export of animal and poultry products to Asian and African countries. The minimum requirements for sustainable export are creation of disease-free zones, organic farming and potable water. These will be made available in selected areas having large marketable surplus. India has a large number of animal markets where livestock are traded but these are not developed on scientific lines. Market facilities are generally inadequate and, if available, are poorly maintained.

Development of organised markets with adequate facilities will, therefore, be taken up. The concept of organic farming can also be extended to animal products. Indian animals are reared in village pastureland and they are not generally treated with hormones, feed-antibiotics, or other drugs, so their products are healthy, wholesome and natural in every sense of the word. In rural India, cow dung and biomass are primarily used as manure. Initiative for export of 'Grassfed' animal products will be taken. Necessary infrastructure for certification procedures related to organic animal farming will be promoted.

## MANAGEMENT OF DAIRY WASTEWATER

### Wastewater Reduction

Surface Water Diversion Barnyard run-off can be reduced by diverting all surface or clean water around the dairy complex using diversion terraces and subsurface drains. Much of the lot run-off is reduced by the growing usage of totally roofed freestall barns and other lounging and paved areas. Guttering of roofs draining onto paved lots is cost-effective, but gutter maintenance can be difficult.

One dairyman reduced the loads of manure that were scraped and hauled by one-third by guttering and preventing mixing of the roof rainwater with manure solids on the lot surface. Spillage and leakage from cow waterers in the lot area should be minimized or eliminated.

All lot run-off should be routed around single-stage manure storages (dry stacks, earthen slurry pits, sumps for above ground tanks, etc.) and handled by a separate wastewater system. Excess water in liquid manure storages increases hauling and spreading costs and tends to hinder the formation of surface mats resulting in greater losses of nitrogen and potential odorous emissions.

### Milking Centre

Water for cleaning the milk centre should be reduced to only that quantity essential for sanitation. Clean water used solely for cooling purposes should be collected and reused for floor cleaning, flushing or to water cows.

Dairies using parlor flush tanks for floor cleaning and/or prep stalls or cow wash sprinklers in holding areas require large amounts of clean water greatly increasing the wastewater to be handled. Wastewater generated from the milking centre should bypass single-stage liquid manure storage pits or tanks and be routed to a separate wastewater handling system except when dilution water is needed for slurry agitation and pumping.

**Collection**

All barnyard run-off and milking centre wastewater must be collected and delivered to a storage or treatment area. Most dairy lots slope in more than one direction sometimes requiring complex collection systems consisting of regrading, curbs, diversions, open channels, pipes, or even lift pumps.

**Retention Pond**

The conventional method for wastewater management consists of an earthen retention pond to collect and temporarily store all wastewater until it can be land applied by irrigation. This system is especially recommended where large wastewater volumes are generated by flush tanks, cow wash sprinklers, or wide expanses of open lot contributing barnyard run-off. A shallow concrete solids settling basin, similar to NCAES Plan 388, is recommended to intercept wastewater from drainlines prior to the retention pond and trap any manure solids. These solids are easily removed by frontend loader and handled with the scraped manure. Addition of manure solids to a wastewater retention pond increases the likelihood of odorous emissions, sludge buildup, or irrigation equipment problems.

A retention pond should have enough capacity to store a 180-day accumulation of wastewater such that field spreading would not be necessary during winter months. Pond liquid levels should be lowered throughout the spring and summer as time permits and wastewater uses exist. The pond should definitely be lowered as much as possible by late fall to allow enough storage capacity for an extended rainy season.

**Second - Stage Lagoon**

Lot scraped manure should never be added to a retention pond. If an earthen manure storage basin is used for the lot scraped manure, then a second stage lagoon is desirable for wastewater storage to facilitate removal and spreading.

**Irrigation**

Retention pond wastewater is most economically and efficiently applied to cropland, pasture, or woodland by irrigation at agronomic rates not exceeding the soil infiltration rate. Irrigation should not occur closer than approximately 25 feet to a streambank or property boundary. The solids content of retention pond wastewater without solids separation should be less than 4% and can be applied through moderate pressure portable irrigation systems with nozzle sizes 1/2 to 3/4-inch or larger.

Where solids have been separated from the wastewater, permanent or solid-set irrigation systems with 1/4 to 9/32-inch nozzles would be more labour-free. This wastewater could also be applied through low-pressure perforated or gated pipe provided the pipe is moved frequently.

**Vegetative Filter**

An alternative to the retention pond - irrigation system is a vegetative filter with a manure solids settling basin. These filters can be pasture, grassed waterways, or even cropland where wastewater is treated by settling, dilution, soil infiltration, and crop uptake of nutrients. Some dairy lots might already have some form of vegetative filter while others could add this component with a minimum of expense and effort.

These systems are planned on the premise that all or a major portion of the lot run-off and wastewater infiltrates into the ground with the remaining run-off filtered to a degree that would have minimal impact on surface waters. Since, these filters have infrequent discharges, the state regulatory agency has taken a wait-and-see attitude before giving a blanket stamp of approval.

Intensive monitoring of a North Carolina dairy farm vegetative filter treatment system as well as performance results from other states indicate that over 95% of the nutrients, solids, and oxygen-demanding materials are removed from the wastewater.

**Settling Basin**

A settling basin to separate manure solids from the wastewater is essential to prevent the upper side of the vegetative filter from clogging with solids and reducing soil infiltration. The most common type of settling basin is a shallow, reinforced concrete structure with a sloping entrance ramp to permit equipment access for solids cleanout. Wastewater flows into the top of the basin where solids settle by gravity and liquid either overflows or filters through an outlet. This outlet should be 3 feet or more wide, the full depth of the basin, and located in a side wall near the bottom of the access ramp.

The outlet may consist of removable boards placed in side wall slots. By remaining in place the boards hold water in the basin allowing liquids to gradually overflow the top of the outlet. Just prior to solids cleanout, the boards are slowly lifted allowing the basin to dewater as much as possible. Solids are removed by tractor front-end loader and field spread with other solid manure. Another outlet type consists of an expanded metal or woven wire screen with 1/2-inch grid openings. This outlet allows continuous dewatering of the basin. All basin outlets are troublesome to some extent, and should be planned to be easily cleaned. Two basins allow one to be used while the other is drying out for cleaning.

Design criteria for basin sizing are based on retaining wastewater in the basin for at least 30 minutes during peak inflow plus a one-foot depth for solids storage between cleanouts. A 1-year, 1-hour rainfall intensity is suggested for determining the feedlot area peak run-off rate.

Performance data from a North Carolina dairy suggests a basin manure solids accumulation rate of 0.05 cubic foot per cow per day. Solids should be removed from the basin monthly or after each heavy rainfall event. Proper construction and management of the settling basin is essential to the success of the vegetative filter.

**Vegetative Filter**

Vegetated areas receiving settling basin liquid overflow consist of either an overland flow plot or a shallow grassed channel or waterway. These areas should be bermed or terraced so that all surface water outside the infiltration area is diverted.

**Overland Flow**

The overland flow system is a wide (up to 100 feet), mildly sloping area in which wastewater is evenly distributed across the filter width and allowed to flow down the length of the filter surface. Filter cross slopes should be relatively flat. Slopes lengthwise should not be flatter than 1% and in most cases not greater than 4%.

If the filter slopes more than 4%, then cross terraces dividing the total filter length into four equal flow segments reduce flow velocities and redistribute the wastewater across the filter width allowing more opportunity for infiltration. Water tends to pond behind these cross terraces eventually infiltrating. Over a period of time, the soil in these areas will likely seal and need renovation.

**Distribution**

The method of distributing liquid overflow from the settling basin across the overland flow filter width is critical. Several methods have been used, all of them, however, requiring some degree of maintenance. The greater the number of discharge points, the better the distribution system operates. One method consists of multiple pipes fanning out from the settling basin with tee outlets at the filter area.

Another method utilizes a pipe split in half lengthwise forming a semicircular trough, laying it level across the filter width, and allowing liquid to fill and overflow this trough uniformly across the filter. Parts of level gated pipe across the filter width can also be used.

Size The size of the overland flow area depends on soil characteristics and generally ranges from 1 to 2 times the feedlot area draining into the filter.

**Channelized Terrace**

The second type of vegetative filter is a channelized flow or grassed infiltration terrace. These terraces have a trapezoidal cross-section with a onefoot depth and a level bottom width of 6-10 feet. The first quarter of the channel length should be sloped approximate 2% to move wastewater away from the settling basin outlet, the second quarter sloped 1%, and the last half sloped 0.5% or just enough to prevent ponding. Successful channel filter treatment lengths in North Carolina have been at least 4 feet per cow. Dual channels allow alternate dosing and drying. These channels should not outlet directly into a stream or drainageway.

**Construction**

Extreme care should be taken during construction of a vegetative filter. Since, infiltration is most important, every effort should be made to maintain soil integrity and permeability. Clay soils, in particular, should not be worked or compacted when wet. If it is impossible to use these precautions during construction, then a subsoiler should be used to break up hardpans or impermeable layers followed by seeding with a grass that has a deep root system. Mulching, fertilizing, liming, and even watering should be utilized to establish a healthy sod as soon after seedbed preparation as possible to prevent soil erosion.

**Management**

Vegetative filter areas should be prepared and seeded at least one growing season before use. A forage combination of fescue and reed canary grass is suggested. When the forage height reaches 12 inches, it should be clipped to about 6 inches and removed from the filter area. Avoid cutting and harvesting when the filter area is too wet. Also do not remove late fall forage to allow a tall forage growth to aid in filtering winter and spring run-off. Cattle should be fenced out of the wettest portions of the filter area.

Alternate dosing and drying of the upper end of the filter appears to be important to maintaining vegetative growth. The settling basin outlet should be managed to release a portion of the liquids into the filter area on a 3-4 day schedule. The outlet then should be closed allowing the filter area to dry between dosings. Soil samples should be analysed from the filter area periodically to monitor buildups of nutrients, salts or other constituents which might become detrimental to forage growth.

**Economics**

Vegetative filters are not adaptable to operations having large amounts of paved feedlot area draining into the filter or to facilities using large amounts of water in the milking centre. However, they can provide a satisfactory, lowcost, low-management means of controlling barnyard run-off and milking centre wastewater for many small and medium-sized dairies. These systems can be constructed for less than $100 per cow for most dairies compared to 3 to 5 times that amount for conventional retention pond-irrigation systems. Given the economy, simplicity and treatment potential of vegetative filters, they are likely to be more readily adopted by dairymen than conventional systems resulting in up to 95% reduction of dairy wastewater inputs to streams.

## COOLING PONDS FOR DAIRY CATTLE

Cattle have used water for cooling probably for as long as there have been cattle. The last survey done in Florida reported that 30 per cent of the dairies had cooling ponds. The reader should be aware that cooling ponds, if not maintained properly, could harbour infectious diseases such as Leptospirosis and many mastitis organisms. The water usage is very high to fill and keep full.

Environmental concerns that must be addressed are the run-off from ponds and ground seepage. Every state seems to have many regulations that must be addressed before building cooling ponds. The benefits of cooling ponds and some suggestions on building and maintaining them. It is the dairymen's responsibility to use them properly and to be aware that ponds can harbour diseases and the pond water must be dealt with according to state and local laws.

What is a cooling pond for dairy cattle? For this discussion they are a man made hole in the ground with a constant inflow of clean fresh water. Usually the ponds drain or overflow from the top. If a series of ponds is used, the overflow water may be run into a retention pond to be irrigated on crops or enter the waste management system. Cooling ponds may also be fed from springs or artesian wells. So cooling ponds for dairy cattle should have constant fresh water in and a constant outflow of water to some place for proper disposal. Cement ponds may also be built. These may drain from the bottom and can be used to flush feed lanes or barns. Bottom draining will help remove some of the solids that have settled to the bottom of the pond. Care must be taken on the entrance and exit to cement ponds. These may be very slippery if the cement is not cross-grooved. A stagnant pond without fresh water entering, a lagoon, a wallow, and a mud hole do not classify as a cooling pond for dairy cattle.

**Site Selection**

A site near the feed and drinking water, ideally with some form of shade for cows, is best. The idea is for cows to cool, leave the pond and goes eat and drink, lay down in the shade and then do it all over again. If cows do not have feed and drinking water near, they will stay in the pond and not eat and we have cool wrinkled cows that do not give much milk.

Cooling ponds should be located close to a water supply as fresh water needs to enter the ponds constantly. There must be a way to dispose of runoff water properly. This will vary by areas of the country. Some slope from the ponds to the waste management area would be helpful, so pumps need not to be used. Cooling ponds should not be too far from the milking parlor as long walks in the sun increase heat stress. Exit lane sprinklers help make the long walk more comfortable.

### Concrete Ponds

Concrete ponds will work and have been used but they are expensive to build. However, they are easier to maintain, as the entrances and exits do not have to be rebuilt. The finish of the concrete on exit and entrance slopes should be cross-grooved to prevent cows from falling. A 1:8 slope would be a safe slope if concrete ponds are constructed.

### Sizing Cooling Ponds

There is no official listing for cooling pond size. If a holding area requires 15/ft$^2$/ cow and cows are driven into a pond and taken out as a group then 15/ft$^2$/ cow might be adequate. If 50/ft$^2$/ cow is recommended for most general animal space, then this might be the correct figure for a cooling pond. This amount of space would allow cows to enter and exit the pond at all times when all cows were not using the pond at the same time. If 50/ft$^2$/ cow for a pond is used, then 5000/ft$^2$ is then needed for the 100 cow group.

### Pond Shapes and Depths

Using the sample of 5000/ft$^2$/100 cows a pond could be 50′ wide × 100′ long, or a circle 80′ in diameter (A= (Pi) r$^2$; A= 3.14 × 40 = 5024ft$^2$). If a 50′ × 100′ pond is used and the sides are fenced so the cows can only enter or exit at each end of the pond, the amount of dirt falling into the pond will be reduced. If a circular pond is made, cow carpet should be used to eliminate the problem of dirt falling in the pond. As cows can swim, pond depth is not a problem. Deeper ponds may allow the settling of organic matter on the bottom of the pond. This organic matter may not be disturbed by cows walking through it as they will swim over the top of it. Preference should be given to depths of 3′ or 4′ as it seems to cool the cows and let them stand and walk in and out at will. While deep ponds allow cows to submerge, they do not seem to like to float too long so they go to where they can stand and may block cow traffic. A circular pond that is deep in the middle lets cows dunk themselves while others enter and exit the pond at will.

### Water Usage

A 100 cow group with 50/ft$^2$/ cow could have a 50′ wide × 100′ long × 3′ deep cooling pond (it may be 4′ in the middle and slope in and out). A cooling pond 50′ wide × 100′ long × an average 3′ deep=15000/ft$^3$. There are 7.48 gallons/ft3, thus the pond requires 112,200 gallons of water.

The pond must be filled and then kept fresh with running water at all times while in use. A 1″ pipe 300 ft. long and water pressure at 35psi will result in a flow rate of about 23.5 gpm. At this rate it would then take 80 hours to fill the pond initially. The dairy water usage would then be 1,410 gph × 24 hours or 33,840 gallons of water per day. This fresh water must be pumped into the pond and there is going to be close to that amount of run off water that will exit the pond for disposal.

### Water Run-off

Disposal of run-off water must be in accordance with whatever local, state, and federal laws that applies. Many dairies run the water into the waste management system, while others add it to retention ponds to be used for irrigation.

### Shading over Ponds

Experience has led to discontinued use of shade over ponds as the cows never leave the ponds. Remember, the object of this exercise is to increase dry matter intake and cows will not eat much soaking in the pond.

**Pond Maintenance**

At least once a year, usually during the winter, the pond should be fenced and the water removed by pumping. The mud and manure on the bottom of the pond should be removed and the pond left empty for the sun to shine on it. In the spring, the pond should be filled again and the fences removed. Some people just fence the pond in the winter, dig a new pond and fill in the old one with new pond's dirt.

Mycoplasma mastitis is often cultured in water from cooling ponds. This is a real problem if pulsators do not work well resulting in damaged teat ends. Many herds with mycoplasma positive ponds, have no mycoplasma in the bulk tank. If the water is filthy, cows should not be permitted in the ponds and the ponds should be pumped dry. The sludge should be cleaned and the ponds filled with water again. Both the sludge and the water shoud be removed from cow areas.

**Cooling Ponds to Reduce Body Temperature**

In the summer of 1986, an experiment was conducted at a North Florida dairy that was using man-made cooling ponds. Ten early lactation Holstein cows were fitted with radio transmitters that transmitted inner ear temperatures every five minutes to a radio receiver and data logger.

Data were collected over a four-day period in mid-August. The cows' activities were also monitored during this time. Entering and exiting the ponds, eating, drinking and laying were recorded.

The cooling ponds lowered the cows' temperature by 1-2°F depending on the time of day they entered the cooling ponds. The average length per stay in the pond was 18 minutes for events from midnight to noon and 12 minutes per visit from noon to midnight. It was obvious that cooling ponds cooled cows.

**Pond Water Quality**

In 1987, samples were taken from a dairy's man-made earthen ponds. The ponds were sampled weekly from May 19,1987 to September 28, 1987. Six to ten ponds were sampled each week.

Total bacteria counts (TBC), varied greatly from week to week. This may have been due to no water entering the ponds. There did not seem to be any great increase in total bacteria counts or coliform counts as time progressed. The total bacteria count averaged 3,133,700 CFU/ml for all ponds for the 20 weeks. The coliform counts averaged 14,340 CFU/ml for the same period.

**Cooling Ponds and Their Effect on Milk Quality**

In a previous study on a dairy in Florida with man-made cooling ponds, it was reported that cows exposed to cooling ponds did not experience more clinical mastitis than cows that did not have access to cooling ponds. In fact, cows exposed to cooling ponds during the trial period were only half as likely to develop a case of clinical mastitis as cows not exposed to cooling ponds.

**Clinical Mastitis Organisms**

The same dairy had provided its clinical mastitis records for several years. The total number of clinical mastitis cases was high in the first quarter of the year and then declined sharply about the time hot weather came and the cows started using the ponds. The incidence stayed low, even in the last quarter of the year when the ponds were not in use. This can be explained many ways. The first quarter of the year was an extremely wet period.

The cows were quite dirty and the cow wash system was available to one-half of the herd. This may explain some of the variation, even though one-half of the herd had never had a cow wash. Another confounding variable was that this herd switched to Clorox for pre- post-teat dipping in April of that year. It had previously pre- and post-dipped with a Chlorhexidine product. From this it could be concluded that Clorox caused the reduction of clinical mastitis. However, there were no controls in this study, one could conclude nothing except that the ponds did not increase clinical mastitis.

This herd was on a lactation treatment study during the summer of 1987. A total of 40 cows were sampled and treated. There were no unusual organisms treated. These 40 cows were not all the cows treated for clinical mastitis during the period the cows had access to the ponds, but the results were encouraging.

**Statewide Effects of Ponds on Milk Quality**

Regulatory samples for all the herds in Florida were obtained from the Division of Dairy Industry for the year of 1987 and were analysed for the effects of no ponds, man-made ponds and natural ponds. The numbers presented are least squares estimates of Standard Plate Counts (SPC) and Direct Microscope Somatic Cell Counts (DMSCC) for each month. The data are not biased by different numbers of dairies with no ponds, natural, or man-made ponds. The data were analysed by herds whose milking cows had access to ponds as indicated on the survey.

The data indicated that milking cows with access to man-made cooling ponds had lower SPC and DMSCC counts than other herds in the state with no access to ponds and those herds with natural ponds were higher in both categories. From these data it could be argued that people who built manmade ponds were better managers and thus had higher milk quality.

❐

# 5

# Processing Techniques of Milk and Milk Products

Milk can be stored longer if it has been processed. Extended storage is possible if you are able to control the growth of micro-organisms. The processing technique used will determine the storage life of the milk and dairy products.

*The following rules should be followed during the production, storage and processing of milk:*

- Always wash your hands and avoid putting them in the milk if not necessary.
- All equipment used during processing is properly cleaned and disinfected if needed.
- Take care that no dirt particles or insects enter into the milk.
- Try to prevent the use of copper utensils. (Copper can give off flavours in butter and milk.)
- Do not expose milk to sunlight; store it in a dark place.
- The use of a thermometer is recommended.
- Make sure that milk used for consumption has always been boiled or pasteurised.
- Never store raw (i.e., unheated) milk if it is not immediately cooled below 4°C.
- Never drink raw milk because it may contain pathogenic bacteria like tubercular bacteria and salmonella.

*The following processing techniques will be dealt with in this chapter:*

- Pasteurisation
- Cooling
- Souring (acidification)
- Creaming.

Heating and cooling are in fact ways to preserve milk, but for convenience as suggested, deal with them under the heading of processing techniques.

## HYGIENE DURING MILKING

There are several possible causes of contamination during milking. In a normal, healthy cow very low numbers of bacteria are found inside the udder and the teats. Cows possess various mechanisms to prevent the entry of bacteria. To avoid problems while milking, it is important that an animal become accustomed to the activity. It will then know that it will be milked, and will react positively to it. Such positive behaviour can start if, for instance, it hears milk cans clanging, feels its udder being cleaned, etc., Then the animal is easier to milk and gives more milk.

Stress and unrest make the cows move too much and kick; consequently more dirt and manure can enter into the milk. When a cow has an udder infection (mastitis), its milk will be contaminated with the bacteria that cause the udder infection, and that may produce pus and sometimes blood. Milk from these animals should not be used in any way. Mastitis can be prevented by maintaining good hygiene and avoiding injury to the teats during milking.

An infected udder is not always easy to see. When an udder infection occurs, it is advisable to remove milk from the udder very frequently (e.g., every 3 hours by hand). The number of microorganisms in the udder is thus reduced. Be aware, however, that milking an infected udder by machine or by hand is often painful for the animal. The animal will kick frequently and this can be an important source of contamination of healthy cows. Bacteria can be transferred from the skin or teats to the milk, even with healthy dairy cattle.

It is therefore important to clean the udder before milking. Wipe the udder clean with a dry, clean, preferably disposable cloth to prevent infection. If the teats or udder are really dirty, they must first be washed with clean, handwarm water and a clean cloth and then dried with a clean towel. Cleaning the udder improves the cleanliness of the milk and makes milking easier. Skin and hair can also be sources of infection. Do not feed animals first before milking, it may create a lot of dust. The floor is clean, and be careful when clearing dung, mud or dust.

A clean, well-illuminated milking place and fresh surrounding air are essential to maintaining good hygiene. Insects such as flies and cockroaches can also be sources of infection. Try to control them as they can carry many bacteria and viruses. When milking, the milk is caught in a pail or bucket. Dirty milking equipment is the main source of infection of milk. If residues of milk remain in the equipment because of improper cleaning and drying, bacteria will develop in these residues. These bacteria are already accustomed to the milk and will multiply rather quickly during transport and storage of milk in the equipment.

Use pails and buckets that are smooth on the inside, for instance seamless metal buckets. All milking equipment should be thoroughly cleaned immediately after each use. Use soap or other detergents if necessary. Make sure that the water used is clean. If you are in doubt, boil it for several minutes or add chlorine. Very important: after cleaning, the equipment should be stored upside down in such a way that the inside of the buckets and cans dry. This prevents the remaining bacteria from growing.

The person milking plays the most important part in maintaining proper hygiene during production. He or she keeps an eye on the condition of the animal, chooses the milking place and cleans all the equipment. He or she should have clean hands and wear clean clothes. If the milker suffers from tuberculosis, salmonella infection, dysentery or some other disease, the risk of contamination of the milk becomes very high; it would be wise to have somebody else take over. This is also the case if the milker has open wounds or ulcers.

### Hygiene during Storage and Processing

By now you should know that milk should be processed as quickly as possible after milking and that it should be properly stored in order to minimise its chances of spoiling. It is best to filter fresh milk through a filter or clean cloth. This will remove visible dirt that might have entered into the milk. Clean or replace the cloth during filtering or filter the milk several times. The cloth should be thoroughly cleaned after use and then left to dry in the sun.

In tropical conditions, raw milk, i.e., non-pasteurised milk, goes off within a few hours. It must therefore be kept cool and quickly pasteurised and again cooled to a temperature of 4°C if possible. Properly pasteurised and cooled milk can be kept for a few days, even in a warm climate. If you are not able to cool milk below 10°C, then do not mix different batches.

Even if the older milk is still good, you will end up with an increase in bacterial growth and reduction of the overall quality. Use clean equipment for storage. Containers that are clear, such as glass, should be stored in the dark as light reduces the quality of milk. Clean your equipment with clean water.

### Cleaning and Disinfection

Utensils must be cleaned in such a way that all dirt, food residues, feed and micro-organisms are removed from the surface of the equipment. Dirty saucepans, jugs, milking equipment and utensils should be cleaned immediately after use. Washing soda (sodium carbonate) dissolved in hot water is an excellent cleaning agent. It may be useful to disinfect equipment in order to kill any remaining harmful micro-organisms. You can use a chloride solution such as bleach (sodium hypochlorite).

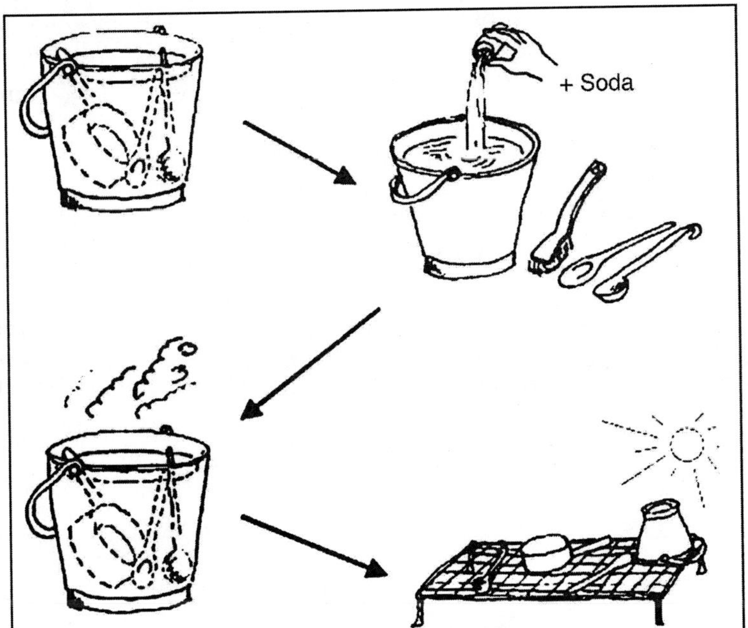


*Fig.5.1: Cleaning Utensils*

*A proper way of cleaning your equipment is the following:*

- Start cleaning immediately after milking, so that milk residues will not dry and stick on the buckets and utensils.
- Rinse well with water.
- Scrub the tools in a hot soda solution (1.5 tablespoons of soda to 5 litres of water), using a small amount of water to dissolve the soda before adding it to the rest of the water.
- Rinse well with hot water.
- Buckets, tubs, etc., should be turned upside down on a rack during storage; the water can then drain and no dirt or dust can enter. Let the utensils dry to prevent bacterial growth.

Well-cleaned tools are nearly sterile, only a small part of the bacteria remains on the tools. If these tools dry during storage hardly any bacteria will be present. In that case disinfection is not necessary. Tools which are used for storage of pasteurised milk or for cheese making and which do not get a heat treatment together with the milk can be disinfected after cleaning or before use.

*Proceed as follows:*

- Clean all your equipment properly. The following step will be ineffective if the utensils are not clean to start with.
- Disinfect in a chloride or bleach solution after cleaning or shortly before use. Add 2 tablespoons of bleach per 4. 5 litres of water.

It is advisable to use stainless steel equipment, cheesecloth and wooden utensils. Tools or any other equipment made from aluminium should not be washed in a strong soda solution, as soda attacks aluminium. Iron utensils will rust in a strong chloride solution. Therefore rinse and dry these utensils immediately after cleaning and disinfection.

*If you have no cleaning agents-like soda-or disinfectants, you can disinfect your equipment as follows:*

- Thoroughly clean the utensils using clean water.
- Rinse with a soap solution.
- Dry the equipment on a rack in the sun upside down or rinse with boiling water.

## PASTEURISATION OF MILK

As you by now know, milk contains certain micro-organisms that can spoil it. These bacteria grow best at temperatures between 10°C and 40°C. It is therefore important to cool milk as quickly as possible. This can be difficult in the tropics if no cold water or refrigerators are available. Most bacteria will be destroyed during heating. The most effective temperature depends on the heating time. In other words, heating for a longer period at a lower temperature can be as effective as heating for a shorter period but at a higher temperature.

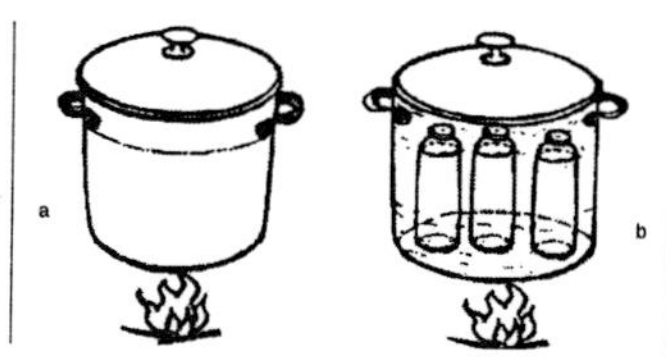


*Fig.5.2: Pasteurisation*

*We see:*

(a) Direct pasteurisation of milk in a saucepan

(b) Pasteurisation of milk in bottles

Pasteurisation improves the safety and storage life of a product, while the taste hardly changes and the loss of vitamins is minimal. A distinction is made between low and high pasteurisation. Although high pasteurisation initially kills more bacteria, the resulting milk can usually not be kept as long, because the high pasteurisation temperature stimulates spores of some bacteria to germinate.

Moreover, the taste of high pasteurised milk has more or less the flavour of boiled milk. Pasteurised milk can be kept for about one week at 4-6°C if no re-infection takes place.

*The pasteurisation temperature to be used depends on the product to be made of the milk:*

- Low pasteurisation is used for milk for direct consumption and cheese.
- High pasteurisation is used for yoghurt, butter and kefir.

**Table.5.1 Time–temperature Combinations for Pasteurising Milk**

| Remarks | Time | Temperature |
|---|---|---|
| Low Pasteurising Quantities>5 litres | 30 minutes | 63°C |
| Small quantities | 3 minutes | 68°C |
| Industrial equipment | 20 seconds | 72°C* |
| High Pasteurising | 2 minutes<br>20 seconds | 82°C<br>85°C* |

*Notes:* * Continuous flow system; not for small-scale processing

If there is no thermometer to measure the exact temperature, heat the milk to its boiling point.

**Pasteurisation Methods**

The following method A is suitable if you are able to accurately control both temperature and time. Method B is more hygienic, if the exact temperature of the milk is unknown.

*You will need:*

- Raw milk, a heat source, a saucepan with a thick bottom that is smooth on the inside, a thermometer and a means of cooling the milk that has been heated
- For method A: a clean wooden spoon
- For method B: glass jars with lids or bottles with tops, or plastic bags and sealing equipment.

**Method A**

Put the milk in a clean saucepan and heat it to 68°C, stirring continuously. Keep the milk at that temperature for at least 3 minutes.

**Method B**

Clean the glass jars with lids or bottles with tops. Fill them with milk and close the lids. Submerge the jars and bottles in a large pan filled with water. Heat everything to 80°C and keep it at that temperature for at least 10 minutes. When using method A, let the milk cool down as quickly as possible. The best storage temperature is 4°C.

If you are using method B but are not able to maintain a constant temperature of 80°C, the best alternative is to heat the water in the pan until it boils and keep it boiling for some time. It is important to store the pasteurised or boiled milk at 4°C. At this temperature it can be kept up to one week. Handle the boiled or pasteurised milk with care to prevent re-infection.

**What is Pasteurization?**

In 1864, a French man named Louis Pasteur discovered that liquids such as milk could be heated to a temperature slightly below boiling and held there for a set amount of time to eliminate the most harmful bacteria. The process of pasteurization is named after Louis Pasteur in recognition of his immense contribution tofood safety and disease theory. Grocery stores carry a wide array of pasteurized goods including milk, juices, non-dairy milks, and other similar food products. Many nations require that foods be pasteurized for safety. Pasteurization relies on the principle that most harmful bacterial can be killed by heat. The most effective way to kill bacteria is boiling, but this compromises the flavour of the liquid. Pasteurization strikes a happy medium, keeping the flavour delicious while making the food safer. In addition to minimizing the risk of sickness, pasteurization also makes foods more shelf stable and less likely to rot, meaning that fresh dairy products and juices are available to more people.

There are two primary methods of pasteurization: the liquid can be heated to 145 degrees Fahrenheit (63 degrees Celsius) and held there for at least thirty minutes, or the liquid can be flash pasteurized at 161 degrees Fahrenheit (72 degrees Celsius) for a minimum of 16 seconds. Pasteurization can be done using a continuous method, where the liquid flows through a pasteurization system, or by using a batch method, where one batch of the liquid is pasteurized at a time. Continuous pasteurization is popular for large producers, because it does not slow the supply line as much as batch pasteurization does.

Pasteurization must be performed on clean equipment. If bacteria is introduced after the liquid has been pasteurized, it can colonize it and potentially cause an outbreak of food borne illness.

For this reason, companies which perform pasteurization are subject to frequent inspections to ensure that the equipment they are using is safe, and that the liquids they are pasteurizing are being handled correctly. After pasteurization, bacteria can still appear. It is important that foods be safely handled and stored at every step of the supply process from animal, fruit or vegetable to stomach. In most cases, after food is pasteurized it should be refrigerated. The food is held in refrigeration until it is shipped out in cooled trucks to grocery stores, which store the food under refrigeration until consumers purchase it. Home consumers are responsible for following directives regarding temperature to ensure that the foods they are consuming are safe.

The process of pasteurization was named after Louis Pasteur who discovered that spoilage organisms could be inactivated in wine by applying heat at temperatures below its boiling point. The process was later applied to milk and remains the most important operation in the processing of milk. The heating of every particle of milk or milk product to a specific temperature for a specified period of time without allowing recontamination of that milk or milk product during the heat treatment process.

*Purpose Ther How do I disinfect my pre are two distinct purposes for the process of milk pasteurization:*

1. *Public Health Aspect:* To make milk and milk products safe for human consumption by destroying all bacteria that may be harmful to health (pathogens)
2. *Keeping Quality Aspect:* To improve the keeping quality of milk and milk products. Pasteurization can destroy some undesirable enzymes and many spoilage bacteria. Shelf life can be 7, 10, 14 or up to 16 days.

The extent of microorganism inactivation depends on the combination of temperature and holding time. Minimum temperature and time requirements for milk pasteurization are based on thermal death time studies for the most heat resistant pathogen found in milk, Coxelliae burnettii. Thermal lethality determinationsrequire the applications of microbiology to appropriate processing determinations. An overview can be found here. To ensure destruction of all pathogenic microorganisms, time and temperature combinations of the pasteurization process are highly regulated:

## ONTARIO PASTEURIZATION REGULATIONS

### Milk

63° C for not less than 30 min.,

72° C for not less than 16 sec.,

Or equivalent destruction of pathogens and the enzyme phosphatase as permitted by Ontario Provincial Government authorities. Milk is deemed pasteurized if it tests negative for alkaline phosphatase.

*Frozen dairy dessert mix (ice cream or ice milk, egg nog):*

- At least 69° C for not less than 30 min;
- At least 80° C for not less than 25 sec;

other time temperature combinations must be approved (e.g., 83° C/16 sec). Milk based products- with 10% mf or higher, or added sugar (cream, chocolate milk, etc) 66° C/30 min, 75° C/16 sec. There has also been some progress with low temperature pasteurization methods using membrane processing technology..

### Methods of Pasteurization

There are two basic methods, batch or continuous.

### Batch Method

The batch method uses a vat pasteurizer which consists of a jacketed vat surrounded by either circulating water, steam or heating coils of water or steam.

In the vat the milk is heated and held throughout the holding period while being agitated. The milk may be cooled in the vat or removed hot after the holding time is completed for every particle. As a modification, the milk may be partially heated in tubular or plate heater before entering the vat.

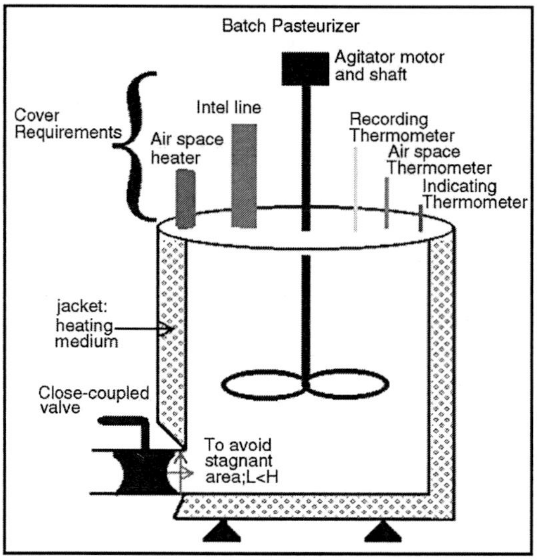


*Fig.5.3: Batch Pasteurizer (26 KB)*

This method has very little use for milk but some use for milk by-products (e.g., creams, chocolate) and special batches. The vat is used extensivly in the ice cream industry for mix quality reasons other than microbial reasons.

**Continuous Method**

Continuous process method has several advantages over the vat method, the most important being time and energy saving. For most continuous processing, a high temperature short time (HTST) pasteurizer is used. The heat treatment is accomplished using a plate heat exchanger. This piece of equipment consists of a stack of corrugated stainless steel plates clamped together in a frame. There are several flow patterns that can be used. Gaskets are used to define the boundaries of the channels and to prevent leakage. The heating medium can be vacuum steam or hot water.

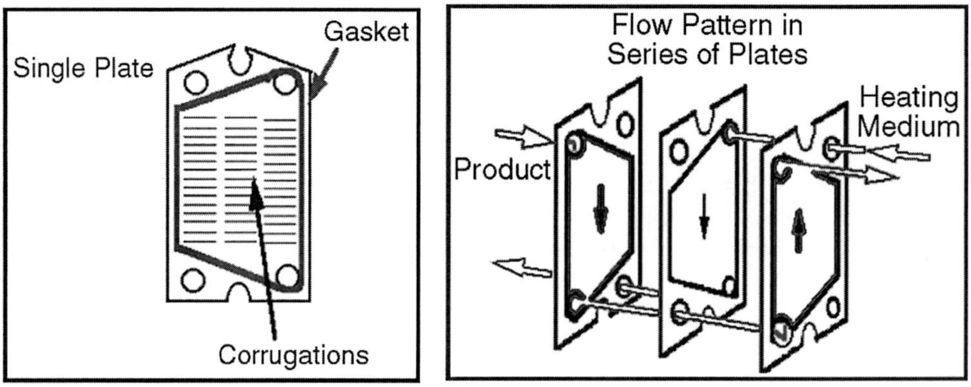


*Fig.5.4: Plate Heat Exchanger 26 KB*

**HTST Milk Flow Overview**

This overview is meant as an introduction and a summary. Each piece of HTST equipment will be discussed in further detail later. Cold raw milk at 4° C in a constant level tank is drawn into the regenerator section of pasteurizer. Here it is warmed to approximately 57° C - 68° C by heat given up by hot pasteurized milk flowing in a counter current direction on the opposite side of thin, stainless steel plates. The raw milk, still under suction, passes through a positive displacement timing pump which delivers it under positive pressure through the rest of the HTST system.

The raw milk is forced through the heater section where hot water on opposite sides of the plates heat milk to a temperature of at least 72° C. The milk, at pasteurization temperature and under pressure, flows through the holding tube where it is held for at least 16 sec. The maximum velocity is governed by the speed of the timing pump, diametre and length of the holding tube, and surface friction. After passing temperature sensors of an indicating thermometre and a recorder-controller at the end of the holding tube, milk passes into the flow diversion device (FDD).

The FDD assumes a forward-flow position if the milk passes the recordercontroller at the preset cut-in temperature (>72° C). The FDD remains in normal position which is in diverted-flow if milk has not achieved preset cut-in temperature. The improperly heated milk flows through the diverted flow line of the FDD back to the raw milk constant level tank.

Properly heated milk flows through the forward flow part of the FDD to the pasteurized milk regenerator section where it gives up heat to the raw product and in turn is cooled to approximately 32° C - 9° C. The warm milk passes through the cooling section where it is cooled to 4° C or below by coolant on the opposite sides of the thin, stainless steel plates. The cold, pasteurized milk passes through a vacuum breaker at least 12 inches above the highest raw milk in the HTST system then on to a storage tank filler for packaging.

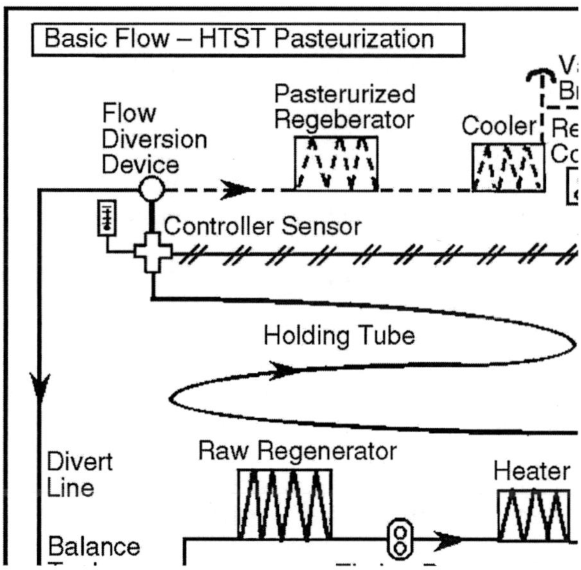


*Fig.5.5: Basic Flow - HTST Pasteurization 17 KB*

**Holding Time**

When fluids move through a pipe, either of two distinct types of flow can be observed. The first is known as turbulent flow which occurs at high velocity and in which eddies are present moving in all directions and at all angles to the normal line of flow. The second type is streamline, or laminar flow which occurs at low velocities and shows no eddy currents.

*The Reynolds number, is used to predict whether laminar or turbulent flow will exist in a pipe:*

Re < 2100 laminar

Re > 4000 fully developed turbulent flow

There is an impact of these flow patterns on holding time calculations and the assessment of proper holding tube lengths. The holding time is determined by timing the interval for an added trace substance (salt) to pass through the holder. The time interval of the fastest particle of milk is desired. Thus the results found with water are converted to the milk flow time by formulation since, a pump may not deliver the same amount of milk as it does water.

*Note:* the formulation assumes flow patterns are the same for milk and water. If they are not, how would this affect the efficiency of the pasteurization process?

**Pressure Differential**

For contiunuous pasteurizing, it is important to maintain a higher pressure on the pasteurized side of the heat exchanger. By keeping the pasteurized milk at least 1 psi higher than raw milk in regenerator, it prevents contamination of pasteurized milk with raw milk in event that a pin-hole leak develops in thin stainless steel plates.

Thispressure differential is maintained using a timing pump in simple systems, and differential pressure controllers and back pressure flow regulators at the chilled pasteurization outlet in more complex systems.

The position of the timing pump is crucial so that there is suction on the raw regenerator side and pushes milk under pressure through pasteurized regenerator.

*There are several other factors involved in maintaining the pressure differential:*

- The balance tank overflow level must be less than the level of lowest milk passage in the regenerator
- Properly installed booster pump is all that is permitted between balance tank and raw regenerator
- No pump after pasteurized milk outlet to vacuum breaker
- There must be greater than a 12 inch vertical rise to the vacuum breaker
- The raw regenerator drains freely to balance tank at shut-down

## BASIC COMPONENT EQUIPMENT OF HTST PASTEURIZER

**Balance Tank**

The balance, or constant level tank provides a constant supply of milk. It is equipped with a float valve assembly which controls the liquid level nearly constant ensuring uniform head pressure on the product leaving the tank. The overflow level must always be below the level of lowest milk passage in regenerator. It, therefore, helps to maintain a higher pressure on the pasteurized side of the heat exchanger. The balance tank also prevents air from entering the pasteurizer by placing the top of the outlet pipe lower than the lowest point in the tank and creating downward slopes of at least 2%. The balance tank provides a means for recirculation of diverted or pasteurized milk.

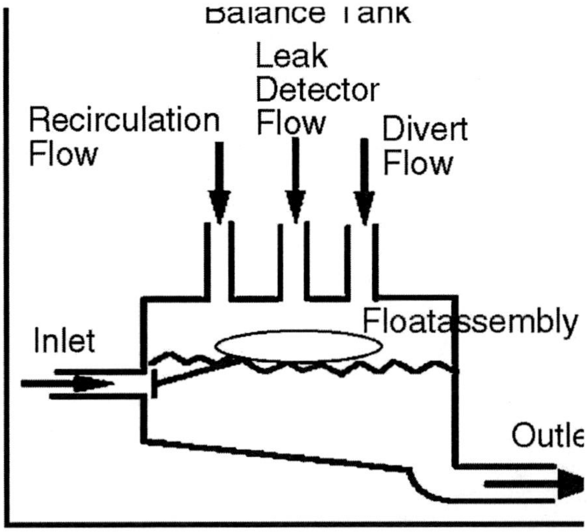


*Fig.5.6: Balance Tank 17 KB*

**Regenerator**

Heating and cooling energy can be saved by using a regenerator which utilizes the heat content of the pasteurized milk to warm the incoming cold milk.

*Its efficiency may be calculated as follows :* per cent regeneration = temp. increase due to regenerator / total temp. increase

*For example :* Cold milk entering system at 4° C, after regeneration at 65° C, and final temperature of 72° C would have an 89.7% regeneration:

$$\frac{65 - 4}{72 - 4} 89.7$$

**Timing Pump**

The timing pump draws product through the raw regenerator and pushes milk under pressure through pasteurized regenerator. It governs the rate of flow through the holding tube. It must be a positive displacement pump equipped with variable speed drive that can be legally sealed at the maximum rate to give minimum holding time in holding tubes. It also must be interwired so it only operates when FDD is fully forward or fully diverted, and must be"fail-safe". A centrifigal pump with magnetic flow metre and controller may also be used.

**Holding Tube**

Must slope upwards 1/4"/ft. in direction of flow to eliminate air entrapment so nothing flows faster at air pocket restrictions.

**Indicating Thermometre**

The indicating thermometre is considered the most accurate temperature measurement. It is the official temperature to which the safety thermal limit recorder (STLR) is adjusted. The probe should sit as close as possible to STLR probe and be located not greater than 18 inches upstream of the flow diversion device.

**Recorder-Controller (STLR)**

The STLR records the temperature of the milk and the time of day. It monitors, controls and records the position of the flow diversion device (FDD) and supplies power to the FDD during forward flow. There are both pneumatic and electronic types of controllers. The operator is responsible for recording the date, shift, equipment, ID, product and amount, indicating thermometre temperature, cleansing cycles, cut in and cut out temperatures, any connects for unusual circumstances, and his/ her signature.

**Flow Diversion Device (FDD)**

Also called the flow diversion valve (FDV), it is located at the downstream end of the upward sloping holding tube. It is essentially a 3-way valve, which, at temperatures greater than 72° C,opens to forward flow. This step requires power. At temperatures less than 72° C, the valve recloses to the normal position and diverts the milk back to the balance tank. It is important to note that the FDD operates on the measured temperature, not time, at the end of the holding period.

*There are two types of FDD:*

1. *Single stem :* An older valve system that has the disadvantage that it can't be cleaned in place.
2. *Dual stem :* Consists of 2 valves in series for additional fail safe systems. This FDD can be cleaned in place and is more suited for automation.

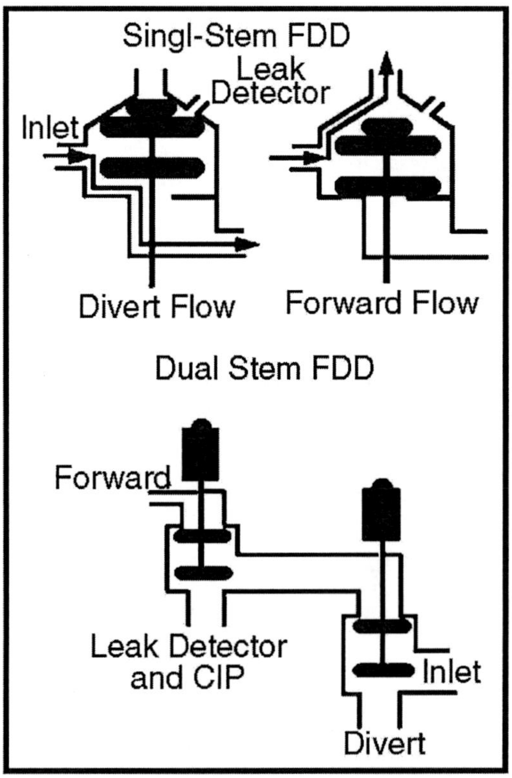


*Fig.5.8: Flow Diversion Devices 17 KB*

### Vacuum Breaker

At the pasteurized product discharge is a vacuum breaker which breaks to atmospheric pressure. It must be located greater than 12 inches above the highest point of raw product in system. It ensures that nothing downstream is creating suction on the pasteurized side.

## AUXILIARY EQUIPMENT

### Booster Pump

It is centrifugal"stuffing" pump which supplies raw milk to the raw regenerator for the balance tank. It must be used in conjunction with pressure differential controlling device and shall operate only when timing pump is operating, proper pressures are achieved in regenerator, and system is in forward flow.

### Homogenizer

The homogenizer may be used as timing pump. It is a positive pressure pump; if not, then it cannot supplement flow. Free circulation from outlet to inlet is required and the speed of the homogenizer must be greater than the rate of flow of the timing pump.

### Magnetic Flow Metre and Centrifugal Pump Arrangements

Magnetic flow metres can be used to measure the flow rate. It is essentially a short piece of tubing (approximately 25 cm long) surrounded by a housing, inside of which are located coils that generate a magnetic field. When milk passes through the magnetic field, it causes a voltage to be induced, and the generated signal is directly proportional to velcoity. Application of the magnetic flow metre in the dairy industry has centred around its replacing the positive displacement timing pump as the metreing device in HTST pasteurizing systems, where with certain products the timing pump rotors reportedly wear out in a relatvely short period of time.

In operation, the electrical signal is sent by the magnetic flow metre to the flow controller, which determines what the actual flow is compared to the flow rate set by the operator. Since, the magnetic flow metre continuously senses flow rate, it will signal the electronic controller if the actual flow exceeds the set flow rate for any reason. If the flow rate is exceeded for any reason, the flow diversion device is put into diverted flow. A significant difference from the normal HTST system (with timing pump) comes into focus at this point. This system can be operated at a flow rate greater than (residence time less than) the legal limit. However, it will be in diverted flow and never in forward flow. Another magnetic flow metre based system with an AC variable frequency motor control drive on a centrifugal pump is also possible in lieu of a positive displacement metreing pump on a HTST pasteurizer.This system does not use a control valve but rather the signal from the magnetic flow metre is transmitted to the AC variable frequency control to vary the speed of the centrifugal pump. The pump, then controls the flow rate of product through the system and its holding time in the holding tube.

Automated Public Health Controllers These systems are used for time and temperature control of HTST systems. There are concerns that with sequential control, the critical control points (CCP's) are not monitored all the time; if during the sequence it got held up, the CCP's would not be monitored. With operator control, changes can be made to the programme which might affect CCP's; the system is not easily sealed. No computer programme can be written completely error free in large systems; as complexity increases, so too do errors.

*This gives rise to a need for specific regulations or computer controlled CCP's of public health significance:*

- Dedicated computer - no other assignments, monitor all CCP's at least once/sec
- Not under control of any other computer system or override system, i.e., network
- Separate computer on each pasteurizer
- I/O bus for outputs only, to other computers no inputs from other computers
- On loss of power - public health computers should revert to fail safe position (e.g., divert)
- Last state switches during power up must be fail safe position
- Programmes in ROM - tapes/disks not acceptable
- Inputs must be sealed, modem must be sealed, programme sealed
- No operator override switches
- Proper calibration procedure during that printing - Public health computer must not leave public health control for > 1 sec and upon return must complete 1 full cycle before returning to printing
- FDV position must be monitored and temperature in holding tube recorded during change in FDV position
- Download from ROM to RAM upon startup
- Integrated with CIP computer which can be programmed e.g., FDV, booster pump controllable by CIP computer when in CIP made only

## PASTEURISED MILK PRODUCTS

**Salmonella**

Salmonellae are not able to survive the typical minimum pasteurisation processes generally prescribed in legislation. Therefore, their presence indicates that the process has not been carried out effectively, or that post-process contamination has occurred. For example, an outbreak of salmonellosis in Kentucky in 1984 was associated with pasteurised milk, but an investigation of the dairy concerned showed that pasteurisation temperatures were inadequate, and could have been as low as 54.5°C for 30 minutes.

An outbreak caused by *Salmonella braenderup* in the UK in 1986 was also associated with pasteurised milk, and on this occasion the pasteuriser was found to be poorly designed and incorrectly operated, probably resulting in the application of an inadequate heat treatment. In 1985, one of the largest outbreaks of salmonellosis in US history occurred in Illinois. Almost 200,000 people were affected, and were associated with pasteurised low-fat 2% milk contaminated with *S. typhimurium.* Investigations at the dairy plant involved revealed no evidence of inadequate pasteurisation, and the outbreak strain was not found to be abnormally heat resistant.

Although the cause of the outbreak has never been completely explained, the investigation did discover a possible cross-connection between raw and pasteurised milk, which may have been the source of contamination. In 1998, an outbreak of salmonellosis in Lancashire, caused by a multiresistant strain of *S. typhimurium* DT104, affected 86 people. This outbreak was also linked to defective pasteurisation of milk at a dairy on a local farm.

Consumption of raw milk or raw milk products have been responsible for 62 and 29 cases of diarrheal illness caused by *S. typhimurium* in 2003 and 2007, respectively, in the states of Ohio and Pennsylvania. Since, salmonellae are occasional contaminants of raw milk, they may sometimes enter the processing environment. It is very important that contamination of the postpasteurisation plant is not allowed to occur and effective precautions and monitoring procedures, based on HACCP principles, are necessary to prevent this.

**Campylobacter Spp.**

*Campylobacter* spp. are not capable of surviving milk pasteurisation treatments, and cannot grow in raw or pasteurised milk, although they are able to survive for long periods in milk at refrigeration temperatures. Nonetheless, outbreaks of campylobacteriosis associated with pasteurised milk have occurred. For example, a large outbreak in thc UK in 1979 caused by *Campylobacter jejuni* was estimated to have affected at least 2,500 schoolchildren, and was associated with free milk provided in schools. Although conclusive evidence was absent, it seems likely that raw milk may have bypassed the pasteurisation process.

A more recent outbreak in 2001 involved 75 people and was linked to the consumption of unpasteurised milk procured thorough a cow leasing programme. Birds are known to be an important reservoir of *Campylobacter* infection, and the tendency of some birds to peck through the foil tops of doorstep-delivered milk bottles is becoming recognised as an important source of infection in parts of the UK.

Some individual cases have been attributed to this cause, and, in one instance in 1990, the organism was isolated from the beaks of jackdaws and magpies as well as the contaminated milk. More recently, an outbreak thought to be associated with bird-pecked milk was reported.

**Listeria Monocytogenes**

There has been some discussion regarding the potential for *L. monocytogenes* in milk to survive pasteurisation. An outbreak of listeriosis in Massachusetts during 1983 resulted in 49 cases, 14 of whom subsequently died. Epidemiological evidence strongly suggested an association with consumption of pasteurised whole and low-fat milk, although this could not be confirmed microbiologically. The investigation failed to reveal any evidence of inadequate pasteurisation and the organism could not be found in environmental samples in the dairy, suggesting that postprocess contamination was unlikely.

However, samples of raw milk taken from farms supplying the plant were found to be positive for *L. monocytogenes* serotype 4b, and the investigators concluded that survival of some organisms through pasteurisation was the most likely cause of the outbreak. Three deaths and a miscarriage in Boston, USA between 2007-8 have been linked to presence of Listeria in pasteurised milk. So far, investigations have found nothing wrong with its pasteurisation process.

Furthermore, in a survey of pasteurised milk conducted in Spain, *L. monocytogenes* was recovered from six out of 28 samples heated at 78°C for 15 seconds. The explanation offered for both these findings was that the organisms might have been protected during heat treatment within leucocytes in the milk. However, this effect has not been conclusively demonstrated, and *L. monocytogenes* has not yet been shown to have survived pasteurisation in milk subjected to minimum HTST pasteurisation requirements of 71.7°C for 15 seconds.

For these reasons, it is currently accepted that existing pasteurisation processes are adequate to inactivate the organism in milk. L. *monocytogenes* is likely to be present in wet dairy processing environments, and post-process contamination is therefore a particular hazard. The organism has been shown to be capable of significantly more rapid growth in pasteurised milk than in raw milk at 7°C, and is also capable of growth at 4°C in pasteurised milk. Therefore, effective HACCP-based controls to prevent post-process contamination are critical, particularly the cleaning and sanitising of all milkcontact surfaces. Adequate temperature control is also important.

**Verotoxigenic Escherichia Coli**

Dairy cattle are an important reservoir for *E. coli* O157: H7 and this organism may therefore be present in raw milk, usually through faecal contamination. For this reason, raw milk is a high-risk food for this serious intestinal pathogen, and there have been a number of small outbreaks of infection associated with its consumption. However, *E. coli* O157: H7 is not a heat-resistant organism and there is no evidence that it is able to survive pasteurisation. Despite this, there have been outbreaks associated with pasteurised milk.

In 1994, an outbreak in Scotland affected over 100 people and was associated with consumption of pasteurised milk from a local dairy. The outbreak strain was eventually recovered from cows on one of the farms supplying the dairy, from a bulk milk tanker, and from a pipe transferring milk from the pasteuriser to the bottling machine. Whether this outbreak was the result of faulty pasteurisation or post-process contamination was unclear, but, in either case, the raw milk is likely to have been the original source of the organism.

In 1999, a serious outbreak occurred in Cumbria in the north-west of England, which was also associated with pasteurised milk from a local dairy. There were at least 60 confirmed cases involved, and the cause was thought to be a fault in the operation of the pasteuriser. The first general outbreak of verocytotoxin-producing *E. coli* in Denmark occurred in 2004 and involved 25 patients; 18 children and seven adults. It was thought to be due to the consumption of a particular kind of organic milk from a small dairy.

Environmental and microbiological investigations at the suspected dairy did not confirm the presence of the outbreak strain, but the outbreak stopped once the dairy was closed and thoroughly cleaned. *E. coli* O157 is not reported to be able to grow in raw or pasteurised milk stored at 5°C, but may grow slowly at higher temperatures. However, since, the infective dose of this pathogen is thought to be very low, effective pasteurisation and the prevention of post-process contamination are critical to ensure product safety.

**Yersinia Enterocolitica**

Although there has been a question about the ability of *Y. enterocolitica* to survive milk pasteurisation, the majority of the evidence indicates that it is inactivated. Three different strains of *Y. enterocolitica* were reported to have D-values of 0.24-0.96 minutes at 62.8°C. Therefore, the presence of the organism in pasteurised milk is likely to be the result of post-process contamination. There have been several *Y. enterocolitica* outbreaks associated with pasteurised milk.

In 1976, an outbreak affecting 36 children was associated with the consumption of contaminated chocolate milk. It was thought that the organism was introduced to the product during mixing of chocolate syrup with pasteurised milk, without any subsequent heat process. Another outbreak in 1982 was the largest foodborne yersiniosis outbreak ever recorded in the USA, and was also associated with pasteurised milk.

It is thought that several thousand people may have developed illness, although the organism was not isolated from milk or environmental samples at the dairy. It was found that surplus milk was used to feed pigs and that the crates used to transport this milk were stored on the ground at the farm and could have become contaminated with pig faeces.

Since, pigs are a well known reservoir for *Y. enterocolitica,* it was thought that inadequate washing of the crates allowed the organism to survive in mud on them, and subsequently contaminate the external surfaces of milk cartons. *Y. enterocolitica* is capable of psychrotrophic growth, and could therefore multiply in pasteurised milk during storage. Measures should therefore be taken to prevent post-process contamination as with *L. monocytogenes.*

**Staphylococcus Aureus**

*Staph. aureus* is only rarely involved in food poisoning associated with consumption of pasteurised milk, although enterotoxigenic strains can be found as contaminants in raw milk. This may be because *Staph. aureus* does not generally grow at temperatures below 7°C, and enterotoxin production is inhibited at low temperatures. The organism is also known to be inhibited by the presence of competing species. Nevertheless, an outbreak in California affecting 500 school children was associated with chocolateflavoured milk. The cause was thought to be growth of *Staph. aureus* in raw milk, and the subsequent persistence of the heat-stable enterotoxin through pasteurisation.

In June and July 2000, a very large outbreak of staphylococcal food poisoning was reported in Japan, associated with consumption of pasteurised low fat milk. Over 14,500 people were said to have been affected. The outbreak was unusual in that the thermal processes had destroyed staphylococci in milk but *Staphylococcus* enterotoxin A had retained enough activity to cause intoxication. SEA exposed at least twice to pasteurisation at 130°C for 4 or 2s retained both immunological and biological activities, although it had been partially inactivated.

**Bacillus Spp**

Psychrotrophic *Bacillus* spp. present in raw milk may survive pasteurisation and then become dominant in the pasteurised milk, potentially causing spoilage. Concerns have been expressed that some psychrotrophic strains of *B. cereus* may be able to produce toxin in milk at refrigeration temperatures, but it seems likely that obvious spoilage would occur before sufficient toxin production had taken place to cause illness. Even so, B. cereus was isolated at levels of 4x105/g from pasteurised milk associated with 280 food poisoning cases in the Netherlands in 1989.

**Mycobacterium Avium Subsp. Paratuberculosis**

MAP is the causative organism of Johne's disease in cattle, a chronic wasting disease, and may occasionally be present in raw milk. Evidence linking MAP to a chronic inflammatory bowel condition in humans, called Crohn's disease, is becoming increasingly compelling. Concerns have been raised that MAP might be able to survive pasteurisation if present at levels above 100 cells per ml, especially if clumps of cells are present, and that pasteurised milk may therefore be a vehicle for Crohn's disease.

On the basis of new heat-resistance studies, many UK dairies have increased pasteurisation times to from 15 to 25 seconds. A survey of the level of contamination of pasteurised milk by MAP over a 17 month period, in 1999-2000, revealed a mean of 1.6% of raw and 1.8% of pasteurised samples were positive for MAP cultures indicating that commercially pasteurised milk may occasionally contain low levels of viable MAP. The potential public health impact of this situation is, however, still uncertain given that an association with Crohn's disease in humans remains unproven.

### Viruses

A number of viruses have been shown to be present in raw milk, although many of these, such as Foot and Mouth Disease Virus (FMDV), are not pathogenic to humans. However, raw milk has been implicated in outbreaks of hepatitis and poliomyelitis. Some viruses, including poliovirus, are completely inactivated by pasteurisation, but this seems not to be the case with others, such as FMDV, if the virus is naturally present rather than inoculated. There is therefore the possibility that other viruses pathogenic to humans may survive at low levels, but, in bulk milk processing systems, it is thought unlikely that sufficient viruses will be present to infect consumers.

### Toxins

Mycotoxins may be present in milk as a result of the ingestion of mouldy and contaminated feed by cattle. Feed contaminated by aflatoxin B1 as a result of the growth of *Aspergillus flavus* or *Aspergillus parasiticus* has been shown to give rise to the presence of aflatoxin M1 in the milk of dairy cows consuming it. However, only a small percentage of the ingested toxin appeared in the milk. Aflatoxins are persistent compounds and are not greatly affected by milk processing, and could therefore be present in pasteurised, packaged milk. However, recent surveys suggest that contamination of the milk supply is very limited and well within acceptable levels.

### Separating Curd and Whey

*Three methods can be followed to separate curd from whey:*

1. Hanging the curd/whey mixture up in a clean cloth;
2. Putting the curd/whey mixture in cheese moulds, or in cylindrical forms with perforated sides;
3. First cutting and stirring the curd/whey mixture, putting the curd in the cheese moulds and then pressing the cheese.

When making fresh cheese, the first or second method is usually used. As the whey drains through the cloth or the mould, the volume of the curd will reduce to 1/2 or 1/3. When making ripened cheese, the last method has to be used to remove sufficient whey from the curd.

*Fig.5.9: Letting Soft Cheese Drain*

### Collection and Preservation of the Curd

The amount of whey (water) in the curd has a great influence on the cheese properties. Maturation time, flavour, consistency, keeping quality of cheese, etc., all depend on the water content. Whey contains milk sugar or lactose. This sugar has to be converted into lactic acid by the lactic acid bacteria of the added starter. If a great deal of the whey is removed from the curd, you get cheese with little moisture, therefore a dry and hard cheese, which has to mature a rather long time. If little whey is removed from the curd, you get cheese with a lot of moisture, therefore a soft cheese. This cheese has in most cases a sour taste.

Since, the curd treatment of fresh cheese and ripened cheese is quite different, they will be discussed separately. It is important during this step of chease making that the curd does not cool down and remains at about 30– 36°C. The curd treatment can be started when the coagulated milk forms a firm mass. You can determine this by moving a small strip through the curd: if a smooth clear cut develops when the curd breaks it has coagulated sufficiently.

### Curd Treatment for Fresh Cheese

As a rule, to make fresh cheese little whey is removed. After curdling the milk, the curd/whey mass is hung in a cloth or placed in cheese moulds. After 24 hours, enough whey has leaked out and the curd is cooled down. The cheese is then ready for consumption. The separation of the whey can be stimulated by piling the cloths or cotton sacks on top of each other so that more whey is pressed out of the cheese.

### Curd Treatment for Ripened Cheese

After coagulation of the milk, the coagulated mass is cut with a sharp knife into square cubes of about 1.5 cm. It is important that the cubes are more or less of the same size and that the cutting is done very gently.

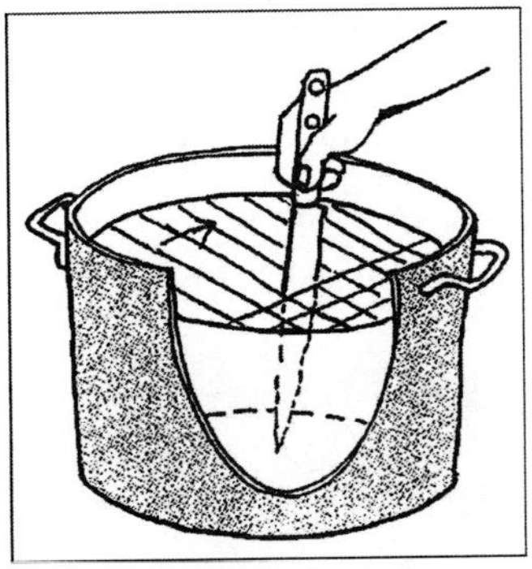

*Fig.5.10: Cutting the Curd*

After cutting, the curd/whey mixture is briefly left to stand, for about 10 minutes, after which it is carefully stirred. After some time it can be stirred a little bit more vigourously. Most of the whey is removed from the cheese vat and the curd is placed in the cheese moulds. The curd is then pressed (0.1 kg/ cm2). After about one hour the pressure can be increased to 0.4 kg/cm2. Other ways of determining the pressure are respectively 2 times and then 5 times the curd's own weight. After being pressed, the cheese is left for some time (4- 20 hours) at 20-25°C.

In the meantime the lactose present in the cheese is completely converted into lactic acid. Then the cheese can be salted. Trying to produce cheese of a Gouda or Edam type in this way will be disappointing, because the cheese will become very firm, crumbly and acid. The reason for this is that the curd–after fermentation by the lactic acid bacteria-contains too much lactic acid.

Therefore Gouda cheese makers add 15 to 20% of hot water to the curd and whey after stirring for about 30 minutes. The temperature of the water is such that after addition of the water the temperature of the curd and whey is 35–36°C. (Water temperature is about 65–70°C. Before adding the hot water, part of the whey (30%) is drained off). After adding hot water the curd-andwhey mixture has to be stirred again for at least 20 minutes.

**Salting the Cheese**

*Salting can be done in several ways:*

- Stir the salt through the curd; add 30 grams of salt per kilogram of curd. This reduces the effect of the bacteria of the starter, but potentially damaging micro-organisms are also inhibited at an early stage.
- After pressing the cheese, rub it in with salt. Rub both sides in and then turn the cheese. This must be done every day for 3 days; in total 20 grams of salt is needed per kilogram of cheese.
- Place the cheese in brine of 200 grams of salt per litre of water at 12-16°C. During this pickling, the cheese absorbs salt and secretes lactic acid. The brine becomes more sour and improves in quality; it should therefore not be thrown away. Salt must be added regularly to the Processing Techniques of Milk and Milk Products 161 brine; 20 grams of salt is removed from the brine by each kilogram of cheese. For a small cheese, e.g., less than 1 kg, pickling time is about 12 hours. During pickling, the cheese must be turned once.

## BUTTER

*You will need:*

- Pasteurised cream, sour cream or sour milk
- A heat source
- A pan
- A thermometer
- Cold water
- Sour milk or a starter culture
- A container for churning
- A sieve
- A bowl
- A tray for kneading
- Wooden spoons
- Fine salt if available (optional)
- Packing material, e.g., greaseproof paper or a jar
- Clean water

*Butter is made by churning one of the following products:*

- Cream,
- Sour cream, or
- Sour milk.

If you do not have enough milk from which to skim off the cream, the milk can be soured and churned as a whole (provided that the fat content of the milk is rather high; above 4%). But sour cream is better to churn than sour milk. It is only possible to manufacture sweet cream butter if the production and handling of the milk, cream and butter are exceptionally hygienic and the cream has undergone after pasteurisation a cold treatment by storing it for at least 12 hours at temperatures below 10°C.

**Heating and Souring**

Heat the milk or cream to a temperature of 85°C. Let it cool down to 18°C as quickly as possible (use a thermometer) using cold running water on the outside of the pan. Add 10-30 ml (about 1-2 tablespoons) of fresh fermented sour milk or a starter culture to one litre of milk or cream and stir. After about 24 hours at 16 to 18°C, the mixture will become thick and sour enough to be churned.

**Churning**

During churning the cream, sour cream or sour milk will be mixed intensively with air. This process causes fat globules to flocculate (or stick together), producing butter and buttermilk. The simplest way to make butter from small quantities of milk is by using a bottle or a jar that can be covered with a well-closing lid or a simple bowl with beaters. If large quantities of milk or cream are available, you should consider acquiring a real churn.

There are several types available. The churn tub is a simple method, which is often used in the tropics. A cheap and practical domestic churn is a glass pot with a paddle attached to a screw top. The paddle can be turned manually. This churn is difficult to clean. It is best to rinse it with water before use, in order to prevent the butter from sticking to the sides.

Churns should not be filled more than one third with soured milk or sour cream. Churn with a regular up and down or sideways movement. Stop churning when the butter particles reach the size of rice grains or peas and the buttermilk looks rather liquid. If, after 30 minutes, no grains have yet been formed, you can change the temperature by adding a little clean cold or warm water. The amount of added water should never be more than 25% of the total amount of churned cream or milk.

The butter particles will float to the top of the buttermilk, because butter is lighter than buttermilk. This makes it easier to separate the two products by pouring off the buttermilk through a coarse sieve. Never add too much water, otherwise the buttermilk will become too watery.

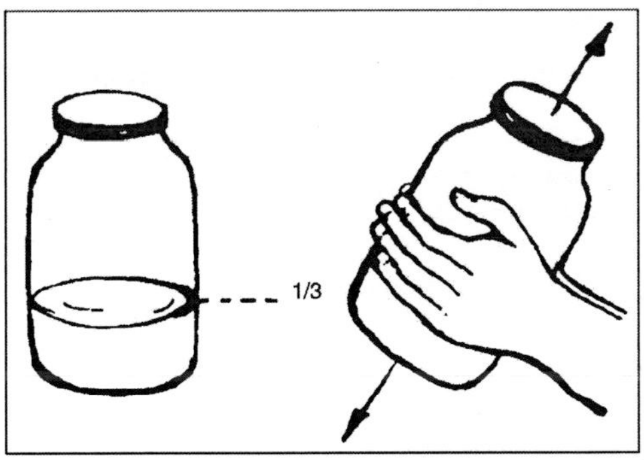


*Fig.5.11: Using a Jar to make Butter*

### Washing

Washing of the butter grains is not necessary. However, if very clean water is available, it can improve butter quality.

*Washing the butter can be done in two ways:*

1. Fill the churn 2/5 full with clean, cold water. Wash the butter by churning it for about 3 minutes. This can be repeated, if necessary. The idea is to remove part of the remaining buttermilk from the butter particles. It is important to remove as much as possible in order to produce butter that can be kept for a longer period. After washing, the butter particles can be skimmed off or the buttermilk can be drained.
2. If small quantities are available, the butter particles can be washed using a sieve. Put the sieve on top of a bowl and pour the mixture through it. Make sure that during churning the butter does not become one big lump, otherwise it will be difficult to wash-in case you want to do this.

### Salting (If Preferred)

Salting is not necessary for preservation; many people, however, like the taste of salted butter. The butter can be slightly salted by kneading in about 10 grams of salt to each kilogram of butter. Mix the butter again the next day in order to allow the salt grains to dissolve.

### Kneading

Kneading the butter is important in order to get a nice, smooth product. It helps to distribute the moisture and this improves quality and shelf life, provided that kneading is done in a hygienic way. Use a clean, well-rinsed kneading board. Knead the butter with the back of two wooden spoons until drops of water and buttermilk are not perceivable any more and the butter has a nice, smooth surface. Remove drops of buttermilk during this process. Instead of a wooden spoon, a wet roller or bottle can be used. If none of these are available, just use clean hands to knead.

### Storage

Butter should be stored in a cool, dark place. Put it in a pot or wrap it up in greaseproof paper or aluminium foil. After some time, one to two weeks, the surface of the butter can be covered with moulds. This mould formation can be partially prevented by sprinkling salt on the surface or by wrapping the butter air tight.

Moulds only grow if oxygen is available. Butter can also be frozen. However, after defrosting the butter will rather soon have an off-taste. It is therefore a good idea to divide the butter into smaller portions before freezing. Salted butter is less suitable for freezing.

### Remarks

- If milk has gone sour without the use of a starter, but it still tastes and smells fresh, it can still be churned.
- Churning can take from 5 to as much as 60 minutes. A number of factors may influence the time needed, for instance:
- Type of animal the milk came from
- The fat content of the cream
- Treatment of the cream; the cream must have had enough time (atleast 12 hours at 10–18°C) before churning for crystallisation of part of the fat to take place
- Feed eaten by the animal; feed influences the crystallisation (=melting point) of the fat

- The temperature of the cream during churning. This last aspect is also dependent on the melting point of the fat. If the cream is too cold, the fat globules do not easily stick together and churning will take longer. If the temperature of the cream is too high, churning will go quickly and the butter grains will not stick together and butter will not be formed. A good churning temperature is 15–20°C.
- Butter has a limited shelf life. It can become mouldy or rancid. An unpleasant cheese-like flavour may develop due to the deterioration of its protein. An alternative is ghee, which does not spoil as quickly as butter. Ghee is produced by removing the last water remnants from butter by heating the butter and letting the water evaporate, or by melting butter and draining the water, which separates from the fat.

## FERMENTED MILKS

### Definitions

Fermented milks have been produced by traditional methods for many centuries, and there are several hundred such products recorded around the world. They are produced as a result of microbial 'souring' of milk, usually cows' milk, but also the milk of other species, including sheep, goat, horse and buffalo. Most are very similar, both in terms of their characteristics, and in the technology used to produce them. Many fermented milk products are distinguished only by their region of origin, and very few have become commercially important.

Interest in these products, particularly yoghurt, has grown rapidly since, the development of flavoured and fruit yoghurts in Europe in the late 1950s, and more recently as a result of the growing demand for, and marketing of, fermented milks as healthpromoting foods. Fermented milks can be conveniently classified on the basis of the type of fermentation they undergo, as lactic, yeast-lactic and mould-lactic. Lactic fermentation products can be further classified, depending on the characteristics of the lactic microflora, as mesophilic, thermophilic and probiotic or therapeutic.

### Lactic acid Fermentaton

Lactic acid fermentation is caused by some fungi and bacteria. The most important lactic acid producing bacteria is Lactobacillus. Other bacteria which produce lactic acid include:

- leuconostoc mesenteroides
- pediococcus cerevisiae
- streptococcus lactis
- bifidobacterium bifidus.

Lactic acid fermentation is used throughout the world to produce speciality foods:

- Western world: yogurt, sourdough breads, sauerkraut, cucumber pickles and olives
- Middle East: pickled vegetables
- Korea: kimchi (fermented mixture of Chinese cabbage, radishes, red pepper, garlic and ginger)
- Russia: kefir
- Egypt: laban rayab and laban zeer (fermented milks), kishk (fermented cereal and milk mixture)

- Nigeria: gari (fermented cassava)
- South Africa : magou (fermented maize porridge)
- Thailand : nham (fermented fresh pork)
- Philippines : balao balao (fermented rice and shrimp mixture)

The presence of lactic acid, produced during the lactic acid fermentation is responsible for the sour taste and for the improved microbiological stability and safety of the food. This lactic acid fermentation is responsible for the sour taste of dairy products such as cheese, yoghurt and kefir.

Lactic acid fermentation also gives the sour taste to fermented vegetables such as traditionally cultured sauerkraut and pickles. The sugars in the cabbage are converted into lactic acid and serve as a preservative.

**Yogurt Fermentation**

Yogurt is made by fermenting milk with friendly bacteria, mainly Lactobacillus bulgaricus and Streptococcus thermophilus. Yogurt fermentation was invented probably by accident by Balkan tribes thousands of years ago. Yogurt remained mainly a food of eastern Europe until the 1900s, when the biologist Mechnikov created the theory that lactobacillus bacteria in yogurt are responsible for the unusually long lifespans of the Bulgar people. The milk sugar or lactose is fermented by these bacteria to lactic acid which causes the characteristic curd to form.

The acid also restricts the growth of food poisoning bacteria. During the yogurt fermentation some flavours are produced, which give yogurt its characteristic flavour. Yoghurt can easily be made at home using a live yogurt as the starter culture. To make you own yogurt use the following process.

Bring the milk (or soymilk) to boiling point and cool down to 40- 45°C. Pour this milk in a sterile container and and per litre milk about 100 ml live yogurt. Mix with a sterile spoon and incubate at 40-44°C during 4 to 6 hours or until the yogurt is set. Put the yogurt in the refrigerator. If you worked under hygienic conditions, you can use your own yogurt as a starter for your next batch.

**Magou Fermentation**

Magou is very popular in South Africa, especially among the Bantu people. Magou is a lactic acid fermented porridge made from maize. To make magua a 10 percent maize meal slurry is cooked, cooled and inoculated with wheat flour, which contains the bacteria. Magou is also produced on industrial scale and is then packed in cartons. In the industrial process the magou is inoculated with lactobacillus delbreuckii cultures.

**Kefir Fermentation**

Kefir fermentation is similar to yogurt fermentation. Yogurt is only fermented by bacteria but kefir fermentation involves the help of bacteria as well as yeasts. These yeast produce some alcohol and carbon dioxide, which gives kefir its typical fizzy aspect. Kefir is inoculated with special kefir grains. These grains are mixtures of bacteria and yeasts in a matrix of proteins, lipids and carbohydrates. Kefir fermentation is done at room temperature, which makes the process easier. On the other hand, not everyone likes the taste of kefir.

**Mesophilic**

The genera of microorganisms that fall into this category include *Lactococcus, Leuconostoc* and *Pediococcus.* The optimal growth temperature is between 25-30 °C.

**Traditional or Natural Buttermilk**

Traditional or natural buttermilk is made from the liquid produced during butter production using a starter culture mixture of *Lactococcus* spp. and *Leuconostoc mesenteroides* subsp. *cremoris.*

**Cultured Buttermilk**

Cultured buttermilk is also produced mostly using a mixed culture of *L. lactis* subsp. *lactis,* L. *lactis* subsp. *cremoris* and the fla-vour-producing organisms *L. lactis* biovar *diacetylactis* and *L. mesenteroides* subsp. cremoris. It is traditionally made from skimmed milk. Ymer is similar to cultured buttermilk, but differs in the sequence of the manufacturing stages.

**Nordic Sour Milks**

Nordic sour milks such as Filmjolk and Nordic ropy milk are made using slimeproducing Bacterium lacticus longi, a synonym of Lactococcus spp. The slimy or ropy consistency of the products is also attributed to Butterwort leaves, which are rubbed on the interior of the pails.

**Cultured Cream**

Cultured cream or sour cream is made using the same starter cultures as cultured buttermilk, but has a much higher fat content.

**Miscellaneous Products**

Miscellaneous products include a range of traditional products that depend on spontaneous fermentation by naturally present lactic acid bacteria in milk. Maziwa lala is made using the same starter culture mixture as buttermilk, but is then sweetened. Susa, made from camel's milk is fermented using heterofermentative mesophilic starter cultures. Lben is similar to buttermilk but its production involves spontaneous fermentation. The microflora of this product mainly consists of *L. lactis* biovar *diacetylactis, Leuconostoc lactis, L. mesenteroides* subsp. *cremoris* and *Leuconostoc mesenteroides* subsp. *dextranicum;* lactobacilli, yeast, mould and coliforms are also present.

**Thermophilic**

This category encompasses those starter cultures whose growth optimum is between 37 and 45°C. The genera of microorganisms that fall into this category include *Streptococcus* and *Lactobacillus.*

**Yoghurt**

Yoghurt is a term used to describe a wide range of related products, which may be classified according to legal standards, gel type and whether or not they are flavoured or if they are subjected to a further process. The usual starter culture employed to produce yoghurt is a mixture of *Streptococcus thermophilus* and *Lactobacillus delbrueckii* subsp. *bulgaricus.*

**Acid Buttermilk**

Acid buttermilk, also known as Bulgarian buttermilk is made using *L. delbrueckii* subsp. *bulgaricus* as the starter culture. *Str. thermophilus* or a cream culture may also be included in the starter culture.

**Probiotic or Therapeutic**

LAB such as enterococci, lactococci, propionibacteria, *Leuconostoc,* and pediococci are used as probiotics, but the principal organisms are of the bacterial genera *Lactobacillus* and *Bifidobacterium.*

**Yakult**

Yakult is a term for a group of therapeutic products originating from Japan. The starter culture used is Lactobacillus casei subsp. casei, an organism naturally present in the normal intestinal microflora of humans. The organism is a probiotic strain that is thought to have a beneficial effect on the host, by improving the intestinal microbial balance. The positive health benefits of probiotics are reported to be of particular value in the treatment of diseases that result in a disturbance of the intestinal microflora.

**Acidophilus Milk**

Acidophilus milk is a traditional therapeutic milk product popular in eastern Europe, but now attracting more attention elsewhere for its perceived beneficial properties. It may be made from skimmed or whole milk, and the starter organism is *Lactobacillus acidophilus.*

**'Bio' Yoghurts**

'Bio' yoghurts are made by very much the same process as traditional yoghurt, and are very similar products, but usually use a mixed starter culture consisting of probiotic strains. *Bifidobacterium* spp. are often used, especially *Bifidobacterium bifidum,* and *Bifidobacterium longum,* together with lactobacilli, such as *L. casei* and *L. acidophilus.* These organisms are all found in the normal intestinal microflora and are considered to have a beneficial effect on human health.

**Yeast-Lactic Fermentations**

Mesophilic LAB, thermophilic LAB and yeast are the main fermentation genera.

**Kefir**

Kefir is a rather foamy and effervescent fermented milk that contains about 1% lactic acid and 0.5-1.0% alcohol, and is popular in eastern Europe and Mongolia. The starter culture consists of small, white 'kefir grains', about 2-10 mm in diameter. These grains contain a complex and quite variable microbial community, but little is known about how they develop. The grains usually contain LAB such as *Lactobacillus* spp. plus *Lactococcus* spp., *Leuconostoc* spp., and *Str. thermophilus,* acetic acid bacteria, contaminants such as mould, and a number of yeast species such as *Saccharomyces and Kluyveromyces,* but the principal yeast species present is *Candida kefir.*

**Koumiss**

Koumiss is traditionally made in central Asia from mares' milk, but is now often made from skimmed, or whole cows' milk with added sugar. Starter cultures contain LAB such as lactobacilli, strains of lactose-fermenting yeasts, non-lactosefermenting and non-carbohydrate-fermenting yeasts. The finished product contains lactic acid, alcohol and carbon dioxide, producing a slightly effervescent drink.

**Miscellaneous Products**

Miscellaneous products such as acidophilus-yeast milk fall under the yeast lactic group of fermented products, but little is known about the technology of these beverages.

## MOULD-LACTIC FERMENTATIONS

Mesophilic LAB and mould are the genera responsible for fermentation.

**Villi**

Villi is a fermented milk product from Finland, which is made from whole milk, using a starter culture of *L. lactis* subsp. lactis biovar *diacetylactis, L. mesenteroides* subsp. *cremoris,* and the mould *Geotrichum candidum.* The mould grows on the layer of fat that forms on the top of the product and produces a felt of mycelium.

**Initial Microflora**

The initial microflora of fermented milk products is determined largely by the microflora of the whole and skimmed milks from which they are made.

**Processing and its Effects on the Microflora**

Although there is a very wide range of fermented milk products, the manufac-turing technology used is generally very similar. The principal differences are in the starter cultures used, the composition and treatment of the milk, and the fermentation conditions. Therefore, for the purposes of this chapter, yoghurt manufacture is used as a representative example of fermented milk processes, since, yoghurt is the most commercially important of these products. An outline of the process is depicted in Figure.

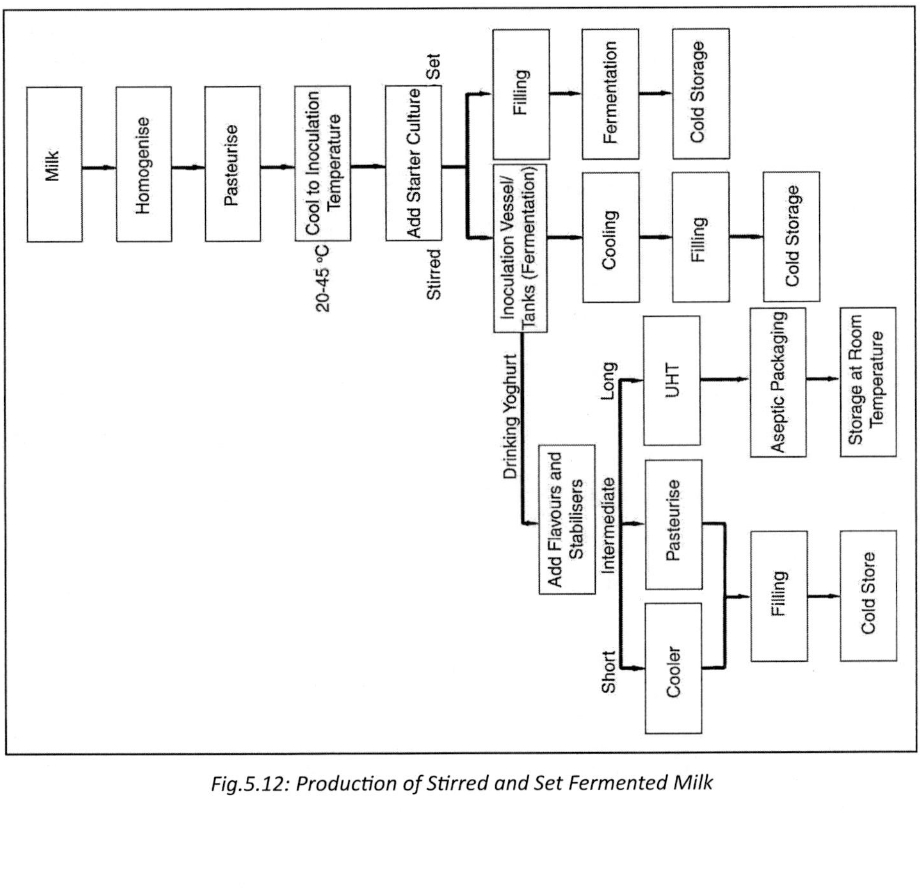


*Fig.5.12: Production of Stirred and Set Fermented Milk*

**Initial Processing**

Several different varieties of yoghurt are produced, but the three main types are: set; stirred; and drinking yoghurt. Yoghurt is most commonly made from cows' milk, but may also be produced from the milk of sheep, goats, and, occasionally, other animal species. The composition of yoghurt varies slightly, and in some countries is regulated by legislation. Both whole milk and reduced-fat milks are used to produce yoghurt, but reduced-fat products have the largest market share in most countries.

A fat content of approximately 1.5% is typical for a low-fat yoghurt, and the milk is usually standardised to control the final fat content. The protein composition and quality of the milk are important, since, they may have a significant effect on texture. Only milk of good microbiological quality should be used, in order to avoid problems of proteolysis associated with bacterial activity, and the production of bacterial proteases by psychrotrophs.

These enzymes may significantly alter the physical properties of the yoghurt, and cause defects. The milk-solids-not-fat content of the milk is usually increased to give a higher viscosity in the finished product. This may be done by fortification with non-fat dried milk or other dairy powders, or by concentration methods, such as evaporation under vacuum, or by membrane filtration. For most yoghurt, an MSNF level of about 15% is typical, but for drinking yoghurt, levels of less than 11% are preferred.

The milk is usually then filtered, to remove undissolved particles, deaerated to provide conditions that favour rapid starter growth, and homogenised to improve texture and help prevent syneresis. Stabilisers may also be added to stirred yoghurts to improve viscosity and further reduce the likelihood of syneresis. Pre-gelatinised starch or plant gums are the most commonly used stabilisers.

**Heat Treatment**

A heat treatment is generally applied to milk for yoghurt manufacture. A process of 80-85°C for 30 minutes is typical for batch processes, but, for continuous processes, a heat treatment of 90-95°C for 5-10 minutes is more usual. In some cases, a full ultra high temperature process may be applied. This relatively severe heat treatment has a number of effects.

Vegetative bacterial cells, which may include pathogens such as Salmonella, are killed, leaving only heat-resistant bacterial spores. Non-pathogenic organisms that might interfere with the growth of the starter culture are therefore reduced to very low levels. The heat treatment also has a significant effect on the final viscosity of the yoghurt, and improves texture by causing denaturation of the whey proteins and the three-dimensional aggregation of casein molecules.

The oxygen concentration of the milk is also further reduced, improving conditions for starter culture growth, since, the starter organisms are generally microaerophilic. Finally, starter culture activity can either be stimulated or inhibited due to the breakdown products of heat-damaged milk proteins.

**Fermentation**

After heat treatment, the milk is cooled to 30 or 45°C and is then inoculated with the starter culture. Most commercial yoghurt production now uses a mixed inoculum containing defined strains of *Str. thermophilus* and *L. delbrueckii* subsp. *bulgaricus*. During fermentation, the two starter organisms grow synergistically. Initially, *Str. thermophilus* grows rapidly and produces lactic acid. As the acidity rises, so *L. delbreuckii* subsp. *bulgaricus* becomes more active and produces more acid along with aroma compounds.

It has been found that the growth of *Str. thermophilus* stimulates the growth of the *Lactobacillus,* probably by the production of a growth factor, thought to be formic acid, which stimulates proteolytic activity. *Lactobacillus* growth is further stimulated by the production of low levels of carbon dioxide from urea. The lactobacilli, in turn, stimulate the growth of *Str. thermophilus* by releasing peptides and, to lesser extent, amino acids as by-products of proteolysis.

The specific strains used are chosen for their effect on product flavour and texture, and strains may be used in rotation to prevent occasional problems with bacteriophage infection. Good hygienic practices after pasteurisation are required to prevent build-up of bacteriophage pools in stagnant whey. It is important that the inoculum contains a balanced population of the two organisms, usually a 1:1 ratio. Both liquid and freeze-dried cultures are used. Most commercial manufacturers use an inoculum of about 2-3% v/v.

Incubation of the inoculated milk at 40-45°C produces a rapid fermentation, which is normally complete within 3-4 hours. During this time, lactic acid is produced, giving an eventual acidity of 0.9-0.95% and a pH of approximately 4.6-5.0. The starter organisms may also produce aroma compounds, such as acetaldehyde, acetone, acetoin and diacetyl, and exopolysaccharides, which improve texture and viscosity, although if too much extracellular material is produced, a 'ropy' texture fault may result. Set yoghurt is fermented in the final container, but stirred yoghurt is fermented in bulk, and stirred slowly, for only a few minutes, during the process.

**Cooling and Packing**

When fermentation is complete, the yoghurt is initially cooled to about 15-20°C, to minimise further acid production. At this point, sweeteners, flavours and/or fruit purees may be added. These additions must be of good microbiological quality, since, for most yoghurts, no further processing is applied. The product is then dispensed into the final containers and further cooled to < 5°C.

A shelf life of about 3 weeks at this temperature is typical, although acid continues to be produced during this time and may affect flavour. Some yoghurt is heat treated after fermentation to destroy starter organisms, and this increases shelf life to several months. Greek-style, concentrated yoghurts are produced by further separation of the yoghurt after fermentation to increase the fat and solids content. Yoghurt may also be frozen, or dried for use as an ingredient.

## COMPONENTS OF MILK FOOD

Milk contains components that are essential to humans such as proteins, carbohydrates, fat, water, all the B-vitamins, vitamins A and D, calcium and phosphorus. It also provides energy.

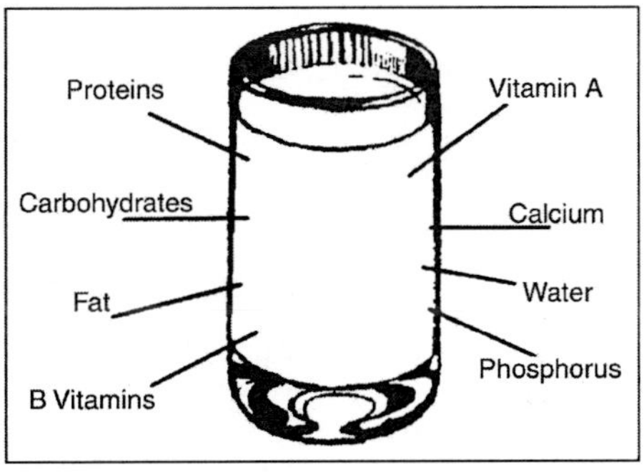


*Fig.5.13: Main Components of Milk*

An important protein in milk is casein (in many cases 80% of the milk protein). This is the base for cheese making. Casein is linked to calcium phosphate, which is why milk contains a relatively large amount of this salt that is a very important nutrient for humans and animals. In addition to casein, milk contains whey proteins (20% of the milk protein). The whey proteins are in most cases not incorporated in the cheese; they remain in the whey. Whey proteins (globulins and albumins) have a very high nutritive value.

Milk protein is of a high quality. This means that the human body can use a large part of the protein efficiently. Proteins in various other foodstuffs have a comple-mentary effect. In combination with cereals, potatoes, meat, eggs or nuts in one meal, the body can use an even greater percentage of the milk protein. Apart from milk, there are other animal protein sources such as fish and meat.

Vegetable protein, which is also important in making the body's proteins, is found in cereals and pulses. Protein is needed by the body for growth, replacement of worn-out body proteins and the production of compounds that the body needs. Milk sugar (lactose) is a carbohydrate, a necessary component to keep the body going. Our bodies burn carbohydrates in the same way an oven burns wood. Through this combustion, energy is released which is used by our bodies for many kinds of activities.

Milk fat is present in the form of small fat globules, which have a lower weight than the other components of the milk. When cow milk is allowed to stand, these globules collect on top of the milk and form a layer of cream. Buffalo milk also forms some cream on top, but other kinds of milk, such as that of sheep and goats, hardly form a layer of fat at all. For these types of milk one needs to separate the cream from the milk.

Milk fat is easy to digest. The body uses fat as a fuel or stores it as fat reserves. Milk is also an important source of minerals and vitamins. It contains large quantities of calcium, which can easily be absorbed by the body after digestion and is important for the formation of bones (the skeleton).

Milk is also an important source of vitamin B2 (Riboflavin), but there is little vitamin C in milk. Therefore a person's diet must also include vegetables and fruits in order to ensure a sufficient supply of vitamin C.

Milk is able to compensate for a lack of certain nutrients in a monotonous diet because of the great diversity of nutrients it contains and the high value of milk protein. It can therefore greatly improve the quality of the diet.

Products derived from milk contain these nutrients to a greater or lesser extent. Milk is especially desirable for vulnerable groups, for instance babies, toddlers, children and pregnant and nursing mothers. Always strive for a healthy, varied diet, which apart from milk also includes cereals, pulses, vegetables, fruits and if possible meat or fish. The various types of milk differ in various ways, including nutritional value.

## COMPOSITION AND CHARACTERISTICS OF VARIOUS TYPES OF MILK

The composition of mother's milk and milk from cow, buffalo, goat, sheep, camel, donkey and lama is shown in table. The figures in table show that the composition of the milk of non-ruminants, e.g., mother's milk and mare milk, differs distinctly from the milk of ruminants (cow, goat, sheep, etc.). This may be partly explained by differences in the digestive system of the two groups.

Apart from the differences in cream formation there are other differences between the various kinds of milk. There is a lot of provitamin A (carotene) in cow milk, giving it its yellow colour, but not in buffalo, goat or sheep milk. In the milk of goats and sheep the carotenoids are already converted into the colourless vitamin A. This is why only cow milk is yellow in colour.

Buffalo milk curdles sooner than cow milk. Unless the preparation is adjusted, cheese made from buffalo milk will mature more slowly and have a drier consistency than cheese made from cow milk. Goat milk can have an unpleasant smell; this can be prevented by boiling the milk as soon as possible after milking. Between some goats or breeds of goats there may be a difference in the taste of the milk. Cow milk accounts for 91% of the world's milk production. Buffalo, goat and sheep milk account for 5.9%, 1.6% and 1.7% respectively.

**Table: Composition of various Types of Milk**

| Milk Source | Fat (%) | Protein (%) | Lactose (%) | Calcium (%) | Energy (cal 100g) |
|---|---|---|---|---|---|
| Human (mother's) milk | 4.6 | 1.2 | 7.0 | 0.0 | 73 |
| Friesian cow | 3.5 | 3.3 | 4.6 | 01 | 62 |
| Guernsey cow | 4.7 | 3.2 | 4.7 | 0.1 | 75 |
| Indian buffalo | 7.5 | 3.8 | 4.9 | 0.2 | 100 |
| Goat | 4.5 | 3.3 | 4.4 | 0.1 | 71 |
| Sheep | 7.5 | 5.6 | 4.4 | 0.2 | 105 |
| Mare | 1.6 | 2.2 | 6.0 | 0.1 | 47 |
| Donkey | 1.5 | 2.1 | 6.2 | 0.1 | 46 |
| Camel | 4.2 | 3.7 | 4.1 | ? | 70 |
| Lama | 3.2 | 3.9 | 5.3 | ? | 65 |

Although there are enormous regional differences we can generally say that, if it is to be drunk, milk from cows or buffaloes is preferred to that from goats and sheep. This is because of the more neutral flavour of cow milk and buffalo milk. Goat and sheep milk are, just like the milk of cows and buffaloes, popular for making cheese and soured milk products (especially sheep milk). Camel milk is usually drunk. Mother's milk is the most ideal food for a suckling infant. Nonetheless, many substitutes have been developed which find a ready demand. We shall pay more attention to infant nutrition in the next section.

**Infant Nutrition**

Mother's milk is best suited to the needs of a baby, and contains certain components that protect an infant against infectious diseases. All the nutrients a baby needs, except iron and vitamin C, are to be found in sufficient quantities in mother's milk. At birth, a baby has a store of iron in its liver, which it uses up during its first 6 months. Any kind of supplementary feeding is only necessary after 3 months, as the mother's milk then no longer supplies all the nutrients the infant needs.

Fruit juice and mashed fruit provide additional vitamin C, which the infant then needs. Supplementary feeding of energy-giving foods is also desirable. Mixing small quantities of milk powder into mashed food can considerably improve the food's value (especially the value of its protein). It is advisable to continue breastfeeding as long as possible because mother's milk is often the only source of animal protein for a baby.

If the mother cannot breastfeed, does not have enough milk or dies, bottle feeding is a solution and the best substitute. However, in practice often too much water is added to the (artificial) baby food, which is usually bought in powder form. It becomes too watery and is therefore not nutritious enough. Moreover, artificial foods are costly and require good hygiene.

Dilution with water is often a cause of infection because the available water may be polluted. Water used for bottle feeding must first be boiled, but sterilising water by boiling uses a lot of fuel, which is often in short supply. By using a cup or a spoon it is easier to maintain the necessary hygiene rather than a bottle because they are easier to clean. Money might be better spent on essential necessities of life than on artificial infant food if the latter is not strictly necessary. If a baby cannot digest milk, you will be forced to use milk products, which do not contain lactose. This is the case with inherited lactose intolerance.

**Lactose Intolerance**

Lactose intolerance means that the human body is almost, or entirely, unable to digest the milk sugar, lactose, which is present in milk because the body lacks the enzyme lactase. Lactase splits the lactose into glucose and galactose. The latter two mono-saccharides can easily be absorbed in the intestine. Undigested lactose can be converted by the microbial flora in the intestine into lactic acid and gases. Consumption of larger quantities of milk thus causes flatulence, stomach cramps and diarrhoea. 'Lactose intolerance' is thus often called 'lactase deficiency'.

*There are different forms of lactose intolerance among children:*

- Congenital lactose intolerance. In this case, a baby cannot digest milk because the baby lacks the enzyme lactase, necessary for the breakdown of lactose into glucose and galactose.
- Lactose intolerance among children who are 2-5 years old. From the age of two years lactase activity in a child decreases and the child may have problems due to insufficient lactase by the time he or she is 4-5 years old. Consumption of small quantities of milk (one glass at a time) usually does not cause any problem. It is also possible to prevent problems by eating fermented milk products, in which part of the milk sugar has been converted, such as cheese, yoghurt and buttermilk.
- Lactose intolerance as a result of intestinal disease and/or malnutrition, especially in babies and toddlers. The lactose activity is temporarily decreased making it necessary to use lactose-free milk products for a short time. Cheese and fermented products like yoghurt, in which milk sugar has been converted, are also suitable.

Apart from lactose intolerance, the use of milk also depends on other factors, which as suggested, now discuss.

**Milk and Dairy Products in the Diet**

Diet refers to the way people feed themselves and the foodstuffs they use to do so. This is strongly influenced by people's traditions and religion, their economic position, their place in society and the possibilities offered by their natural surroundings. It is not surprising that each population group has its own diet. The use of milk and dairy products can also be looked at when examining the diet.

*Here are a few examples of how the factors can influence the role and form of milk and dairy products in the diet :*

- The cow is a sacred animal in India; therefore the rennet used in cheese making may not be taken from a calf's stomach.
- If milk or dairy products have to be bought, money is needed.
- In densely populated areas, people are forced to use all available land for crops that give a maximum yield, or crops that can be directly consumed by the people. This limits the land available for dairy farming.
- It may not be possible to keep cattle in certain regions, e.g., the humid tropics, due to the natural environment. For example, in humid areas of West Africa cattle cannot be kept because they are the host of the tsetse fly, which transmits sleeping sickness.

For these reasons, milk and dairy products in the diet can be of greater or lesser importance in one area or another. Economic and social situations are especially subject to change and dietary patterns change with them. New foodstuffs may be introduced to (partly) substitute others. Adoption of new products is often no easy matter; sometimes centuries-old traditions may have to change. Also, taste and other characteristics such as texture are important in the acceptance of new kinds of food. Something that may be considered very tasty in one place, may not be appreciated elsewhere.

*Fig.5.14: Camel Milk is a very Popular Food in Parts of Africa and the Middle East*

## RAW MILK TRANSPORT AND STORAGE

In developed countries, raw milk on the farm is usually cooled quickly and stored in refrigerated bulk tanks at <7 °C prior to collection. Collection by insulated tanker is often on alternate days, or sometimes less frequently, and therefore some of the milk in the tank could be 48 hours old at the time of collection. Temperature control is thus critical to minimise microbial growth, and tanker drivers are usually permitted to refuse milk stored at too high a temperature, or which has an abnormal appearance or odour.

Bacterial numbers in the milk may increase during transport, either as a result of contamination from inadequately cleaned tankers or from the growth of psychrotrophic organisms, particularly Pseudomonas spp.. Milk temperature and duration of the transport stage are therefore important factors. On arrival at the processing site, the milk is transferred to bulk storage tanks, or silos, prior to processing.

The milk may be stored in the silos for 2-3 days, and further growth of psychrotrophic bacteria is likely during this period. The degree of growth is dependent on the initial microbial load, and the storage time and temperature. Pseudomonads are the predominant organisms present in stored raw milk, with *Pseudomonas fluorescens, Pseudomonas fragi,* and Pseudomonas lundensis being commonly isolated, but Enterobacteriaceae, *Flavobacterium, Alcaligenes,* and Gram-positive species can also be found.

The growth of psychrotrophic bacteria may also be accompanied by the production of heat-stable, extracellular proteolytic and lipolytic enzymes. These enzymes are often capable of surviving pasteurisation and, in some cases, ultra high temperature processing, and they may subsequently cause spoilage in the processed milk. A number of techniques have been used to limit the growth of psychrotrophs during raw milk storage.

**Thermisation**

The most commonly used technique is to apply a mild heat treatment by heating to around 57-68 °C for 15-20 seconds and then cooling rapidly to <6°C. This reduces the psychrotrophic population significantly and can extend the storage life of the raw milk by several days. However, thermisation cannot eliminate vegetative pathogens, and is therefore not a reliable control for the hazard. For example, *L. monocytogenes* can survive the process and could then grow during chilled storage.

**Deep Cooling**

As the storage temperature is a key factor for the rate of growth of psychrotrophic spoilage organisms, storing milk at as Iow a temperature as possible can also extend the storage life significantly. Reducing the storage temperature from 6°C to 2°C has been shown to give a 2-day gain in storage life for milk of good microbiological quality.

**Carbon Dioxide Addition**

There has been some interest in extending the storage life of raw milk by the addition of carbon dioxide at a concentration of 20-30 mM. Three mechanisms are thought to be involved in carbon dioxide inhibition of microorganisms: the first is by the displacement of oxygen; the second is a lowering of the pH of the milk due to the dissolution of carbon dioxide and formation of carbonic acid, particularly for Gram-negative psychrotrophic aerobes; and the third is a direct effect on the metabolisms such as inhibiting the production of enzymes by these organisms.

It has also been suggested that the technique could be used to extend the shelf life of pasteurised milk, but concerns have been raised that the use of carbon dioxide addition could allow growth and toxin production by psychrotrophic *Clostridium botulinum.* However, recent work indicates that the risk of botulism is not increased by the use of this treatment. Following storage, the milk then undergoes further processing.

**Separation**

If necessary, the milk is separated into skimmed milk, cream and sediment fractions, using centrifugal separators. The sediment may contain a comparatively high number of microorganisms and must be carefully discarded. The agitation involved may also break up clumps of bacteria, potentially producing an apparent increase in the number of colony-forming units. This process also allows the milk to be standardised to a specified fat content by adding back the correct quantity of cream.

**Homogenisation**

The fat globules in milk can coalesce and form a cream layer. Homogenisation reduces the size of the milk fat globules by using a pump to force milk through a valve under pressure. The fat globules are then small enough to remain in suspension. This process has little microbiological effect, although clumps of bacterial cells may be broken up. Homogenisers used for pasteurised milk may be linked to the pasteuriser, and run at raised temperature in order to minimise possible microbial contamination. UHT processed milks are homogenised in sterile conditions after heat treatment and before aseptic filling. Effective cleaning and sterilising of the homogeniser are then critical to product safety.

**Pasteurisation**

Some form of heat process is commonly applied to milk to ensure microbiological safety, and to extend shelf life. In the UK, the most commonly used process is pasteurisation. Time-temperature requirements for pasteurisation vary between countries, and are often specified in legislation. In the UK, both low-temperature, long time and high-temperature, short time minimum processes are permitted. However, in practice, the HTST process is now generally used. Recent concern about the possible survival of MAP in pasteurised milk has seen many dairies increase the length of the HTST process to 25 seconds.

Higher processes may also be applied to products with high fat and solids content. Plate heat exchangers are the most common method for milk pasteurisation, but it is essential that they are designed, constructed and operated in such a way as to minimise the possibility of recontamination of the pasteurised milk by raw milk. Most commercial pasteurisers are fitted with sensors that continuously monitor the pasteurisation temperature, and are linked to automatic divert valves.

If the pasteurisation temperature falls below a specified value, the valve opens and diverts the under-processed milk away from the post pasteurisation section of the plant and the filling line, into a divert tank. The correct operation of these monitoring systems is critical and should be regularly checked. It is also essential that there are no cross-connections between the raw and pasteurised sides of the process, and this should include separate clean-inplace systems. It is also usual to maintain a higher pressure in the pasteurised milk to minimise the risk of cross contamination in the heat exchanger.

Recontamination of this kind may have serious public health consequences. Accepted pasteurisation processes are designed to reduce the numbers of vegetative microbial pathogens to levels that are considered acceptable, although bacterial spores are not destroyed. Most of the potential psychrotrophic spoilage bacteria are also eliminated. However, certain heatresistant mesophilic organisms, referred to as thermoduric, are able to survive pasteurisation.

Thermoduric species commonly isolated from pasteurised milk include *Micrococcus* spp., *Enterococcus faecium* and *Enterococcus faecalis, Bacillus subtilis, Bacillus cereus,* and certain lactobacilli. Psychrotrophic strains of these organisms may be able to grow slowly in the pasteurised milk at 5°C, and, if present initially in high numbers, could eventually cause spoilage. Effective cleaning of the cooling sections of pasteurisers is important to ensure that these organisms do not build up on surfaces.

**Uht or Sterilisation Processes**

Milk may also be subjected to more severe heat processes sufficient to achieve "commercial sterility". This may be done by batch heating in closed containers, or continuously with aseptic filling into sterile containers. Both conventional retort sterilisation and UHT processes must achieve a minimum Fo of 3 minutes to ensure product safety. These processes destroy all vegetative cells in the milk, and the majority of spores, although certain very heat-resistant spores may survive. This results in a long shelf life without the need for refrigeration, but also causes organoleptic changes in the milk, such as browning.

Conventional sterilisation processes involve heating the milk in thickwalled glass bottles, closed with a crimped metal cap, at about 120 °C for approximately 30 minutes. However, modern large-scale production methods often use an initial UHT treatment prior to filling the container, followed by retorting for a reduced time and then a rapid cooling process. This is said to give a product with improved organoleptic properties. UHT processes may be direct or indirect. Direct systems inject high-pressure steam directly into the milk to obtain the desired temperature, and then employ flash cooling under vacuum to remove the resulting excess water.

Indirect systems utilise heat exchangers and holding tubes. Direct systems are said to give better organoleptic properties, as the heating and cooling processes milk involves preserving milk by holding at a temperature of 140- 150 °C for 1-2 seconds. Heat treatment is usually followed by aseptic filling into sterile cartons or other containers. The maintenance of sterility in filling is vital to prevent recontamination of the treated milk.

As with pasteurised milk, it is also vital to ensure that raw milk cannot recontaminate the UHT-treated milk. Certain very heat-resistant spores of mesophilic bacilli, classified as *Bacillus sporothermodurans* are able to survive UHT processes and may subsequently grow in the final product. However, this organism has been shown not to be pathogenic and does not seem to cause any detectable changes to the product. Thermoduric *Bacillus stearothermophilus* are able to survive UHT processes and cause flat-sour spoilage.

## PROCESSING AND ITS EFFECTS ON THE MICROFLORA

Examples of processes used to produce condensed, evaporated and dried milk products are shown in Figures. In each case, the initial steps of milk storage, transport, separation and standardisation are the same as those used for fresh milk. The first key stage is therefore the pasteurisation or pre-heating process. The time and temperature applied depends on the intended use of the product, but, as a minimum, will correspond to milk pasteurisation. Much higher processes are used in some instances. For example, in large-scale continuous production of evaporated milks, temperatures as high as 121°C may be applied for several minutes to stabilise milk proteins.

Condensed milk is also subjected to processes more severe than milk pasteurisation, with the exact process being determined by the nature of the product required. This preheating helps to increase viscosity and improve other characteristics. These processes may be less controlled than conventional pasteurisation, but it is important that a safe minimum process is always applied. As with fresh milk, most vegetative bacteria will be destroyed during heating, but some thermoduric types and bacterial endospores are likely to survive all but the most severe processes. The second common process in the manufacture of all types of concentrated milk products is the removal of water, usually by evaporation.

The most common type of evaporator used in the dairy industry is the falling film evaporator, which is both energy-efficient and readily controllable. It is common to link several evaporators together in series to form what is known as a 'multiple effect evaporator', with a common condenser and vacuum source. The vapour produced in the first effect heats the second, and so on, producing a stepwise decrease in temperature from 70-80°C in the first effect, to about 40°C in the last. The vacuum, however, is greater in the lowest temperature effect, so that the milk flows from high to low temperature.

This process is very efficient and produces milk at the required concentration without a second pass. The temperatures within the lower temperature effects of the evaporator are low enough to permit the growth of thermophilic and some mesophilic spores, and quite high numbers may develop in the effects during prolonged production runs. Growth of certain thermophilic species has even been reported in milk at temperatures as high as 70°C. The growth of thermophiles must be controlled, by limiting the lengthof production runs, effective plant cleaning and sanitation, and ensuring thatadequate standards of plant hygiene are applied.

**Concentrated Milk**

Raw milk is given a heat treatment approximating that of pasteurisation. It is then concentrated at a low temperature, followed by standarisation, homogenisation and pasteurisation before packaging. Pasteurisation is usually done at 79.4°C for 25 sec; the product is stored at 10°C to prevent growth of thermoduric bacteria and any post-pasteurisation contaminants.

**Bulk Condensed Milk**

In the manufacture of bulk condensed milk, the milk is first separated, if ecessary, and standardisation of fat content is often carried out after concentration. Unless skimmed milk is used, homogenisation is also usually carried out at this stage. A pre-heating process is then applied, using a continuous heater or a 'hot well'. Temperatures of 65.6–76.7°C are often used, but higher temperatures of 82.2-93.3°C for as much as 15 minutes may be applied to obtain a higher viscosity product and to impart other desirable characteristics.

These processes will greatly reduce the number of vegetative bacterial cells in the milk, but they are not under the same degree of control as conventional pasteurisation. The heater or 'hot wells' can act as incubators for thermophilic bacteria, especially if the product is held in the lower temperature range, allowing bacterial numbers to build up; it is also possible that pathogens may survive some lower pre-heat temperatures. Therefore, a further HTST pasteurisation step should be applied to eliminate this hazard.

The preheated milk is then concentrated in a vacuum-pan or in a multipleeffect evaporator at a temperature range of 54.4-57.2°C After evaporation, the product is not sterile and will support rapid microbial growth. It is also likely that post-process contamination could occur during standardisation or packaging. Therefore, effective post-process hygiene procedures, and rapid cooling to <5°C are necessary to achieve the required shelf life. The process is depicted in Figure.

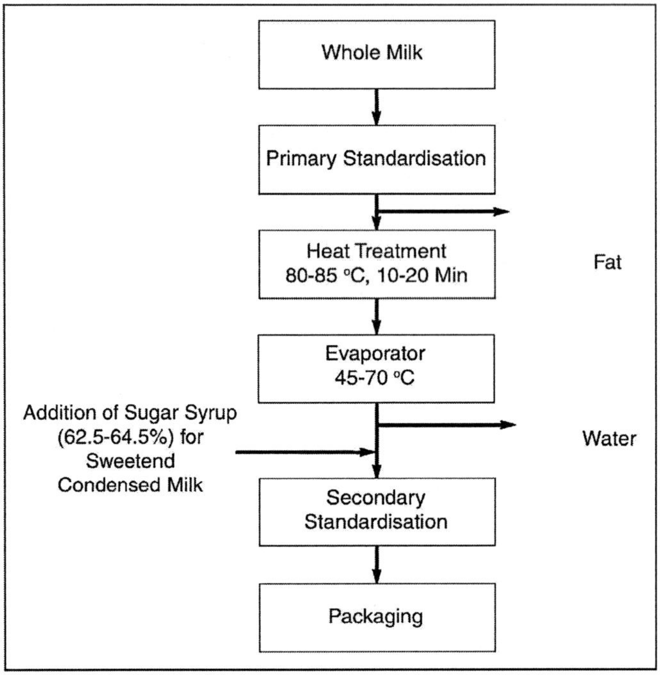


*Fig.5.15: Production of Condensed Milk*

**Sweetened Condensed Milk**

In the manufacture of sweetened condensed milk, the milk is preheated, and may also undergo superheating. Temperatures within the range 82-100°C for 10-30 minutes are used, and these processes are sufficient to destroy vegetative cells. For bulk, sweetened condensed milk, sugar can be added before concentration at varying levels depending on the end use. This material is not usually microbiologically stable and has a limited shelf life.

In the production of sweetened condensed milk for retail sale, sugar is added during the later stages of evaporation. The sugar is normally added as a 65% solution, and the finished product then contains a high enough solute concentration to give an aw of 0.83-0.86. It is this reduced aw, rather than a heat process, that confers microbiological stability, and a long shelf life when packed in pre-sterilised cans or tubes. However, some osmophilic yeasts and moulds are able to grow in the product, and may cause spoilage.

Evaporation is carried out at a temperature of around 57.2°C, but can drop to 48-9°C late in the cycle. Partially cooled milk is seeded with very fine lactose crystals to force crystallisation. A high standard of hygiene during the later handling and filling stages is necessary to prevent contamination. A particular problem with sweetened condensed milk is its high viscosity, and 'sticky' nature, which makes cleaning processing equipment difficult. This high viscosity means that positivedisplacement, plunger-type fillers are needed to fill the product. These are complex and difficult to clean and may become heavily contaminated with micrococci and yeasts if not properly maintained.

## Evaporated Milk

The manufacture of canned evaporated milk is very similar to that of bulk condensed milk, but the product is given a long shelf life by applying a heat process designed to give commercial sterility. Because of this, the milk has to be stabilised to prevent coagulation during processing and to minimise 'age thickening' during storage. Stabilisation is achieved by the addition of permitted salts, including phosphates, citrates and bicarbonates, which are used to maintain the pH of the milk at 6.6-6.7.

Pre-heating is also important, and temperatures of 120-122 °C for several minutes are used to denature whey proteins. Only a few bacterial spores are likely to survive such a process. Condensation is usually performed at a temperature lower than 54.5°C. After evaporation, the milk is homogenised, cooled and stored. It is then standardised, and further stabilising salts may also be added at this point. It is important to ensure that cooling is rapid and sufficient to minimise any microbial growth during this procedure.

The milk is then filled into cans, hermetically sealed, and sterilised using batch retorts or continuous sterilisers. Processing at 115°C for 15-20 minutes, or 120°C for 10 minutes, has been traditionally applied, but recently there has been a move towards UHT processing followed by aseptic filling into presterilised cans or cartons.

Processing at 130°C for 30 seconds, to 150°C for less than one second may be used. Retorted canned milk is commercially sterile, and only extremely heat-resistant spores of organisms such as Bacillus stearothermophilus are likely to survive. These spores do not germinate unless the cans are then stored at high ambient temperatures. Aseptically filled evaporated milk may become recontaminated during filling, unless stringent hygiene procedures equivalent to those used in filling other UHT milk products are used. The process is depicted in Figure.

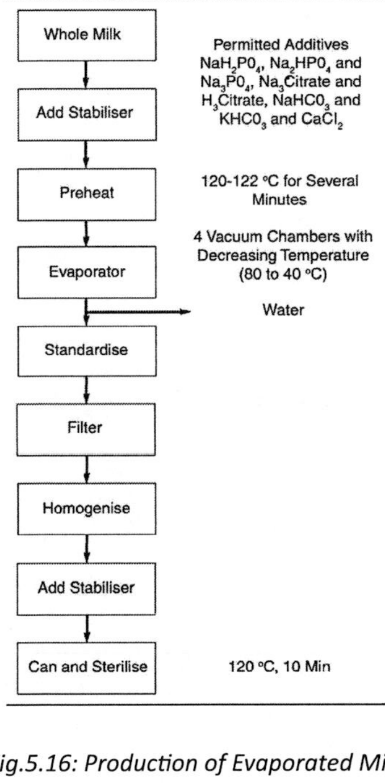


*Fig.5.16: Production of Evaporated Milk*

**Dried Milk**

Drying is used, after evaporation, to produce a stable, powdered product with a residual moisture content of 2-5%. Most dried milk powders are now spraydried, and drum and roller dryers are little used. Spray drying is a more energy-efficient process and causes less heat damage to the product. Therefore, only spray drying will be considered further. Before evaporation and drying, the milk is standardised, if required, and heattreated.

Vegetative bacteria, including Enterobacteriaceae and *Listeria monocytogenes* have been shown to survive the drying process, and therefore all raw milk should receive a process at least equivalent to pasteurisation. Skimmed milk may also be subjected to low, medium and high heat processes to give varying degrees of protein denaturation as required. Typically, a low heat process will be 74°C for 30 seconds, a medium heat process 80-100°C for 1-2 minutes, and a high heat process may be equivalent to an ultra high temperature treatment. Milk for dried whole milk powders is heated at 85-95°C for several minutes.

UHT heating units result in products that have excellent microbiological quality, which is important when dried milk is to be used as an ingredient in baby food. The heat-treated milk is then evaporated to about 50% total solids before drying. As the drying process does not kill all vegetative bacterial cells, effective cleaning and hygiene procedures are required to ensure that the heattreated milk does not become recontaminated. The current practice is to link the evaporation plant and dryer as a single integrated unit. Two systems of spray drying are used: jet or nozzle dryers, and rotary atomiser dryers.

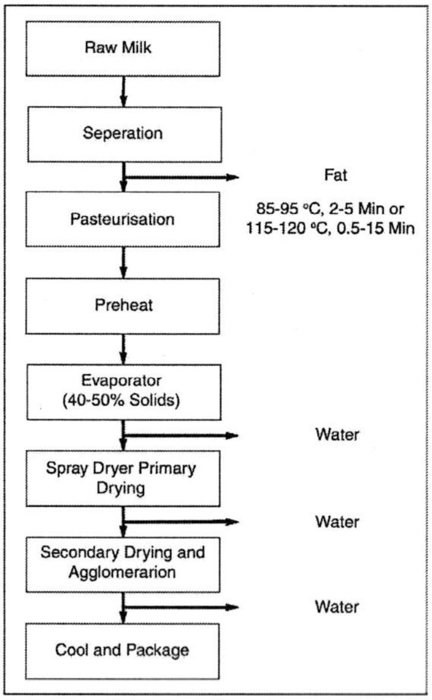


*Fig.5.17: Production of Skimmed Milk Powder*

Each dryer produces powders with specific characteristics. In the case of jet dryer systems, milk is fed to a high-pressure pump, then pumped under pressure to a series of jets or nozzles within the drying chamber. The impact of hot air on the milk causes the liquid to break up into fine droplets that form milk powder. In the rotary atomiser, the milk enters the drying chamber through slots or holes located at the periphery of a circular disc fixed to a rotating shaft.

# 6

# Dairy Products

Dairy products are generally defined as foods produced from cow's or domestic buffalo's milk. They are usually high-energy-yielding food products. A production plant for such processing is called a dairy or a dairy factory. Raw milk for processing mostly comes from cows and to a lesser amount from domestic buffalos, but occasionally from other mammals such as goats, sheep, yaks, or horses. Dairy products are commonly found in European, Middle Eastern and Indian cuisine, whereas they are almost unknown in East Asian cuisine.

The dairy products vary greatly. Some cows give richer milk than others. Butter may be almost pure fat, or it may contain much water and salt. The cheeses are rich or poor in protein and fats according to method of making. Cottage cheese may be well drained or quite watery. Therefore, this table gives only approximate contents.

| | **Protein** | **Fat** | **Carbohydrates** | **Ash** | **Calories** | **Per Ib.** | **Water** |
|---|---|---|---|---|---|---|---|
| Whole milk | 87.00 | | 3.3 | 4.0 | 5.0 | 0.7 | 325 |
| Cream | 74.00 | 2.5 | | 18.5 | 14.5 | 0.5 | 910 |
| Buttermilk | 91.00 | 3.0 | | 0.5 | 4.8 | 0.7 | 165 |
| Butter | ... | .. | | 82.4 | .. | .. | 3475 |
| Cheese, whole milk | 33.70 | 26.0 | 34.2 | 2.3 | 3.8 | 1965 | |
| "skimmed milk | 45.70 | 31.5 | 16.4 | 2.2 | 4.2 | 1320 | |

Milk is not a beverage. It is a food. A quart of milk contains as much food and fuel value as eight eggs or twelve ounces of lean beef. That is, a cupful is equal to two eggs or three ounces of lean beef. This shows that milk should not be taken to quench thirst, but to supply nourishment. Milk is one of our most satisfactory and economical albuminous foods, even at the present high prices. In many foods from 5 to 10 per cent of the protein goes to waste. In milk the waste does not ordinarily amount to more than about 1 per cent.

This fluid generally leaves the stomach within one or one and one-half hours after being ingested. In spite of its merits as a food some writers on dietetics advocate that adults stop using it, giving it only to the young. Milk is an excellent food when properly used. When abused it tends to cause discomfort, disease and death, and so does every other food known to man. Milk is given in fevers and in other diseases, when the digestive and assimilative processes are suspended. This is a serious mistake and has caused untold numbers of deaths. When the digestion has gone on a strike all feeding is destructive.

Milk and meat broths, which are generally given, are about the worst foods that could be selected under the circumstances, for they decay very easily, and are excellent food for the numerous bacteria that thrive in the digestive tract during disease. These foods must decay when they are not digested, for the internal temperature of the body during fevers is over one hundred degrees Fahrenheit. When bacteria are present in excess they give off considerable poison, which makes the patient worse. If circumstances are such that it is necessary to feed during acute disease, which is always injurious to the patient, let the food be the least harmful obtainable, such as fruit juices.

Even they do harm. In our country cow's milk is used almost exclusively. In other lands the milk of the mare, the ass, the sheep, the goat and of other animals is used. The objection voiced against cow's milk is that it is an unnatural food for man, only fit for the calf, which is equipped with several stomachs and is therefore able to digest the curds which are larger and tougher than the curds formed from human milk. It is said that the curds of cow's milk are so indigestible that the human stomach cannot prepare them for entry into the blood. This is probably true, but it is also true of other protein-bearing foods. The digestion and assimilation of proteins are begun in the stomach and completed in the intestines, and the protein in milk is one of the most completely utilized of all proteins.

To call a food unnatural means nothing, for we can call nearly all foods unnatural and defend our position. A natural food is presumably a nutritious and digestible aliment that is produced in the locality where it is consumed, one that can be utilized without preparation or preservation. So we may say that a resident of New York should not use figs, dates, bananas and other products of tropical and semi-tropical climates, for they are not natural in the latitude of New York. We can take the position that it is unnatural for people to eat grains, which need much grinding, for the birds are the only living beings supplied with mills.

We can further say that it is unnatural to eat all cooked and baked foods. But such talk is not helpful. The more a person uses his brain the less power he has left for digestion and therefore it is necessary to prepare some of the foods so that they will be easy to digest. Man is such an adaptable creature that we are not sure what he subsisted on before he became civilized and are therefore unable to say what his natural food is. We know that in the tropics fruits play an important part in nourishing savages, while in the frozen north fat flesh is the chief food. Perhaps there is no natural food for man. Some of those who advocate the disuse of milk have a substitute or imitation to take its place, nut milk made from finely ground nuts and water. Like all other imitations, it is inferior to the original.

It is more difficult to digest than real milk and the flavour is quite different. The objection that milk is indigestible is not borne out by the experience of those who give it under proper conditions. It is true that milk disagrees with a few, but so do such excellent foods as eggs, strawberries and Concord grapes, and many other aliments which are not difficult to digest. This is a matter of individual peculiarity. Some can take boiled milk, but are unable to take it fresh, and vice versa. Outside of the few exceptions, milk digests in a reasonable time and quite completely. It is easier to digest than the legumes which are rich in protein.

It is also easier to digest than nuts, which contain much protein. The milk sugar causes no trouble and cream is one of the easiest forms of fat to digest, if taken in moderation. The protein in milk will cause no inconvenience if the milk is eaten slowly, in proper combinations and not to excess. The rennet in the stomach curdles the casein. The hydrochloric acid and the pepsin in the gastric juice then begin to break down and dissolve the clots, and the process of digestion is completed in the small intestines.

Those who overeat of milk in combination with other foods will derive benefit from omitting the milk. They will also be benefitted if they continue using milk and omit either the starch or the meat. When foods disagree, in nearly every instance it is due to the fact that too much has been eaten and too many varieties partaken of at a meal. Some may single out the milk or the meat as the offenders.

Others may point to the starches, and still others to the vegetables with their large amount of indigestible residue. They are all right and all wrong, for all the foods help to cause the trouble. However, such reasoning does not solve the problem. If the meals cause discomfort and disease, reduce the amount eaten, take fewer varieties at a meal and simplify the cooking. Those who eat simple meals and are moderate are not troubled with indigestion. Those who eat such mushy foods as oatmeal and cream of wheat usually take milk or cream and sugar with them. This should not be done, for such dressing stimulates the appetite and leads to undermastication. Neither children nor adults chew these soft starchy foods enough. The result is that the breakfast ferments in the alimentary tract. After a few months or years of such breakfasts, some kind of disease is sure to develop.

Mushy starches dressed with rich milk and sugar are responsible for a large per cent of the so-called diseases of children, which are primarily digestive disturbances. Colds, catarrhs and adenoids are, of course, due to improper eating extending over a long period of time.

Nothing should be eaten with mushy starches except a little butter and salt. After enough starch has been taken, a glass of milk may be eaten. If parents would only realise that they are jeopardizing the health and lives of their dear ones when they feed them habitually on these soft messes, which ferment easily, there would be a remarkable decrease in the diseases of childhood and in the disgraceful infant and childhood mortality, for several hundred thousand children perish annually in this country.

Milk is often referred to as a perfect food, and it is the perfect food for infants. The young thrive best on the healthy milk given by a female of their own species. Every baby should be fed at the breast. The milk contains the elements needed by the body. The ash is composed of the various salts necessary for health, containing potassium, chlorine, calcium, magnesium, iron, silicon and other elements. For the nourishment of the body we need water, protein, fat, carbohydrates and salts, so it will be seen that milk is really a complete food. However, as the body grows the nutritive requirements change and milk is therefore not a balanced food for adults.

It may be interesting to note that there is no starch in milk and that infants fed at the breast exclusively obtain no starchy food. Many babies get no starch for nine, ten or even twelve months, and this is well, for they do not need it. They grow and flourish best without it. Milk is an emulsion. It is made up of numerous tiny globules floating in serum. The size of the globules varies, but the average is said to be about 1/10,000 of an inch in diameter. These globules are fatty bodies. There are other small bodies, containing protein and fat, which have independent molecular movement. The milk is a living fluid. When it is tampered with it immediately deteriorates. Without doubt, nature intended that the milk should go directly from the mammary gland into the mouth of the consumer, but this is not practicable when we take it away from the calf. However, if we are to use sweet milk it is best to consume it as nearly like it is in its natural state as possible.

It is quite common to drink milk rapidly. This should not be done. Take a sip or a spoonful at a time and move it about in the mouth until it is mixed with saliva. It is not necessary to give it as much mouth preparation as is given to starchy food. If it is drunk rapidly like water large curds from in the stomach. If it is insalivated it coagulates in smaller curds and is more easily digested, for the digestive juices can tear down small soft curds more easily than the large tough ones. Milk should not form a part of any meal when other food rich in protein is eaten. Our protein needs are small, and it is easy to get too much. Whole wheat bread and milk contain all the nourishment needed. On such a diet we can thrive indefinitely. This is information, not a recommendation. The bread should be eaten either before or after partaking of the milk. Do not break the bread into the milk. If this is done, mastication will be slighted. Bread needs much mastication and insalivation. When liquid is taken with the bread, the saliva does not flow so freely as when it is eaten dry.

Fruit and milk make a good combination, but no starchy foods are to be taken in this meal. Take a glass of milk, either sweet or sour, and what fruit is desired, insalivating both the fruit and the milk thoroughly. If you have read that the combination of fruit and milk has proved fatal, rest assured that those who made such reports only looked at the surface, for other foods and other influences were having their effects on the system.

Many people die of food-poisoning and apoplexy. These bad results are due to wrong eating covering a long period and it is folly to blame the last meal. It would be queer if fruit and milk were not occasionally a part of the last meal. In winter, figs, dates or raisins with milk make an excellent lunch or breakfast. These fruits take the place of bread, for though they are not starchy, they contain an abundance of fruit sugar, which is more easily digested than the starch. Starch must be converted into sugar before the system can use it. On hot days milk and acid fruit make a satisfying meal. Many believe that milk and acid fruit should not be taken in the same meal, because the acid curdles the milk.

As we have already seen, the milk must be curdled before it can be digested. If this step in digestion is performed by the acid in the fruit no more harm is done than when it is performed by the lactic acid bacteria. Fruit juices and milk do not combine to form deadly poisons. If fruit and milk are eaten in moderation and no other food is taken at that meal the results are good. However, if fruit, milk, bread, meat, cake and pickles make up the meal, the results may be bad. Such eating is very common. But do not blame the fruit and the milk when the whole meal is wrong.

Likewise, if a hearty meal has been eaten and before this has had time to digest a lunch is made of fruit and milk, trouble may ensue. All the foods may be good, but a time must come when the body will object to being overfed. In summertime much less food is needed than during the cold months. Nevertheless, barring the Christmas holidays and Thanksgiving, people overeat more in summer than at any other time of the year. Picnics often degenerate into stuffing matches. We should expect many cases of serious illness to follow them, and such is the case.

Sometimes the milk is so carelessly handled that it becomes poisonous and at other times the fruit is tainted, but generally bad combinations and overeating are the factors that cause trouble when the fruit and milk combination is blamed. Buttermilk and clabbered milk are more easily digested by many than is the fresh milk. In Europe sour milk is a more common food than in this country. Here many do not know how excellent it is.

Two glasses of milk, or less, make a good warm-weather lunch. Those who have a tendency to be bilious should use cream very sparingly. Bilious people always overeat, otherwise their livers would not be in rebellion. The fat, in the form of cream, arouses decided protest on the part of overburdened livers.

A theory has found its way into dietetic literature, sometimes disguised as a truth, to the effect that boiled or hot milk is absorbed directly into the bloodstream without being digested. This is contrary to everything we know about digestion and assimilation, and although it is a fine enough theory it does not work out in practice. We have seen bad results when nothing but a small amount of the hot milk was fed to patients with weak digestive power. Perhaps others have had better results. When the system demands a rest from food, nothing but water should be given. Boiled or natural milk is then as bad as any other food, and worse than most, for in the absence of digestive power it soon becomes a foul mass, swarming with billions of bacteria. The system is compelled to absorb some of the poisons given off by the micro-organisms and the results are disastrous.

Every food we take must be modified by our bodies before entering the circulation, and milk is no exception. When milk is allowed to stand for a while the sugar ferments, through the action of the lactic acid bacteria. The sugar is turned into lactic acid, which combines with the casein and when this process has continued for a certain length of time the result is clabbered milk or sour milk. The length of time varies with the temperature and the care given the milk. If milk remains sweet for a long time during warm weather, discharge the milkman and patronize one whose product sours more quickly, for milk that remains sweet has been subjected to treatment.

All kinds of preservative treatment cause deterioration. If extraordinary care is taken with the milk and it is kept at a temperature of about forty-two degrees Fahrenheit, it may remain sweet five or six weeks, provided it is not exposed to the air, but such care is at present not practicable in commercial dairies. The milk contains unorganized ferments which spoil it in time without exposure to bacterial influences. These ferments cause digestion or decay of the milk.

Fresh butter is a palatable form of fat, which digests easily. Like all other milk products, it must be kept clean and cold, or it will soon spoil. Butter absorbs other flavours quickly and should therefore not be placed near odourous substances. It is best unsalted and in Europe it is very commonly served thus. When people learn to demand unsalted butter they will get good butter, for no one can palm off oleomargarine or other imitations under the guise of fresh unsalted butter.

Unsalted butter must be fresh or it will be refused by the nose and the palate. Salt and other preservatives often conceal age and corruption of foods. Butter combines well with starches and vegetables, in fact, it can be used in moderation with any other food, when the body needs fat. Butter should not be used to cook starches or proteins in. Greasy cooking should be banished from our kitchens.

Milk is a complex food, highly organized, and therefore is easily injured or spoiled. The general rule is that the more complex a food is, the more easily it spoils. It is rather difficult at present to get wholesome milk enough to supply the people of our large cities. When it is boiled, the milk keeps longer, but boiled milk is spoiled milk. The fine flavour is lost, the casein, which is the principal protein of milk, is toughened, the milk, which is normally a living liquid, is killed, the chemical balance is lost, the organic salts being rendered partly inorganic. Milk that is unfit to eat without being boiled is not fit to eat afterwards, for the poisonous end products of bacterial life remain.

The milk is soured by the bacteria it contains. The lactic acid bacteria are harmless. When there is a lack of care and cleanliness, other bacteria get into the milk, and these are also harmless to people in good health, and most of them are not injurious to sick people. The bacteria do not cause disease, but when disease has been established, they offer their kindly offices as scavengers. Bacteria thrive in sick people, especially when they are fed when digestive power is lacking.

Boiling retards the souring of milk, but when fat and protein are boiled together the protein becomes hard to digest. Milk is rich in both fat and protein. Excessive heat turns the milk brown, the milk sugar being carameled. Babies do not thrive on boiled milk. They may look fat, but instead of having the desirable firmness of normal children, they are puffy. Children fed on denatured milk fall victims to diseases very easily, especially to diseases which are due to lack of organic salts, such as rickets and malnutrition.

Pasteurization of milk is very popular. This is objectionable for the same reasons that boiling is condemned, though not to the same extent. Pasteurization is heating the milk to about 140 to 150 degrees Fahrenheit. This kills many of the bacteria, but many escape and when the milk is cooled off they begin to multiply and flourish again. It is estimated that pasteurized milk contains one-fourth as many bacteria as natural milk. So nothing is gained, and the milk is partly devitalized.

The advocates of pasteurization give statistics showing that milk so treated has been instrumental in decreasing infant mortality. But please bear in mind that previously a great deal of milk unfit for consumption was fed to the babies. Those who pasteurize milk generally are careful enough to see that they get a good product in the first place. If we can't get good milk we can do without it, for it is not a necessary food, but we can get good milk if we make the effort. If the milk is filthy, boiling or pasteurizing does not remove the dirt. Gauthier says of pasteurization: "Sometimes it is heated up to 70 degrees with pressure of carbonic acid. But even in this case pasteurization does not destroy all germs, particularly those of tuberculosis, peptonizing bacteria of cowdung, and the dust of houses and streets, etc."

Even boiling does not kill the spores of bacteria unless it is continued until the milk is rendered entirely unfit for food. To kill these spores it is necessary to boil the milk several times. The spores are small round or oval bodies which form within the bacterial envelope when these micro-organisms are subjected to unfavourable conditions.

The spores resist heat and cold that would kill almost any other form of life. When conditions are favourable they develop into bacteria again. After heating, the cream does not rise so quickly nor does it separate so completely as it does in natural milk. This is due to the toughening of the casein in the milk. Heating partly disorganizes the delicately balanced salts contained in the milk.

The result is that they can not be utilized so easily and completely by the body, for the human organism demands its food in an organic state, that is, in the condition built up by vegetation or by animals.

We may consume iron filings and remain anemic, in fact, the effect the iron medication has is to ruin the teeth, digestive organs and other parts of the body as a consequence. But if we partake of such foods as apples, cabbage, lettuce and spinach, the necessary salt is taken into the blood. Heating milk also makes it constipating. True, normal people can take boiled milk without becoming constipated, but how many normal people are there? We are sorely enough afflicted in this way now. Let us have a supply of natural milk or go without it.

It is not my desire to convey the impression that it does any harm to scald or boil milk occasionally, but if done daily it does harm, especially to the young. Scalded milk has its proper place in dietetics. Occasionally we find a person who has persistent chronic diarrhaea. If he is in condition to eat anything, this annoying affliction is usually overcome in a reasonable time if the patient will take boiled or scalded milk in moderation three times a day, and nothing else except water. How are we to obtain good milk? We can do it by using common sense, care and cleanliness.

It is well to remember that there are bacteria in all ordinary milk, and that if the milk is from healthy cows and is kept clean and cold these bacteria are harmless. Most of them are the lactic acid bacteria, which change the milk sugar into acid. When the milk has attained a certain degree of acidity, the lactic acid bacteria are unable to thrive and the souring process is slowed up and finally stopped. Most of the other bacteria in milk perish when lactic acid is formed.

This is why stale sweet milk is often harmful, when the same kind of milk allowed to sour can be taken with impunity. If the milk is kept in a cold place the bacteria multiply slowly. If it is kept in a warm place they increase in numbers at a rate that is marvelous, and consequently the milk sours much sooner. Even if the milk is kept cold, bacterial growth will soon take place, but it will perhaps not be lactic acid bacteria. It may be a form that causes the milk to become ropy and slimy or one that gives it a bad odour.

Bacteria are like other forms of vegetation, such as grass, weeds, flowers and trees, in that some flourish best under one condition and others under dissimilar conditions, and they struggle one against the other for subsistence and existence. Like flowers there are thousands of different forms of bacteria and they vary according to their food and environment. Peculiar odours in milk generally come from certain kinds of food given to the cows, such as turnips; from bacterial action; or from flavours absorbed from other foods or from odours in the air. Milk should not be exposed to odourous substances, for it becomes tainted very quickly.

Sometimes yeast finds its way into milk and causes decomposition of the sugar with the formation of carbon dioxide and alcohol. A count of the bacteria in milk often serves a good purpose, for it shows whether it is good and has had proper care. The consumers have a right to demand milk low in bacteria, for if no preservatives have been used, that means clean milk. If we could live in our pristine state of beatific bliss, if such it was, we would not have to use milk after childhood is past, but our present condition demands the use of easily digested foods and to many milk is almost a necessity.

The milk in the udder of a healthy cow is almost surely free from bacteria, but the moment it is exposed to the air these little beings start to drop into the fluid. The bacterial standards given by various city health departments vary. Those who are mathematically inclined may find the following figures interesting: In some great cities they allow 500,000 bacteria to the cubic centimetre of milk.

A cubic centimetre contains about twenty-five drops. In other words, they allow 20,000 bacteria per drop. This may seem very lively milk, but these bacteria are so small that about 25,000 of them laid end to end measure only about an inch, and it would take 17,000,000,000,000 of them to weigh an ounce, according to estimates. These are the tiny vegetables we hear and read so much about, that we are warned against and fear so much.

Truly the pygmies are having their innings and making cowards of men. The bacteria multiply by the simple process of growing longer and splitting into two, fission, as it is called, and the process is so rapid that within an hour or two after being formed a bacterium may be raising a family of its own.

Some of the milk brought to the cities contains as many as 15,000,000 bacteria per cubic centimeter, that is, about 600,000 per drop. This milk is either very filthy or it has been poorly cared for and should not be given to babies and young children. The filthiest milk may contain several billion bacteria to the cubic centimetre. By using care milk containing but 100, or even fewer, bacteria per drop can be produced.

From the standpoint of cleanliness this is excellent milk. Of course, the dairyman who takes pride enough in his work to produce such milk will sell nothing but what is first-class, and if he has business acumen he can always get more than the market price for his product.

The talk about germs has been overdone, but no one can deny that the study of bacteriology has made people more careful about foods. The filthy dairies that were the rule a few years ago are slowly being replaced by dairies that are comfortable, well lighted and clean. Do not allow the germs to scare you, for if ordinary precautions are taken no more of them will be present than are necessary, and they are necessary.

They thrive best in filth, and they are dangerous only to those who live so that they have no resistance. Wholesome milk can be produced only by healthy animals. Bovine health can be secured by the same means as human health. The cows must be properly fed and housed. They must have both ventilation and light. They must not be unduly worried. If a nursing of an angry mother's milk is at times poisonous enough to kill a baby, you may be sure that the milk from an abused, irritated and angry cow is also injurious.

If the animals are kept comfortable and happy they will do the best producing, both in quality and quantity. It may sound far-fetched to some to advocate keeping animals happy in order to get them to produce much and give quality products, but it is good science and good sense. Happy cows give more and better milk than the mistreated ones. The singing hens are the best layers. Cows should have fresh green food all the year, and this can be obtained in winter time by using silage.

It is a mistake to give cows too much of concentrated foods, such as oil meals and grains. Cattle cannot long remain well on exclusive rations of too heating and stimulating foods. When fed improperly they soon fall prey to various diseases, such as rheumatism and tuberculosis. It is the same with other domestic animals. The horse when overfed on grain develops stiff joints. The hogs that are compelled to live exclusively on concentrated, heating rations are liable to die of cholera. Young turkeys that have nothing but corn and wheat to eat die in great numbers from the disease known as blackhead. It is the same law running all through nature, applying to the high and to the low, that improper nourishment brings disease and death. When cattle roam wild, the green grasses are their principal source of food. Man should be careful not to deviate too much, for forced feeding is as harmful to animals as it is to man.

*The following excellent recommendations for the care of milk are given by Dr. Charles E. North of the New York City Milk Commission:*

- "No coolers, aerators, straining cloths or strainers should be used.
- "The hot milk should be taken to the creamery as soon as possible. 100 Dairy Farming
- "The night's milk should be placed in spring or iced water higher than the milk on the inside of the can. It should not be stirred, and the top of the can should be open a little way to permit ventilation.
- "The milking pails and cans will be sterilized and dried at the creamery, and should be carefully protected until they are used.

- "Brush the udder and wipe with a clean cloth; wash with clean water and dry with a clean towel.
- "Whitewash the cow stable at least twice yearly.
- "Feed no dusty feed until after milking.
- "Remove all manure from cow stable twice daily.
- "Keep barnyard clean and have manure pile at least 100 feet from the stable.
- "Have all stable floors of cement, properly drained.
- "Have abundant windows in cowstables to permit sunlight to reach the floor.
- "Arrange a proper system of ventilation.
- "Do not use milk from any cows suspected of gargot or of any udder inflammation. Such milk contains enormous numbers of bacteria.
- "Brush and groom cows from head to foot as horses are groomed.
- "Use no dusty bedding; wood shavings or sawdust give least dust.
- "Use an abundance of ice in water tank for cooling milk."

Perhaps some will take issue with the doctor on the first paragraph of his recommendation. If straining cloths are used they should be well rinsed in tepid water, washed and then boiled. However, if his recommendations are carried out in letter and spirit no straining is necessary.

Herr Klingelhofer near Dusseldorf, Germany, runs a model dairy. The cows, stables, milkers, containers, in fact, all things connected with the dairy are scrupulously clean. The milkers do not even touch the milk stools, carrying them strapped to their backs. The milk is strained through sterilized cotton and cooled. The cows are six and seven years old and are milked for ten or twelve months and they are not bred during this time. The first part of the milk drawn from each teat is not used, for that part is not clean, containing dirt and bacteria. This milk is practically free from bacteria, for without adding preservatives it will remain sweet, for as long as thirteen days.

If ordinary milk fails to sour in two or three days it shows that it has been treated. According to the Country Gentleman, it will cost from one cent and a quarter to one cent and three-quarters extra per quart to produce clean milk. Healthy adults can take milk teeming with bacteria without harm, but for babies it is best to have very few or none in the milk. At Dusseldorf the babies used to die as they do here when fed unclean milk.

Herr Klingelhofer says that when fed on his product "sterben keine". This is submitted to those who advocate pasteurizing the milk. Denatured milk makes sickly babies. Clean natural milk makes healthy babies. The extra cost of less than two cents a quart is not prohibitive. Most fathers, no matter how poor, waste more than that daily on tobacco and alcoholics.

The extra cost would be more than saved in lessened doctor bills, to say nothing of funeral expenses. The recompense that comes from the satisfaction of having thriving, sturdy, healthy children can not be figured in dollars and cents. Dr. Robert Mond, of London, after investigating for years, has come to the cease that sterilized milk predisposes to tuberculosis, instead of preventing it. He believes that milk so treated is so inferior that he would not personally use it. That sterilized milk predisposes to tuberculosis, as well as to other diseases which can attack the body only when it is run down, is natural.

Any food that has been rendered inferior can not build the robust health that comes to those who live on natural food. Adults who use sterilized milk should counteract its bad effects by partaking liberally of fresh fruits and vegetables. If the milk is clean, put into clean containers by careful milkers and is then kept cold until delivered, it will reach the consumers in good condition. Do not let the fact that when you consume a glass of milk you are also engulfing some millions of bacteria bother you, for bacteria are necessary to our existence. If all the bacteria on earth should perish, it would also mean the end of the human race.

Today the progressive farmer is coming to the fore. He is a man who is justly proud of his work, so it will probably not be long before all city people who desire clean milk can get it. The milk cure consists in feeding sick people on nothing but milk for varying periods. Generally the patient is told to either take great quantities three or four times a day, or to take smaller quantities perhaps every half hour. The milk cure has no special virtue, except that it is a monotonous diet.

The body soon rebels if forced to subsist on an excessive amount of but one kind of food. The individual loses his desire for food and even becomes nauseated. If the advocates of the milk cure would prescribe milk in moderation, instead of in excess, they would have better success. The benefit derived from the milk cure comes from the simplicity, not from the milk. A grape cure, an orange cure or a bread and milk cure would be as beneficial. The milk cure is ancient. It was employed twenty-five centuries ago.

## TYPES OF DAIRY PRODUCTS

- Milk after optional homogenization, pasteurization, in several grades after standardization of the fat level, and possible addition of bacteria Streptococcus lactis and Leuconostoc citrovorum
  - Crème fraîche, slightly fermented cream
    - (a) Smetana, Central and Eastern European variety of sour cream
    - (b) Clotted cream, thick spoonable cream made by heating
  - Cultured buttermilk, fermented concentrated (water removed) milk using the same bacteria as sour cream
  - Kefir, fermented milk resembling buttermilk but based on different yeast and bacteria culture
  - Kumis/Airag, slightly fermented mares' milk popular in Central Asia
  - Milk powder (or powdered milk), produced by removing the water from milk
    - (a) Whole milk products
    - (b) Buttermilk products
    - (c) Skim milk
    - (d) Whey products
    - (e) Ice Cream
    - (f) High milk-fat and nutritional products (for infant formulas)
    - (g) Cultured and confectionery products
  - Condensed milk, milk which has been concentrated by evaporation, often with sugar added for longer life in an opened can
  - Evaporated milk, (less concentrated than condensed) milk without added sugar
  - Ricotta cheese, milk heated and reduced in volume, known in Indian cuisine as Khoa

- Infant formula, dried milk powder with specific additives for feeding human infants
- Baked milk, a variety of boiled milk that has been particularly popular in Russia

- Butter, mostly milk fat, produced by churning cream
  - Buttermilk, the liquid left over after producing butter from cream, often dried as livestock food
  - Ghee, clarified butter, by gentle heating of butter and removal of the solid matter
  - Smen, a fermented clarified butter used in Moroccan cooking.
  - Anhydrous milkfat
- Cheese, produced by coagulating milk, separating from whey and letting it ripen, generally with bacteria and sometimes also with certain molds
  - Curds, the soft curdled part of milk (or skim milk) used to make cheese (or casein)
  - Whey, the liquid drained from curds and used for further processing or as a livestock food
  - Cottage cheese
  - Quark
  - Cream cheese, produced by the addition of cream to milk and then curdled to form a rich curd or cheese made from skim milk with cream added to the curd
  - Fromage frais
- Casein
  - Caseinates
  - Milk protein concentrates and isonates
  - Whey protein concentrates and isonates
  - Hydrolysates
  - Mineral concentrates
- Yogurt, milk fermented by Streptococcus salivarius ssp. thermophilus and Lactobacillus delbrueckii ssp. bulgaricus sometimes with additional bacteria, such as Lactobacillus acidophilus
  - Ayran
  - Lassi
- Clabber (food), milk naturally fermented to a yogurt-like state
- Gelato, slowly frozen milk and water, lesser fat than ice cream
- Ice cream, slowly frozen cream and emulsifying additives
  - Ice milk
  - Frozen custard
  - Frozen yogurt, yogurt with emulsifiers that is frozen
- Other
  - Viili
  - Kajmak
  - Filmjölk
  - Piimä
  - Vla
  - Dulce de leche

## HEALTH RISKS OF CONSUMING DAIRY PRODUCTS

Most dairy products contain large amounts of saturated fat. Some dairy products may cause health issues for individuals who have a lactose intolerance and milk allergies. Some dairy products such as blue cheese may become contaminated with the fungus Aspergillus fumigatus during ripening, which can trigger asthma and other respiratory problems in susceptible individuals.

Vegans and some vegetarians avoid dairy products due to a variety of ethical, dietary, environmental, political, and religious concerns.

## MILK PROCESSORS

In order to estimate the potential success of these new product concepts, a survey instrument was sent to U.S., dairy processors. Participants were informed of the particulars of the new product concept and supplied with the estimated cost of manufacturing the new dairy product. Background information was requested in a variety of areas including the respondent's opinion as to why customers purchased their existing dairy products, the importance of private-label products, the size of the firm, and the frequency of the respondent's contact with end-customers.

The survey also asked whether the firm presently employed any membrane technology for dairy purposes (only 10 per cent did so), whether the respondent thought consumers would buy the new product, and requested suggestions for increasing the probability of the new product's commercial success.

A total of 179 firms were contacted, of which 63 completed the survey for a total response rate of 35 per cent.

These 63 firms included 26 fluid milk processors, 21 ice cream manufacturers, and 16 yogurt manufacturers. The individuals surveyed were plant managers and/or those designated by each firm's receptionist as being most likely to make new product and/or new equipment decisions.

The survey instrument presented the new product idea, the equipment needed, the capital cost, the operating cost, and the increase in milk-component cost. Most of the interviews were initiated with a telephone call and then carried out by fax communication. Copies of the survey instruments are available from the authors upon request.

### Anecdotal Findings

Anecdotes reported by survey respondents are presented below. In all product areas, these comments illustrate a high level of cost and price sensitivity.

Based upon the results, one would expect this to be true for fluid milk. However, price sensitivity is also evident in the case of ice cream and even in the case of yogurt.

*Comments received included:*

- "Our current business isprice-driven, thus the supplier would have to absorb any cost increase." (From a bottler in the State of Washington.)
- "This product would have acceptance from only a small group of consumers." (From a bottler in Texas.)
- "We make a NFDM [Nonfat Dry Milk]-fortified product. At standard retail price it sells well. However, with a $0.05/gal. premium it does not sell well." (From a bottler in the State of New York.)
- "It takes a lot of consumer education and advertising to market a value-addedproduct at a premiumprice."(From a bottler in Kentucky.)

- "Adds cost. Our market area could not support this." (From an ice cream maker located in the North Central U.S.,)
- "I am not sure customers would understand or care" (From an ice cream maker located in Wisconsin.)
- "This would take advertising." (From an ice cream maker in the High Plains.)
- "Customers currently love indulgence."(From an ice cream maker in California.)
- "Superiorflavour and texture at a competitive price will be a new product requirement." (From a yogurt maker in Ohio.)
- "I do not thinkyou can produce aproduct with enough improvement in taste/ mouthfeel tojustify cost increase to the consumer." (From a yogurt maker in Michigan.)
- "Shelfplacement is critical." (From a yogurt maker in Illinois.)

**Study Implications**

These anecdotal findings reveal extreme concerns from dairy food manufacturers regarding highly elastic demand as well as the ability of consumers to perceive and/or pay for product differentiation. Because of cost, membrane technology investments for the purpose of producing a new product are likely to be scrutinized with great caution.

Among the three types of processors studied, statistical findings indicate that yogurt manufacturers are the most likely to consider a new functional-food formulation involving membrane technology. Concern about enhancing taste would likely be the motivation for making such a new product investment. This study has simply scratched the surface of an evolving industry process. Should membrane manufacturing technologies for new consumer dairy products become more widespread in the future, opportunities will then exist for economists to gain a greater understanding of this technology and its associated cost.

## MILK DRINKING ITEMS

There is but one real beverage and that is water. The other so-called beverages are foods, stimulants or sedatives. Milk is a rich food, one glass having as much food value as two eggs. Coffee, tea, chocolate and cocoa are stimulants, with sedative after-effects. Their food value depends largely on the amount of milk, cream and sugar put into them. Chocolate and cocoa are both drugs and foods. Alcohol is a stimulant at first, afterwards a sedative, and at all times an anaesthetic. When we think of drinking for the sake of supplying the bodily need of fluid, we should think of water and nothing else. If other liquids are taken, they should be taken as foods or drugs. Water is the best solvent known.

The alchemists of old spent much time and energy trying to find the universal solvent, believing that thereafter it would be easy to discover a method of making base metals noble. But they never found anything better than water. Water is the compound that in its various forms does most to change the earth upon which we live, and it is more necessary for the continuation of life than anything else except air. Pure water does not exist in nature, that is, we have never found a compound of the composition H2O. Water always contains other matter.

The various salts are dissolved in it and it absorbs gases. The nearest we come to pure water is distilled. Pure water is an unsatisfied compound, and as soon as it is exposed it begins to absorb gases and take up salts and organic matter. Pure water differs from clean water. Clean or potable water is a compound which contains a moderate amount of salts, but very little of organic matter. Bacteria should be practically absent.

Water that contains much of nitrogenous substances is unfit to use. If the water is very hard, heavily loaded with salts, it should not be used extensively as a drink, for if too much of earthy and mineral matter is taken into the system, the body is unable to get rid of all of them. The result is a tendency for deposits to form in the body. In places where the water is excessively charged with lime it has been noticed that the bones harden too early, which prevents full development of the body.

If the bones of the skull are involved, it means that there will not be room enough for the brain. Such diseases are rare in this country, but in parts of Europe they are not uncommon. If the water is very hard, a good plan is to distill it and then add a little of the hard water to the distilled water. People who partake of an excessive amount of various salts can perhaps drink distilled water to advantage, but those who take but a normal amount of the salts in their foods should have natural water. Water forms three-fourths of the human body, more or less. It is needed in every process that goes on within the body. "To be dry is to die."

Water keeps the various vital fluids in solution so that they can perform their function. Without water there would be no sense of taste, no digestion, no absorption of food, no excretion of debris, and hence, no life. The water is the vehicle through which the nutritive elements are distributed to the billions of cells of the body, and it is also the vehicle which carries the waste to the various excretory organs.

We can live several weeks without food, but only a few days without water. Hot water and ice-cold water are both irritants. Water may be taken either warm or cool. It is best to avoid the extremes. The amount of water needed each twenty-four hours varies according to circumstances. Two quarts is a favourite prescription. Those who eat freely of succulent fruits and vegetables do not need as much as those who live more on dry foods. Salt in excess calls for an abnormal amount of water, for salt is a diuretic, robbing the tissues of their fluids and consequently more water has to be taken to keep up the equilibrium.

Naturally, more water is required when the weather is hot than when it is cool. On hot days warm water is more satisfying and quenches thirst more quickly than ice water. Warm water also stimulates kidney action, which is often sluggish in summer. Ice water is the least satisfactory of all, for the more one drinks the more he wants. A normal body calls for what water it needs, and no more. An abnormal body is no guide for either the amount of food or drink necessary. Many people do not like the taste of water, especially in the morning.

This means that the body is diseased. To a normal person cool water is always agreeable when it is needed, and it is needed in the morning. People with natural taste do not care for ice water, but other water is relished. The common habit of drinking with meals is a mistake. Man is the only animal that does this, and he has to pay dearly for such errors. Taking a bite of food and washing it down with fluid lead to undermastication and overeating, and then the body suffers from autointoxication. A mouthful of food followed by a swallow of liquid forces the contents of the mouth into the stomach before the saliva has the opportunity to act. The best way is to drink one or two glasses of water in the morning before breakfast. Partake of the breakfast, and all other meals, without taking any liquid. Sometimes there is a desire for a drink immediately after the meal is finished. If so, take some water slowly. If it is taken slowly a little will satisfy. If it is gulped down it may be necessary to take one or two glasses of water before being satisfied.

Those who have a tendency to drink too much during warm weather will find very slow drinking helpful in correcting it. If there is any digestive weakness, the liquid taken immediately after a meal should be warm and should not exceed a cupful. Those with robust digestion may take cool water.

Cold water chills the stomach. Digestion will not take place until the stomach has reached the temperature of about one hundred degrees Fahrenheit again, and if the stomach contents are chilled repeatedly the tendency is strong for the food to ferment pathologically, instead of being properly digested. For this reason it is not well to drink while there is anything left in the stomach to digest.

As stomach digestion generally takes two or three hours at least, it is well to wait this long before taking water after finishing a meal, and then drink all that is desired until within thirty minutes of taking the next meal. If the thirst should become very insistent before two or three hours have elapsed since, eating, take warm water. Those who eat food simply prepared and moderately seasoned are not troubled much with excessive thirst. Two quarts of water daily should be sufficient for the adults under ordinary conditions. Here, as in eating, no exact amount will fit everybody. Make a habit of drinking at least a glass of water before breakfast, cleaning the teeth and rinsing the mouth before swallowing any, and then take what water the body asks for during the rest of the day. Taking too much water is not as injurious as overeating, but waterlogging the body has a weakening effect.

To drink with the meals is customary, not because it is necessary, but because we have a number of drinks which appeal to many people. Water is the drink par excellence. A food-beverage that is used by many is cambric tea, which is made of hot water, one-third or one-fourth of milk and a little sweetening. Children generally like this on account of the sweetness. It may be taken with any meal, when fluid is needed, but the amount should be limited to a cupful. It is not well to dilute the digestive juices too much.

The water taken in the morning helps to start the body to cleanse itself. Water drinking is a great aid in overcoming constipation. Constipated people generally overeat. Less food and more water will prove helpful in overcoming the condition. Unfortunately for the race, we have accustomed ourselves to partake of beverages containing injurious, poisonous substances. Inasmuch as this is the place to discuss the drugs contained in coffee and tea, we shall take the liberty of dwelling upon other habitforming substances. They are all a part of the drug addictions of the race. For scientific discussion of these various substances we refer you to technical works. Coffee, tea and chocolate contain a poisonous alkaloid which is generally called caffeine. The theine in tea and the theobromine in cocoa are so similar to caffeine that chemists can not differentiate them. These drinks when first taken cause a gentle stimulation under which more work can be done than ordinarily, but this is followed by a reaction, and then the powers of body and mind wane so much that the average output of work is less than when the body is not stimulated.

The temporary apparently beneficial effect is more than offset by the reaction and therefore partaking of these beverages makes people inefficient. Coffee is very hard on the nerves, causing irritation, which is always followed by premature physical degeneration. Experiments of late indicate that children who use coffee do not come up to the physical and mental standard of those who abstain. The effect on the adults is not so marked because adults are more stable than children.

Those who are not used to coffee will be unable to sleep for several hours after partaking of a cup. Some people drink so much of it that they become accustomed to it. Coffee is not generally looked upon as one of the habit-forming drugs, but it is. However, of all the drugs which create a craving in the system for a repetition of the dose, coffee makes the lightest fetters.

It is surprising how often health-seekers inform the adviser that they "can not get along without coffee". If they would take a cup a few times a year, it would do no harm, but the daily use is harmful to all, even if they feel no bad effects and make it "very weak," which is a favourite statement of the women. Smoking, drinking beer and drinking coffee have a tendency to overcome constipation in those who are not accustomed to these things, but their action can not be depended upon for any length of time and the cure is worse than the disease. Tea drinking has much the same effect as coffee drinking, except that it is decidedly constipating. Perhaps this is because there is considerable of the astringent tannin in the tea leaves.

Chocolate is a valuable food. Those who eat of other aliments in moderation may partake of chocolate without harm, but if chocolate is used in addition to an excess of other food, the results are bad. The chocolate is so rich that it soon overburdens some of the organs of digestion, especially the liver. The Swiss consume much of this food and it is valuable in cases where it is necessary to carry concentrated rations.

Alcohol in some form seems to have been consumed by even very primitive people as far back as history goes. The Bible records an early case of intoxication from wine, and beer was brewed by the ancient Egyptians.

So much has been consumed that some people have a subconscious craving for it. There are cases on record where the very first drink caused an uncontrollable demand for the drug. Fortunately these cases are very rare. Alcohol is really not a stimulant, though it gives a feeling of glow, warmth and well-being at first, but this is followed by a great lowering of physical power, which gives rise to disagreeable sensations. Then the drinker needs more alcohol to stimulate him again. Then there is another depression with renewed demand: There is no end to the craving for the drug once it has mastered the individual. The lungs, heart, digestive organs, muscles, in fact, every structure in the body loses working capacity. Alcohol seems to have a special affinity for nervous tissue. A glass of beer or wine taken daily is no more harmful than a cup of coffee per day, but the coffee drinker does not make of himself such a public nuisance and menace as the man often does who drinks alcohol to excess. Formerly, it was respectable to drink. Some of our most noted public men were drunkards. Now a drunkard could not maintain himself in a prominent public position very long. To drink like a gentleman was no disgrace. Now real gentlemen do not get drunk.

In backward Russia they are becoming alarmed about the inroads of vodka, and are trying to decrease its consumption. France is trying to teach total abstinence to its young men because it disqualifies so many of them from military service to drink. Scandinavia is temperance territory. The German Kaiser has recently given a warning against drinking. The United States discourages drinking in the army and navy. Field armies are not supplied with alcoholics. Drinking is becoming disreputable.

It is very difficult to prove the harm done by excessive drinking of tea and coffee, also by the use of much tobacco, even if we do know that it is so. Everyone knows something about the deleterious effect of alcohol upon the consumer. Solomon wrote: "Wine is a mocker, strong drink is raging, and whosoever is deceived thereby is not wise. Who hath wounds without cause? Who hath redness of eyes?" Alcohol permanently impairs both body and mind. Depending on how much is taken, it may cause various ills, ranging from inflammation of the stomach to insanity. It reduces the power of the mind to concentrate and it diminishes the ability of the muscles to work. It reduces the resistance of the body and shortens life. Its first effect is to lull the higher faculties to sleep.

Most drunkards do not recover from their disease, for drunkenness is a disease. The various drugs given to cure the afflictions are delusions. Strengthening the body, mind and the will and instilling higher ideals are the best methods of cure. Suggestive therapeutics, and the awakening of a strong resolve for a better life are powerful aids. Proper feeding should not be overlooked, for bad habits do not flourish in a healthy body.

Civilization necessitates self-control and considerable self-denial. Those who go in the line of least resistance are on the road to destruction. It is often necessary to overcome habits which produce temporary gratification of the senses. Warden Tynan of the Colorado Penitentiary, 96 per cent of the prisoners are brought there because they use alcohol. It is also well known that moral lapses are most common when the will is weakened through the use of liquor.

Those who have the welfare of the race at heart are therefore compelled to give considerable thought to this subject. Past experience, it will not help to try to legislate sobriety into the people. Education and industrialism are the factors which it seems to me will be most potent in solving the alcohol problem. Morality, which in the last analysis is a form of selfishness, will teach many that it is poor policy to reduce one's efficiency and thereby reduce the earning capacity and enjoyment of life.

More and more the employers of labour will realise that the use of alcohol decreases the reliability and worth of the worker. Many will take steps like the following: "In formal recognition of the fact, established beyond dispute by the tests of the new psychology, that industrial efficiency decreases with indulgence in alcohol and is increased by abstinence from it, the managers of a manufacturing establishment in Chester, Penn., have attacked the temperance problem from a new angle. "Unlike many railways and some other corporations, they do not forbid their employees to drink, but they offer 10 per cent advance in wages to all who will take and keep—the teetotaler's pledge. Incidentally, a breaking of the promise will mean a permanent severance of relations, but there is no emphasizing of that point, it being confidently expected that the advantage of perfect sobriety will be as well realised on one side as on the other."

Business has during the past two centuries been the great civilizer, the great moral teacher. It has found that honesty and righteousness pay and that injustice is folly. Business has led the way to the acceptance of a new ethics, and new morals. What has been said about alcohol applies to tobacco in a much smaller degree. The use of tobacco seems to lead to the use of alcohol. It retards the development of children. It is surely one of the causes of various diseases. Tobacco heart, sore throat and indigestion are well known to physicians. Tobacco contains one of the deadliest of poisons known. Onesixteenth of a grain of nicotine may prove fatal. The reason there are so few deaths from acute tobacco poisoning is that but very little of the nicotine is absorbed. Men who chew tobacco make themselves disagreeable to others. Smoking of cigarettes is to be condemned not only because it poisons the body, but causes inattention and inability to concentrate on the part of the smoker, as well.

Every little while he feels the desire to take a smoke, and if smoking is forbidden he devises means of getting away. He robs his employer of time for which he is paid and injures himself. The ability to work is decreased by indulgence in smoking. Recent experiments show that for a short time there is increased activity after a smoke, but the following depression is greater than the stimulation, so there is an actual loss.

A few years ago, according to Mr. Wilson, who was then Secretary of Agriculture, there were about 4,000,000 drug addicts or "dope fiends" in the United States. Without doubt this estimate was too high, for the proportion of addicts in the country is not as great as in the large cities. The drugs chiefly used are cocaine, opium, laudanum, morphine and heroin. These drugs are much more destructive than alcohol. Cocaine and heroin are the worst. It is very difficult to stop using any of them once the habit has been formed. Nearly every "fiend" dies directly or indirectly from the effect of his particular drug. Every one weakens the body so that there is not much resistance to offer to acute diseases. Every one destroys the will power so that a cure is exceedingly difficult.

It is well to bear in mind that all are not possessed of strong enough will power to resist their cravings and that some take to cocaine when they can not get liquor. Cocaine is far worse than alcohol. People should be very careful about taking patent medicines. There is no excuse for taking them. The most popular ones have as their basis one of the habit-forming drugs. Most of the soothing syrups contain opium in some form. To give babies opiates is a grave error, to speak mildly. It weakens the child, may lay the foundation for a deadly habit later in life, and often an overdose kills outright. Well informed mothers avoid such drugs and keep their children reasonably quiet by means of proper care. Many of the remedies for nasal catarrh and hay fever contain much cocaine. Cocaine is an astringent and a painkiller and people mistake the temporary lessening of discharge from the nose and disappearance of pain for curative effects. But there is nothing curative about it. In a short time the mucous membrane relaxes again and then the discharge is re-established. The nerves which were put out of commission resume their function and then the pain reappears.

Opium or one of its derivatives is generally present in the patent medicines given for coughs. Opium is also an astringent and will suppress secretions, but this is not a cure. Excessive secretions are an indication that the body is surcharged with poison and food. Let them escape and then live so that there will be internal cleanliness and then there will be no more coughs and colds. The unfortunate people who get into the habit of using these drugs degenerate physically, mentally and morally. They need more and more of their drug to produce the desired effect until they at last take enough daily to kill several normal men. Sometimes they are able to keep everybody in ignorance of what they are doing for years. They develop slyness and secretiveness.

They become very suspicious. They are nearly always untruthful, and those who deal with them are surprised and wonder why those who used to be open and above-board now are furtive and dishonest. They often lie when there is not the slightest excuse for it. The moral disintegration is often the first sign noticed. After habitually using any of these drugs for a while the body demands the continuation and if the victim is deprived of his accustomed portion there will be a collapse with intense suffering. Every tortured nerve in the body seems to call out for the drug. The victim will do anything to get his drug. He will lie, steal, and he may even attack those who are caring for him. For the time being he is insane. Many professional men use cocaine. It is a favourite with writers. It often shows in their work. Those who write under the inspiration of this drug often do some good work, but they are unable to keep to their subject. Their writings lack order.

We have enough of such writings to have them classified as "cocaine literature". If there are 4,000,000, or even fewer, of these people in our land, it is a serious problem, for every one is a degenerate, to a certain degree. If the medical profession and the druggists would cooperate it would be easy enough to prevent the growth of a new crop of dope fiends. Of course, people would have to stop taking patent medicines, which often start the victims on the road to degeneration.

Then the physicians should stop prescribing habit-forming drugs, as well as all other drugs, and teach the people that physical, mental and moral salvation come through right living and right thinking. Unfortunately the medical profession is careless and is responsible for the existence of many of the drug addicts. A patient has a severe pain. What is the easiest way to satisfy him? To give a hypodermic injection of some opiate. The patient, not realizing the danger, demands a pain-killer every time he suffers. He soon learns what he is getting and then he goes to the drug store and outfits himself with a hypodermic outfit and drugs, and the first thing he knows he is a slave, in bondage for life.

This is no exaggeration. There are hundreds of thousands of victims to the drug habit who trace their downfall to the treatment received at the hands of reputable physicians, who do not look upon their practice with the horror it should inspire because it is so common. Doctors do not always bury their mistakes. Some of them walk about for years. In spite of laws against the sale of various drugs, they can be obtained. There are doctors and druggists of easy conscience who are very accommodating, for a price. There is no legitimate need for the use of one-hundredth of the amount of these drugs that is now consumed. A local injection of cocaine for a minor operation is justifiable, but none of the habit-forming drugs should be used in ordinary practice to kill pain, for the proper application of water in conjunction with right living will do it better and there are no evil after effects. Massage is often sufficient.

To show a little more clearly how some people become addicted to drugs, let us consider one of the latest, heroin: A few years ago this drug, which is an opium derivative, was practically unknown. It is much stronger than morphine and consequently the effect can be obtained more quickly by means of a smaller dose. Physicians thought at first that it was not a habit-forming drug, for they could use it over a longer period of time than they could employ morphine, without establishing the craving and the habit.

So they began to prescribe heroin instead of morphine, and many a morphine addict was advised to substitute heroin. All went well for a short while, until the victims found that they were enslaved by a drug that was even worse than morphine. Now, thanks chiefly to the medical profession, it is estimated that we have in our land several hundred thousand heroin addicts. Sallow of face, gaunt of figure, looking upon the world through pin-point pupils, with all of life's beauty, hope and joy gone, they are marching to premature death.

The medical profession furnishes more than its proportion of drug addicts. They know the danger of the drugs, but familiarity breeds contempt. If the public but knew how many of their medical advisers, who should always be clear-minded, are befuddled by drugs, there would be a great awakening. One eminent physician who has now been in practice about forty-five years and has had much experience with drug addicts, has said that according to his observations, about one physician in four contracts the drug habit. I believe this is exaggerated, but I am acquainted with a number of physicians who are addicts.

Physicians who smoke do not condemn the practice. Those who drink are likely to prescribe beer and wine for their patients. Those who are addicted to drugs use them too liberally in their practice. Those who have watched the effects of the various drugs, from coffee to heroin, must condemn their use. It is true that an occasional cup of coffee or tea, a glass of wine or beer does no harm. A cigarette a week would not hurt a boy, nor would on occasional cigar harm a man.

But how many people are willing to indulge occasionally? The rule is that they indulge not only daily, but several times a day, and the results are bad. One bad habit leads to another, and the time always comes when it is a choice between disease and early death on one hand, and the giving up of the bad habits on the other, and when this time comes the bonds of habits are often so strong that the victim is unable to break them. We realise that knowledge will not always keep people out of temptation and that some individuals will take the broad way that leads to destruction in spite of anything that may be said. Youth is impatient of restraint and ever anxious for new experiences.

Regarding this serious matter of destructive drug use, much could be done by teaching people their place in society: That is, what they owe to themselves, their families and the public in general. In other words, teach the young people the higher selfishness, part of which consists of considerable self-control, self-denial and self-respect.

Drugs are too easy to obtain today. Some day people will be so enlightened that they will not allow themselves to be medicated. This is the trend of the times. Until such a time comes, society should protect itself by making it very difficult to get any of the habit-forming drugs. If necessary, the free hand of the physician should be stayed. Much of the confidence blindly given him is misplaced.

## CHEESE PRODUCTS

Cheese is a product that has been made for centuries. Virtually all the nutrients present in milk are concentrated in cheese. There is a huge assortment of cheeses. They can have various compositions; we make a rough distinction between fresh cheese and matured cheese, and between soft cheese and hard cheese. Fresh cheese can be consumed immediately after production, whereas matured cheese has to be stored after processing to develop flavour and a good consistency. Soft cheese has a higher water content than hard cheese; moreover hard (or semi-hard) cheese generally has a clean, dry rind. Soft cheeses and hard cheeses can be matured for some weeks or even up to a number of years.

**Table. Rough Composition of Milk and Some Types of Cheese**

| Product | Content (in% Weight) of | | | |
|---|---|---|---|---|
| | Water | Fat | Protein | Salt (Sodium Chloride, NaCl) |
| Milk | 87.5 | 3.5 | 3 | less than 0.1 |
| Skimmed milk | 91 | 0.1 | 3 | less than 0.1 |
| Fresh cheese (whole fat) | 73 | 10 | 10 | less than 0.1 |
| Fresh cheese (low fat) | 83 | 0.2 | 13 | less than 0.1 |
| Cream cheese (fresh) | 57 | 32 | 9 | 0.5 |
| Soft cheese | 51 | 25 | 19 | 2 |
| Semi-hard cheese | 42 | 30 | 25 | 2–2.5 |
| Hard cheese | 30 | 35 | 30 | 2–2.3 |

Cheese production in the tropics is typified by specific problems; consequently, production processes and end products differ from those in Western Europe:

- Outside the temperate zones, high temperatures and very high air humidity must be taken into consideration. Both these factors are unfavourable for cheese making, in particular for the maturation of cheese.
- Milk is often available in small quantities, while its quality may not be up to standard. In particular, its hygienic quality and composition may leave much to be desired.
- Hard and semi-hard cheeses require good-quality milk and hygienic processing. Moderate temperatures are needed for good ripening and storage of these cheeses. In warm and hot climates most cheeses are produced on a small scale and cannot be stored for a long time. Therefore generally these are soft cheeses.
- In many tropical and subtropical countries, very matured cheese is not very popular. Most consumers are not used to the distinct flavour and smell of such cheese.

The shelf life of cheese can vary from several days to some months and even to some years, depending on its processing. Fresh cheese can, like fermented products, be stored for only a short time; it must be consumed immediately or within a few days. The keeping quality of such cheese can be improved by cold storage and salting. Fresh cheese generally does not have a rind and is packed in a wrapping or a package.

Most of the fresh cheese has been curdled using only an acid; it cannot be ripened and it should be consumed within a couple of days. Soft cheese is processed by using acid and rennet, in most cases it matures for some weeks or even some months. Soft cheese generally has a rind and often also a microbiological flora on the surface of the rind (like Camembert and Brie). Semi-hard and hard cheese can be kept well for 3-4 months or more. Cheese which is able to continue ripening should not be kept in a refrigerator, but in a cellar or cool place at 10-15°C.

*Cheese making has three main goals:*

1. Concentration of the milk into curd, whereby a great deal of the liquid part of the milk, the whey, is removed.
2. Preservation of the curd. Acidification of the curd and the salting process are important, along with a well-closed cheese rind or effective wrapping of the cheese.
3. Maturation of the cheese, in order to get a good taste, flavour and consistency.

*The cheese-making process has some essential steps, these are:*

- Coagulation of protein of the milk, whereby the fat is incorporated in the coagulated protein
- Draining of the whey
- Aacidification of the curd
- Collection of the curd and combined growth into a cheese
- Salting
- Maturation
- The processing of fresh cheese follows steps 1 to 3; matured cheese needs steps 1 to 6. The basic operations in cheese making will be discussed in this chapter: the treatment and quality of the milk used to make cheese (pasteurisation and/ or standardisation)

- The coagulation (curdling) of the milk using acid or enzymes
- The separation of the curd and whey
- The collection and preservation of the curd (heating, collection, pressing and salting)
- The maturation (ripening) of the cheese.

**Maturation of the Cheese**

During the maturation of the cheese, protein and fat are partly broken down, causing a change in structure and flavour. The older the cheese, the more flavour it will have. Sometimes, after more than one year the structure becomes crumbly because of the protein breakdown. Maturation is caused primarily by the enzymes in the cheese. To mature cheese, it can be stored in a cool room.

This is a good method but technically rather difficult in the tropics. After salting or pickling, cheese is ripened on a wooden shelf in a cool environment (12-20°C) with a not too high relative humidity (about 80%). Cheese must be turned regularly: initially, i.e., during the first 2 to 3 weeks, daily and later once a week. If mould grows on the cheese, it can be removed with water or vinegar.

*In addition to this method, the following treatments can be carried out on curd:*

- Curd can be smoked over a fire.
- Curd can be boiled in brine.
- You can salt curd, make little balls of it and leave them to dry in thesun.

*Fig.6.1: Smoking Curd over a Fire*

The products which result are particularly suitable to be processed in other foods. After boiling, cheese will not ripen anymore because the enzymes inside the cheese are destroyed by heating.

**Separating Curd and Whey**

*Three methods can be followed to separate curd from whey:*

1. Hanging the curd/whey mixture up in a clean cloth;

2. Putting the curd/whey mixture in cheese moulds, or in cylindrical forms with perforated sides;

3. First cutting and stirring the curd/whey mixture, putting the curd in the cheese moulds and then pressing the cheese.

*Fig.6.2: Letting Soft Cheese Drain*

When making fresh cheese, the first or second method is usually used. As the whey drains through the cloth or the mould, the volume of the curd will reduce to 1/2 or 1/3. When making ripened cheese, the last method has to be used to remove sufficient whey from the curd.

**The Use of Cheese Whey**

Whey is the by-product of cheese making. The acidity and the composition vary widely with the type of cheese and manufacturing process used. Whey from rennet-coagulated cheeses is less acid than whey of acid-coagulated cheeses. Also, the content of solids varies depending on the method of cheese making. If the content of solids is high, e.g., in the case of the processing of sheep cheese or in the case of rough curd treatment, the solids of the whey can be processed to a whey cheese. A rather well-known type of whey cheese is the Italian product Ricotta.

**Manufacture of Ricotta from Cheese Whey**

- Heat the acidified whey till at least 85°C or boil it for some time till the whey proteins have coagulated.
- Add some salt (0.1%) if desired.
- Collect the coagulated curd by filtering the mass through a towel or a filter.
- If you press the curd you will get a hard cheese; if the curd is pressed lightly or not at all, the cheese is consumed fresh.
- Add some salt if you like (if you did not do so before)
- Store the cheese in the fridge.

**Whey as Animal Feed**

If whey is discarded it can cause serious problems as a dairy effluent. Therefore it is far better to use the whey as an animal feed. It has a good feeding value because of the presence of some of the whey proteins. It can be used for feeding pigs or young animals like calves or lambs. Even adult cows or fattening cows can be fed with whey. It is important that the whey used for animal feed is acid (completely acidified) at the moment of feeding, otherwise the animals can get intestinal problems because of the lactose content of the whey.

**Utensils for Making Cheese**

When making cheese, you will not always need all the utensils described below. Decide beforehand which you will use, and make sure that they are clean and rinsed with clean water. It is preferable to use utensils made of stainless steel or glass.

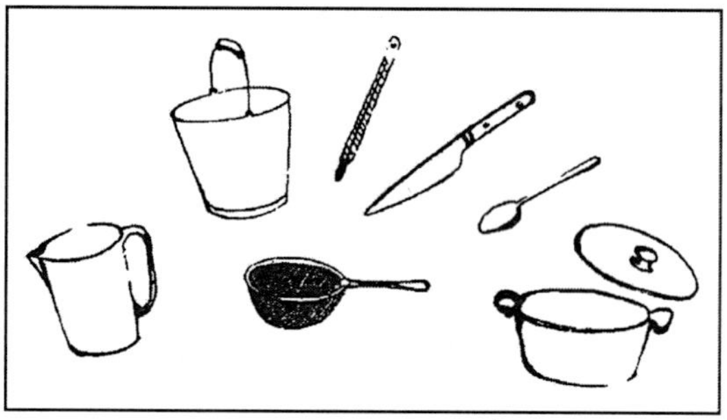

*Fig.6.3: Utensils for Cheese Making*

*The utensils used during cheese making are:*

- A thermometer with a range of 20–100°C
- A measuring cup
- A bucket for coagulation of the milk
- Cheese moulds, which can be made in various ways
- Cheesecloth, its size depends on the size of the mould
- Cutlery and other tools such as:
  - Spoons to measure rennet and/or acids
  - A knife to cut curdled milk
  - A skimmer to scoop curd out of whey, or a colander.

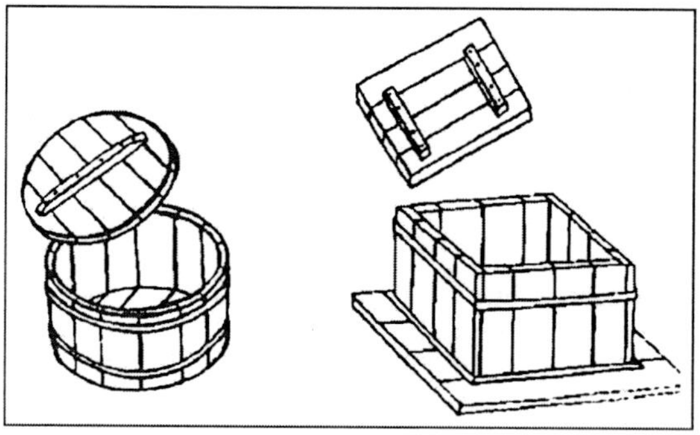

*Fig.6.4: Cheese Moulds*

Cheese moulds can be made from various materials , *e.g.,* wood, plastic or metal. Metal materials should be non-rusting. Do not use plastic tubing used in construction as it can release poisonous substances. Cut the moulds lengthwise and drill holes from the inside out. Plastic moulds for the production of soft cheese are also commercially available. Wooden cheese moulds can be used as well. Cheese that will have a closed rind after pressing is never placed directly into a mould. Instead, a clean cloth of linen or cotton is first placed in the mould and it is then filled with curd. The cheesecloth is then folded closed.

*To make hard or semi-hard cheese you will also need the following:*

- A curd knife to cut the renneted milk
- A cheese press

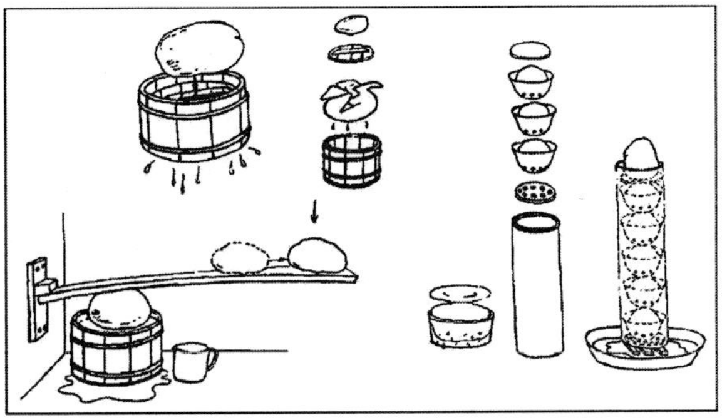

*Fig.6.5: Some Examples of Cheese Presses*

*Buy these second-hand if possible or make your own simple press, paying special attention to the following:*

- The materials used must not be poisonous.
- It must be possible to easily clean the materials.
- It must be possible to build up sufficient pressure (0.1 to 0.4 kg/cm2 or 2-5 x the weight of the cheese).

**The Quality of Milk Used to Make Cheese**

Cheese making begins with hygienic milking. The quality of the milk used greatly influences the smell, taste and keeping qualities of cheese. The composition of milk can vary greatly. Just before a cow is set dry–the period in which a cow is not milked–and just after calving, the cow milk has a different taste and composition. Milk from a cow with an udder infection is not suitable for human consumption, and therefore cannot be used for making cheese.

*Apart from the usual measures taken to ensure good hygiene during milking, attention must be paid to the following points:*

- Clean the equipment very well.
- Disinfectants and cleaning agents must never be left in or on equipment. Disinfectants inhibit the growth of the bacteria of the starter or souring agent.
- The room in which cheese is prepared must be kept properly clean.
- The milk used for cheese making should preferably be pasteurised (15 seconds at 72°C or 30 minutes at 63°C). More intense heating is not desirable because it reduces the curdling of milk. More rennet or calcium chloride (CaCl2) is then needed.
- For the above reasons, milk powder which is strongly heated during its production (high-heat milk powder) is less suitable for cheese processing. Only low-heat milk powder can be used.
- Sour milk neutralised with sodium bicarbonate will not curdle well.

**Coagulation of the Milk**

The principle of cheese processing is based on the coagulation of the protein in milk, during which about 90% of the milk fat is encapsulated. The coagulated mass is called curd, the remaining liquid is called whey. Curd consists mainly of milk proteins (casein) and milk fat; while whey mainly contains water, milk sugar (lactose), protein (serum proteins) and B-vitamins.

*There are two basic ways to cause milk to coagulate:*

1. Using an acid
2. Using a rennet (enzyme coagulation)

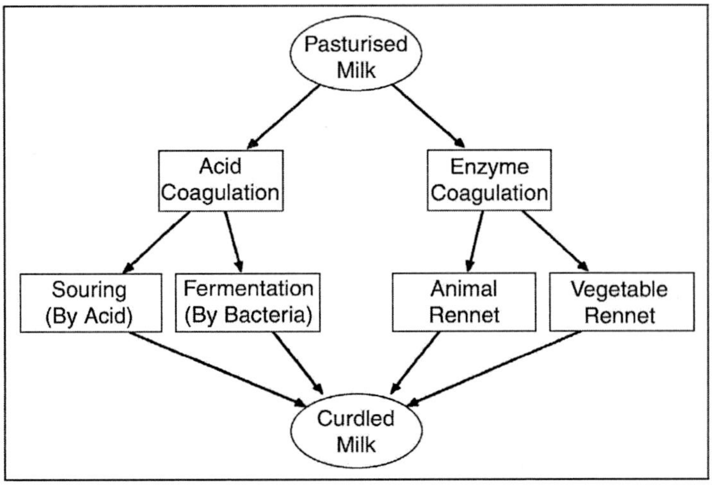


*Fig.6.6: Four Methods of Curdling Milk*

**Acid Coagulation**

This is mainly used to make fresh cheese. The acid can come from bacteria from the starter culture or from an acid added to the milk. When using a culture, pasteurised milk is inoculated. Inoculating agents can be a specific cheese starter culture, whey or sour milk. Curdling time depends on the amount of inoculating agent added (0.1-5% of the milk used to make cheese), temperature (20-35°C) and the starter culture used. It takes 2-16 hours. When the curd is firm, the curdling is finished.

When using an added acid, you can use pure vinegar acid, lactic acid, citric acid or any other harmless organic acid. Sometimes a natural acid such as lemon juice is added. The acid can be added drop by drop to warm milk (about 80- 90°C, just after boiling). Milk curdles much quicker at a high temperature. The curd is collected by straining the curdled milk through a coarse cloth. Sometimes the collected curd is pressed a little bit, and sometimes no pressure is applied. These products are consumed fresh.

**Rennet**

Rennet used in cheese processing can be of animal, vegetable or microbial origin.

*The rennet in cheese has two functions:*

- Rennet causes the milk to coagulate.
- During ripening, rennet causes milk protein to break down, giving the typical cheese taste.

Rennet is available in liquid form and as a dried powder. As it is an enzyme and therefore a biological product, the strength of the liquid product decreases during storage. Therefore, it is preferable to use the dried form. The concentration of the rennet is written on the package.

The amount of rennet to be added depends on the strength of the rennet and on the kind of cheese you are going to make. When making soft cheese, sometimes no rennet is needed; if rennet is added, only a little is needed (0.1 ml of rennet to 10 litres of milk). For hard or semi-hard cheeses, about 1.5 ml of rennet is added to 10 litres of milk; assuming the rennet concentration is 1:10,000. A starter is almost always added before or while adding rennet.

*A number of factors influence coagulation:*

- Amount of rennet or acid added.
- *Curdling Temperature :* When using rennet a small rise in temperature (for example from 30°C to 33°C) can significantly reduce coagulation time.
- Intensity of pasteurisation. Curdling is reduced when milk has been strongly heated. This effect can be neutralised by adding a small amount of CaCl2; for example 7 grams of CaCl2 per 100 litres of milk.
- *Fat Percentage of the Milk :* A high fat percentage means more fat must be encapsulated and curdling occurs a little bit slower.

**Preparation of Rennet**

Rennet from animal origin is prepared from the stomach of suckling calves or lambs. It is obtained by extraction of the stomachs in a salt solution with a preservative.

*A traditional method formerly used in The Netherlands can be applied in the tropics:*

- Take 9 litres of boiled water.
- Add 26 carved calf stomachs, 500 gram sodium chloride (salt) and 200 gram boric acid.
- Store these for at least 10 days and stir once per day.
- After ten days, remove the stomachs from the solution, add another 500 gram salt to the solution and store it for some days more.
- Then, pour it into clean bottles, close these and store the bottles in a cool and dark place. Your rennet is ready.

You have to try out the strength of the rennet. Also, the keeping quality of these rennets is usually poor. Sometimes the stomachs of the young animals are kept after cleaning, salting and drying. The dried stomachs are easy to transport and are used by some nomadic tribes. In cheese making a piece of dried stomach is then added to the milk.

## CHEESE RECIPES

There are many variations in cheese making. To make a good product, it may be necessary to adjust the recipe. Therefore you should have a good method of recording exactly how the cheese is made.

*Your records can include the following aspects:*

- Date and surrounding temperature
- Quality of the milk and pasteurisation temperature
- Aamount of milk

- Ingredients, amount of starter culture, acid or rennet added
- Temperature at which starter culture, acid or rennet was added
- Coagulation time
- Temperatures during the cheese making process
- Temperature at the end of coagulation
- Pressure applied, length of time applied, etc.
- Salting time
- Storage time and conditions during storage

The following recipes should be seen as guidelines for making cheese. Instead of cow milk, you can often use goat, sheep or buffalo milk. Start by making rather simple products like yoghurt, fresh cheese, etc.

**Fresh Cheese**

Fresh or unripened cheese has a high moisture content of about 75%; it can be consumed directly after preparation. It is made by removing the whey from soured, skimmed milk. The milk is usually coagulated by souring. Sometimes a small amount of rennet is added; this is done to facilitate the draining of the whey. However, addition of rennet is not essential.

A well-known kind of fresh cheese is curd, known in various countries by the following names: *Frischkäse, fromage frais,* quarg, and baker's cheese. The differences between these cheeses are their fat levels. You can make curd by souring fresh milk, cream or skimmed milk into sour milk, sour cream or sour skimmed milk and then draining the thick sour milk in a bag or cloth. Sometimes bags are placed on top of each other to increase the removal of whey.

After draining, the curd has a crumbly structure. By stirring or using a blender you can make the product smooth again. There are various kinds of curd cheese in which moisture, fat and salt content and size of curd particles vary. Fresh cheese has a fresh sour taste, especially when it is prepared from skimmed milk. By adding cream, the taste will become milder and richer. Curd can be kept for only a short time and must be stored at cool temperatures. During storage, further whey separation can occur; this is the result of further souring of the product.

**Curd from Whole Milk**

Pasteurise the milk 30 minutes at 63°C and then cool it to 20°C. Add per 10 litres of milk ¼-½ litre of starter culture or fresh sour milk or buttermilk; yoghurt can be added if desired. Add 2 drops of rennet-if available. It is advisable to dilute this small amount of rennet with several ml of water to improve its distribution through the milk. After stirring well, leave the inoculated milk to stand for 24 hours at 18–20°C.

During those 24 hours, souring and coagulation will take place; the milk becomes a rather firm mass. This thick mass is subsequently poured into a cotton or linen cloth or a bag so that the whey can drain through the cloth. The cloth is placed into a large colander or cheese mould beforehand so that the whey can thoroughly drain.

After 24 hours, sufficient whey will have leaked out and the remaining curd can then be mixed, for example with a spoon or blender, until it becomes a homogenous mass. The curd can now be consumed. When kept in a refrigerator, curd can be stored for 1-2 weeks.

**Bag Cheese**

You will need a sieve, small basket or cheese mould and a cheesecloth or tea towel.

*Fig.6.7: Bag Cheese*

Let 10 litres of buttermilk with low fat content drain through a cheesecloth until 1.5 litres of bag cheese, or curd, remain. Place a cheesecloth in a sieve, small basket or cheese mould and press the curd firmly into it. Let the curd drain for several hours, then turn it. About 1.5 kg of bag cheese has then been made, which contains no salt and hardly any fat. It can be kept for only a rather short time: 1 to 2 weeks. Keep it cool, preferably in a refrigerator.

**Krut**

For making krut one needs buttermilk, cheesecloth and salt. This is a way to make cheese from any leftover milk. Add some sour milk or buttermilk to the leftover milk and mix. Boil the mixture until the milk curdles. Separate the curd from the whey by pouring it through a cheesecloth. The curd is then kneaded with 2-4% salt and dried in the sun.

**Rasagollas**

You will need raw milk, a fire, pan, spoon, lemon juice or sour whey, cheese-cloth, bowl, knife and concentrated sugar water. Rasagollas is a sweet dairy product originally from India. Traditionally it was formed into sweet curd balls, but because of the way it is prepared here, the curd can only be cut into cubes and not formed into balls. The milk is boiled with lemon juice (10 tablespoons or 150 ml per 10 litres of milk) or sour whey (1.5 litres per 10 litres of milk) while stirring continuously. Sour whey can be obtained from drained sour milk after the production of curd.

The curd is separated from the whey by pouring the mixture into a cheesecloth, which has been placed over a bowl. The slightly elastic curd is cut into cubes with sides of about 2.5 cm. These are then boiled for about an hour in a sugar solution of 600 g per litre of water. 1 litre of sugar solution is needed for each kilogram of curd. The cubes can be stored quite some time and are very sweet.

**Feta**

You will need sheep, goat or cow milk, starter culture or fresh sour milk, rennet, cooking-salt, knife, cheese moulds, cheesecloths and cans or a plastic container to store the cheese. Feta is a sharp, salty cheese originally from Greece that is made of sheep and goat milk. You can also use a mixture of sheep and cow milk, but then the cheese will not have its typical white colour.

Feta is kept in a solution of whey and brine. Heat 10 litres of pasteurised milk mixed with 200 ml of a starter culture, sour milk or buttermilk to 30°C. After 1-2 hours, rennet is added; use 2 ml of rennet per 10 litres of milk. After allowing it to coagulate for about one hour, the curd is cut into cubes of about 2.5 cm, after which it is carefully stirred for another 20 minutes. The curd must then be carefully transferred to the tubs covered with cheesecloth.

This can be done either by scooping the curd directly out of the whey into the moulds lined with cheesecloth, or by letting the curd settle, pouring off the whey and only then putting the curd in the cheese moulds. After a few hours the cheese must be turned. The curd mass is carefully removed from the cheesecloth and replaced upside down. After one day, the lumps of curd are cut into cubes of about 10 cm.

Salting can be done by sprinkling the blocks several times with salt or by placing the blocks in brine for 24 hours. If the cheese is kept for several days at about 18°C, it must be turned regularly and washed with cold water at the end of the storage period. The cheese can be kept for some time by piling blocks of cheese closely on top of each other and covering them with brine. The cheese should have a smooth and soft consistency.

**Queso Blanco**

The so-called *queso blanco* is manufactured in many ways in Latin America. Typical for this cheese is that salt is added directly to the whey/curd mixture. This has the advantage that slightly soured milk can be used to make *queso blanco.*

*.A much-used method is the following:*

- Take raw (unheated) soured milk of 32°C, or take 10 litres of pasteurised milk and add 50 ml of sour milk, buttermilk or starter culture. Add 1.5 ml of rennet. After 45 minutes the curd is cut and stirred. Leave the whey/curd mixture to settle for another 30 minutes at 30-36°C. Pour off the whey and compress the curd to remove more whey. Mix 30-50 grams of salt through the curd. The salt can also be dissolved in water before being added. 100 grams of salt dissolved in 50 ml of water must then be added for each 10 litres of milk.

Transfer the salted curd into cheese moulds and press the cheese. During the first hours, turn the cheeses occasionally. Press them until the following day. To improve rind formation, pour whey heated at 50°C over the cheese while being pressed (after one hour). Cheese made with rennet can be kept for 2 months at 10-15°C. As a variation to this method, you can add acid instead of a starter culture and use no rennet. Take raw milk, which may already be a little bit sour. Heat it to almost boiling. Acidify it with 300 ml vinegar per 10 litres of milk until a precipitate is formed. The acid can be partly neutralised with the addition of some sodium bicarbonate (double soda). Pour off the whey.

**Fresh Goat Cheese (in Oil)**

You will need pasteurised goat milk, a heat source, a pan with lid, a thermometer, sour milk (or buttermilk or starter culture), rennet, a spoon, an insulated box or blanket or newspapers, cheesecloth, salt, cheese moulds, a cool storage place, greaseproof paper (if available), a large pot, herbs and olive oil. Bring the pasteurised goat milk to a temperature of 20°C. Per 10 litres of milk, add 0.5 litre of fresh starter or sour milk or buttermilk.

Take 20 drops of rennet per litre of milk, dilute this in a little water and stir this through the milk. Place the pan in the insulated box or in the blanket or the newspapers to prevent it from cooling down. Check the next day to see if the milk has curdled sufficiently; a little whey on top is acceptable. Cut the curd into cubes the size of a matchbox. After 2 hours transfer the mass into a cheesecloth and let it drain for 12 hours at room temperature.

Mix the dry curd with some salt and put the cubes into cheese moulds. Press the curd into the moulds so that no air holes remain and place the moulds in a cool (15°C) place. The next day remove the cheese carefully from the cheesecloth and replace it upside down in the cheesecloth and mould. Leave the cheese for a further 24 hours in a cool place.

Remove the cheeses from cloth and mould and turn them daily. Should they become too dry, wrap them tightly, for example in greaseproof paper. If you wish to store the fresh goat cheese cubes for several weeks, place them in a large (glass) jar, which can be closed. Sprinkle a mixture of different herbs over them, such as rosemary, basil, thyme, bruised juniper berries, a finely chopped piece of garlic, several pepper kernels and a chopped up hot pepper.

Other herbs can also be used. Pour olive oil over the cheeses until they are just covered and add a few twigs of dill or rosemary to the oil. Close the jar and put it away in a cool and dark place. Before using the cheeses, let them drain well. Use the leftover oil for salad dressing.

**Fresh Goat Cheese (Salted)**

You will need pasteurised goat milk, a heat source, pan with lid, thermometer, sour milk (or buttermilk or starter culture), acid, spoon, rennet, knife, colander or cheesecloth, cheese moulds, pressing equipment and salt. Heat the pasteurised milk in a pan to 30°C, stirring continuously. For each 10 litres of milk, add 0.2-0.5 litres of sour milk or buttermilk or 0.2 litres of a starter culture and 30 drops of rennet (diluted in water).

After 45 minutes, cut the coagulated curd with a knife; after another 10 minutes, the curd will be the size of a marble. The top layer of whey can be poured off after leaving the mixture to stand a bit. Leave the curd in the carefully closed pan with the rest of the whey for a further 30-45 minutes. Then transfer the curd into cheese moulds in which cheesecloth has been placed. Press the curd; one hour is sufficient. The cheeses mustthen be pickled in brine. For a cheese of 500 grams, 10 hours of pickling is long enough.

**Fresh Sheep Cheese**

You will need pasteurised sheep milk, a heat source, a pan, a thermometer, a starter culture or fresh sour milk or buttermilk, rennet, a spoon, a knife, a cheesecloth, some salt (if desired) and cheese moulds. Sheep milk contains more fat and protein than cow milk and therefore only 4-4.5 litres of sheep milk are needed to make 1 kg of cheese. Because of the higher content of dry matter in the milk, sheep milk coagulates firmer than cow milk.

Heat the pasteurised milk to about 30°C, stirring continuously. Add 300 ml of a starter culture and 40 drops of rennet to each 10 litres of milk. After 45 minutes the milk will have coagulated sufficiently to be cut. Cut the curdled, thick mass carefully; continue till the curd particles have the size of a pea. Bring the curd into a cheesecloth. If desired mix in some salt, and let the cloth hang until the cheese has the desired firmness.

You can speed up the draining of the whey by opening the cheesecloth after several hours, scraping the thick part from the cloth, and mixing it in with the rest of the curd. You may want to make a less sour sheep cheese, which is a little bit firmer and with some lower moisture content. For this, you must leave the curd for a longer time: about 15-30 minutes in the cheese vat where the curd treatment is done. After a short period of rest, pour off part of the whey, stir the curd carefully again and fill the cheese mould using a cheesecloth. Add some salt to the curd, if desired. Press the curd: about 4 hours of light pressing is sufficient. Store in a cool place. Sheep cheese can be kept for at least one week in the refrigerator.

**Matured Sheep Cheese**

You will need pasteurised sheep milk, a heat source, a pan, a thermometer, sour milk (buttermilk or starter culture), rennet, a spoon, a knife, colander, a cheesecloth, cheese moulds and pressing equipment, salt, a tightly sealed pickling tub, coarse cheesecloth and a cool storage place. 10 litres of sheep milk yields about 2 kg of ripened cheese. After adding 60 ml of starter culture or sour milk (or buttermilk), leave the milk to stand at 30°C for 30-45 minutes.

Only then add 60 drops of rennet, diluted with a little water, per 10 litres of milk, and stir it thoroughly through the milk. After allowing it to curdle for 1 hour, cut the coagulated milk for about 15 minutes until it is divided into particles of about 1-2 cm. Then stir it for 10 minutes, pour half of the whey off and heat the curd to 35°C by adding hot water with a temperature of 80-100°C.

Stir the mixture again for about 15 minutes, after which time the curd must be left to stand for 30 minutes in the pan. Keep the pan warm as well as possible but never place it on a fire. Remove the whey that has separated, and pour the curd with the remaining whey into a colander. After the first draining, the curd must be transferred by hand into cheese moulds covered with cheesecloth.

## FLAVOUR LEXICONS FOR DAIRY PRODUCTS

M.A. Drake and G.V. Civille have reviewed lexicon history, methods and applications. A flavour lexicon is a set of word descriptors that describe a product's flavour. While the panel generates its own list to describe the product array under study, a lexicon provides a source of possible terms with references and definitions for clarification. Development of a representative flavour lexicon requires several steps, including appropriate product frame-of- reference collection, language generation and designation of definitions and references, before a final descriptor list can be determined.

Once developed, flavour lexicons can be used to record and define product flavour, compare products and determine storage stability, as well as to study correlations of sensory data with consumer liking/acceptability and chemical flavour data. Good flavour lexicons should be both discriminating and descriptive.

The language should be developed from a broad representative sample set that exhibits all the potential variability within the product. For example, Drake collected 220 samples of Cheddar cheese varying in age, milk heat treatment and geographical origin to identify a descriptive language for Cheddar cheese.

**Table: Cheddar Cheese Lexicon with Identified References**

| Term | Definition | Reference |
|---|---|---|
| Cooked | Aromatics associated with cooked milk | Nonfat milk heated to 85°C for 30 min. |
| Whey | Aromatics associated with Cheddar cheese whey | Fresh Cheddar whey |
| Diacetyl | Aromatics associated with diacetyl | Diacetyl |
| Milkfat/ heavy cream d-Lactone | Aromatics associated with milkfat | Fresh coconut meat, dodecalactone |
| Fruity | Aromatics associated with different fruits | Fresh pineapple, canned pineapple juice |
| Sulfur | Aromatics associated with sulfurous bubbled | Boiled mashed egg, H2S compounds through water, struck match |
| Free Fatty Acid | Aromatics associated with short-chain fatty acids | Butyric acid |
| Brothy | Aromatics associated with boiled meat or vegetable soup stock | Canned potatoes, commercial low-sodium, beef broth |
| Nutty | Nutlike aromatic associated with nuts, wheat germ, unsalted wheat crackers | Lightly toasted unsalted different nuts |
| Catty | Aroma associated with tomcat urine | 2 mercapto-2 methyl-pentan-4-one |
| Cowy/ phenol Phenolic | Aromas associated with barns and stock | p-cresol, BandAids, trailers |
| Bitter | Fundamental taste sensation elicited by caffeine, quinine | Caffeine (0.08% in water) |
| Salty | Fundamental taste sensation elicited by salts | Sodium chloride (0.5% in water) |
| Sweet | Fundamental taste sensation elicited by sugars | Sucrose (5% in water) |
| Sour | Fundamental taste sensation elicited by acids | Citric acid (0.08% in water) |
| Umami | Chemical feeling factor elicited by certain peptides and nucleotides | MSG (1% in water) |
| Prickly | Chemical feeling factor of which the sensation of carbonation on the tongue is typical | Soda water |

The sample set was screened to 70 cheeses prior to language generation. In creating a lexicon, the panel will frequently review the list, merging like terms, eliminating redundancies and organizing the list so that the attributes appear in most products being tested. It is important that multiple terms are not used to describe the same flavour; conversely, it is also important that one term doesn't represent or overlap with several other flavours.

As an example of this type of lexicon problem, Drake reported that use of the term "aged" in a Cheddar cheese flavour lexicon was in fact a meta term that comprised three flavours and one basic taste.

An optimized lexicon can relate consumer acceptance/rejection and instrumental or physical measurements. The use of chemical components, particularly those isolated from the product under study, can make a lexicon clearer and more grounded, establishing a link to the formulation and/or production of that product.

Creating this type of link can be time-consuming and challenging. However, even without such chemical references, a lexicon can be discriminating and precise. Several diff e rent flavour lexicons have been developed to study cheese aroma and flavour development, the effects of fat reduction and the effects of different starter or adjunct bacteria. Muir described nine aroma terms for characterization of aroma profiles of hard and semi hard cheeses.

For studying flavour development in Cheddar cheese during maturation, Piggot and Mowat determined 23 descriptive flavour terms, and Roberts and Vickers developed a flavour lexicon. Muir and Drake used descriptive sensory panels to determine the effect of starter culture and adjunct cultures on Cheddar cheese flavour. Banks used descriptive analysis to determine sensory properties of low fat Cheddar cheese.

## APPLICATION OF SENSORY ANALYSIS TO DAIRY PRODUCTS

Following are specific examples of how QDA and/or other types of sensory analysis techniques have been applied to dairy research studies funded by Dairy Management Inc. ™ (DMI).

### Optimization of Cheddar Cheese Taste in Model Cheese Systems

Cheddar cheese, the most popular natural cheese in the United States, has a very complex flavour system. While much information has accumulated during the past century, the industry is still seeking to fully understand Cheddar cheese flavour and has not been able to replicate it in model systems. The nonvolatile sensory attributes of Cheddar cheese are important for providing the character of Cheddar cheese.

While much work has been published on volatile components of Cheddar, far less is known on how nonvolatiles impact Cheddar flavour. Yang, a Kraft Foods researcher, and Vickers, at the Minnesota-South Dakota Dairy Foods Research Center, used sensory analysis to better understand the importance of nonvolatile compounds to Cheddar flavour.

A descriptive panel was trained to evaluate real and model cheese for a variety of taste attributes and for Cheddarlike taste. Sodium chloride, lactic acid, citric acid and monosodium glutamate were added to the model systems using mixture designs and response surface methodology to determine optimum levels of these components.

*The three model systems investigated were:*

1. A dairy model system (containing milk isolate, anhydrous milk fat, water, annatto colour and chymosin);
2. A nondairy model system (containing gelatin, gum acacia, modified starch, sunflower oil, water and annato colour); and
3. A mozzarella base.

While the mozzarella base did present tastes, it was used because the other two model systems were too unlike Cheddar cheese (or any cheese) texture. Less sodium chloride and fewer acids were required to simulate the taste of mild Cheddar compared with aged Cheddar. None of the model systems mimicked the texture of real Cheddar. The researchers were able to match approximately, but not exactly, the taste of aged Cheddar using a mozzarella base.

Panelists generally rated the optimized taste in the dairy model system as more Cheddar-like than the optimized tastes in the nondairy model. Two methods were used to measure how close a sample was to the Cheddar concept. One was by measuring the similarity of the sample to either mild Cheddar cheese taste or aged Cheddar cheese taste on an unstructured scale.

The left end of the line was marked with "not at all like Cheddar taste" and the right end was marked with "exactly like mild Cheddar taste" or "exactly like aged Cheddar taste." The other method was by concept matching using an R-index methodology. For the mild group, the panel evaluated whether the samples were "MC" (mild Cheddar taste and sure), "MC?" (mild Cheddar taste but not sure), "N?" (no Cheddar taste but not sure) or "N" (no Cheddar taste and sure). For the aged group, "MC" and "MC?" were changed to "AC" (aged Cheddar taste and sure) and "AC?" (aged Cheddar taste but not sure).

A model system for studying Cheddar taste should be as bland-tasting as possible, and also have a texture and composition similar to that of real Cheddar cheese. The characteristic flavour of a food depends not only on the flavour compounds present and their levels but also the rate and extent to which they are released in real time, which in turn are affected by the amounts of proteins, fat and other matrix components of the sample.

By using a trained descriptive analysis panel, Yang and Vickers were able to evaluate the flavour impact of several nonvolatile Cheddar cheese components (i.e., salt, lactic acid, citric acid and monosodium glutamate) in model systems that attempted to mimic real Cheddar cheese. They achieved the most Cheddar-like taste with the mozzarella cheese base, and panelists found the optimal concentration of salts and acids in the model to be nearly indistinguishable from real Cheddar cheese.

**Cheddar Cheese and Powdered Milk Lexicons**

M. A. Drake, at the Southeast Dairy Foods Research Center, developed and validated a descriptive language for Cheddar cheese flavour. For the project, 240 representative cheese samples were collected. Fifteen individuals from industry, academia and government participated in roundtable discussions to generate descriptive flavour terms. A highly trained descriptive panel (n=11) refined the terms and identified references.

Identification of chemical references was conducted with the assistance of K. Cadwallader at the University of Illinois. Instrumental analyses (gas chomatography/ mass spectrometry, or GC/MS) were conducted to identify many flavour compounds that were responsible for specific flavours and offflavours in Cheddar cheese. Twenty-four Cheddar cheeses were then presented to the panel to validate the proposed lexicon.

The panel differentiated the 24 Cheddar cheeses as determined by univariate and multivariate analysis of variance. Twenty-seven terms were identified to describe Cheddar flavour. Seventeen descriptive terms were observed in most Cheddar cheeses. Drake's standard sensory language for Cheddar cheese today is facilitating training and communication among different research groups.

The Cheddar cheese lexicon is helping cheese-makers and cheese users accurately and consistently characterize the flavour of their cheese products and improve quality issues by measuring and controlling the presence of compounds that have been associated with flavour defects.

Following development of the Cheddar cheese lexicon, Drake developed a similar language to help characterize another food industry staple: dried dairy ingredients, including whey proteins and nonfat dry milk. Global production of nonfat dry milk tops 3.3 million tons and whey protein demand still outstrips production, which increases annually.

A sensory lexicon describing the flavour of these ingredients helps dairy processors maximize the quality of these ingredients and allows food technologists to identify the exact attributes or flavour notes these ingredients contribute to formulations. Drake said she was surprised by the number of descriptive terms that the panel uncovered for application to the dried dairy ingredients lexicon. The panel discovered 21 flavour terms that could be applied to milk powders. Examples included cooked/milky flavour, cake mix or vanillin, sweet and sour, earth and cereal.

Each of these flavours was linked to a key aroma compound, many of which were identified by Drake and Cadwallader with GC/MS. For example, lactones tend to lend a sweet, coconut like flavour, while various free fatty acids can simulate a waxy flavour. Many different factors contribute to flavour variability. The source of the powder, processing/ packaging methods and materials, as well as storage time and conditions, are just a few.

The dried dairy ingredient lexicon, linking responsible chemical factors and causal agents, provides common ground for processors and ingredient suppliers to discuss ingredient characteristics. Figure shows how descriptive analysis results based on Drake's dried dairy ingredient lexicon can be analysed by PCA. This two-dimensional PCA plot shows the attribute variability among 27 low-heat skim milk powders less than three months old. Rehydrated milk powders are represented by numbers. PC1 = principal component 1; PC2 = principal component 2.

## PROCESSING OF OTHER CREAMS

### Whipped Cream

Whipped cream contains added sugar and stabilisers. The stabilised cream is then pasteurised and held at 5°C for 24 hours. Compressed air or nitrogen is then introduced into the mix. This provides an excellent aerobic medium for microbial growth, thereby increasing the chances of spoilage in comparison with liquid cream.

### Frozen Cream

Frozen cream is pasteurised at ≥ 75°C for 15 seconds. It is then quickly cooled to 1°C before being frozen in containers, as sheets or pellets, or by direct contact with liquid nitrogen. It is then stored at-18 to-26°C.

### Clotted Creams

Clotted creams are traditionally made by putting milk in a pan 30 cm in diameter and 20 cm deep where it is held for 12 hours to allow the cream to rise. The pan is then put on a steamer until a layer of solidified cream is formed around the edge.

*Modern methods involve:*

- Heating double cream over a layer of skimmed or whole milk, in a large, shallow jacketed tray until a crust is formed or
- Heating a thin layer of high-fat cream (54–59% milk fat) at 77–85°C, to form a crust. The more severe heat treatments result in aerobic spore-formers being the predominant microflora.

However, slow cooling and poor hygiene are more likely to lead to the growth of spoilage moulds, coliforms and other contaminants.

### Cream-Based Desserts

Cream-based desserts typically undergo heat treatments above pasteurisation, in order to allow cooking of other ingredients such as starch.

### Spoilage

The spoilage of cream is generally similar to that described for liquid milk products. However, because of the difference in purchasing patterns, cream is often required to have a longer shelf life than milk (up to 14 days for pasteurised cream), and containers may be opened and then used by the consumer over several days. The keys to obtaining sufficient shelf life are the microbiological quality of the raw milk, good hygiene in processing, and effective temperature control during distribution and storage.

Cream usually receives more severe heat processes than milk, and the post-heat treatment microbial population therefore consists almost entirely of relatively heat-resistant species. Aerobic spore-forming bacteria survive pasteurisation, and psychrotrophic strains of *Bacillus cereus* may cause 'sweet curdling' and 'bitty cream'. Other, more heat-resistant species, such as *Bacillus licheniformis, Bacillus coagulans,* and Bacillus subtilis, may survive sterilisation and even UHT processes, and may cause bitterness and thinning in sterilised creams.

*Bacillus pumilus* and *Bacillus sporothermophilus* are now recognised as potential contaminants in cream, primarily carried over from raw milk. Under UHT conditions, *B. sporothermophilus* has D-values of 3.4-7.9 sec and z-values of 13.1-14.2. Heat-resistant lipases produced by psychrotrophic bacteria growing in the raw milk may also survive high-temperature processing and cause spoilage in UHT cream. The keeping quality of cream is greatly affected by the introduction of postprocess contamination.

Psychrotrophic bacteria such as pseudomonads may contaminate pasteurised cream during processing and are important spoilage organisms. The high fat content of cream means that lipolytic species, such as *Pseudomonas fluorescens* and *Pseudomonas fragi,* are a particular problem. A study of pasteurised double cream showed that pseudomonads were the predominant spoilage organisms. Psychrotrophic members of the Enterobacteriaceae are also sometimes involved.

Yeasts and moulds are rarely implicated in the spoilage of cream. Few yeasts are able to ferment lactose, but species such as *Candida lipolyticum* and *Geotrichum candidum* may occasionally spoil bakers' whipping cream where sucrose has been added. If, however, other organisms hydrolyse lactose, then the yeast can grow rapidly to produce yeasty or fruity flavours and gas; *Torula cremoris, Candida pseudotropicalis* and *Torulopsis sphaerica* have been implicated with such defects. Where cream is stored at very low temperatures (0-1°C) to prolong the shelf life, mould growth, usually *Penicillium* spp. may develop on the cream surface.

Defective cans or leaking seams could cause spoilage of cream due to entry of bacteria from cooling water or other sources, *e.g.*, a waterborne organism, for example *Proteus*, can cause bitterness and thinning, coliforms can produce gas, and lactococci could result in acid curdling.

In the case of cream-based desserts, thermoduric organisms are most likely to be an issue due the more aggressive heat treatments that are used. In addition, the added sugar increases the range of contaminants that could grow in the product. Fruit conserves, if added, will lower the pH of the product thus favouring the growth of yeasts and moulds. With multi-component desserts, both individual components, and blends obtained from their mixing could be responsible for microbial spoilage.

**Pathogens: Growth and Survival**

In practice, to overcome the protective effect of the higher fat content, cream usually receives a more severe heat treatment than milk. This means that pathogens present in the raw cream are more likely to be destroyed. Unpasteurised cream carries a high risk from the presence of foodborne pathogens, as does raw milk, but the recent safety record of pasteurised cream is good. Although foodpoisoning outbreaks have been associated with cream, they are often linked to products filled with, or prepared with cream. In these cases, it is probable that poor hygiene during manufacture, and temperature abuse during storage have been important contributory factors.

**Salmonella Spp.**

Salmonellae will not survive the heat treatment applied to cream, and therefore their presence is likely to be due to post-pasteurisation contamination. The cells are likely to survive for extended periods in contaminated cream, but growth is not possible unless significant temperature abuse occurs. Storage at temperatures below 5°C will prevent multiplication. Most of the relatively recent outbreaks recorded have been associated with foods prepared with cream. For example, in 1986 an outbreak of *Salmonella typhimurium* DT40 infection affecting 24 people in the UK was linked to consumption of creamfilled profiteroles.

A much larger outbreak occurred in Navarra in Spain in 1991, and was reported to have affected approximately 1,000 people. The causative organism was *Salmonella enteritidis,* and the outbreak was associated with the consumption of contaminated confectionery custard and whipped cream.

In 1992, an outbreak of S. *enteritidis* PT4 infection in Wales was associated with fresh cream cakes, and was found to be a result of contamination of the factory environment by the organism, and inadequate cleaning of the nozzles used to pipe cream into the cakes. More recently, in 1998, an outbreak of S. *typhimurium* DT104 infection affected 86 people in Lancashire. The outbreak was linked to inadequately pasteurised milk from a local dairy, but cream from the same dairy was also recalled.

**Listeria Monocytogenes**

There has been some concern that L. *monocytogenes* might be able to survive cream pasteurisation processes and then grow during chilled storage. However, *L. monocytogenes* strain Scott A recorded a D-value of 6 seconds at 68.9 °C in raw cream with a fat content of 38%, indicating that pasteurisation is likely to be effective. The D-value increases to 7.8 sec in inoculated 'sterile' cream. Z-values were calculated as 6.8°C and 7.1°C, respectively.

A later study, using two strains of *L. monocytogenes* suspended in different dairy products, including half and double cream, showed that, although heat resistance did vary, minimum pasteurisation processes would be adequate to eliminate the organism in all products. An investigation into the fate of several strains of *L. monocytogenes* in whipping cream at various storage temperatures recorded generation times of 29-46 hours at 4°C.

Populations of approximately 107 cells/ml were reached after incubation for 30 days, and, at 8°C, hazardous levels were reached in only 8 days. This indicates that post-pasteurisation contamination of cream could be a potentially serious problem. The same post-process hygiene precautions should be applied for cream as for other high-risk chilled products. Despite this, although L. monocytogenes infection is reported to have been linked to cream on epidemiological evidence, such cases have not been confirmed by microbiological investigation.

**Yersinia Spp.**

*Yersinia enterocolitica* is a common contaminant of raw milk, although the majority of the strains isolated are not pathogenic to humans. The organism is heat-sensitive and does not survive pasteurisation, but is capable of psychrotrophic growth. Therefore, it is a potential hazard in cream if introduced as a post-pasteurisation contaminant. A survey of dairy products in Australia recorded an isolation of Y. *enterocolitica* from pasteurised cream, but the organism was not detected in cream sampled in the UK over the course of a 3-year survey to determine its incidence in foods. There have been no reported outbreaks of *Y. enterocolitica* infection associated with cream.

**Staphylococcus Aureus**

Although *Staph. aureus* can often be isolated from raw milk, and is a common cause of mastitis in cows, it does not survive pasteurisation, and cases of staphylococcal food poisoning from pasteurised dairy products are now uncommon. It may be introduced into cream as a post-process contaminant, particularly from infected food handlers. However, it is incapable of growth below about 7 °C, and high numbers will only develop following significant temperature abuse. An investigation of growth and enterotoxin.

A production by *Staph. aureus* in whey cream showed that growth was limited and that enterotoxin was not produced at detectable levels. Despite this, between 1951 and 1970, six outbreaks of staphylococcal poisoning associated with cream were recorded in England and Wales. There have been few recent reports of outbreaks, following significant improvements in hygiene and temperature control. As with *Salmonella*, products prepared or filled with cream are now more likely to be implicated as vehicles of staphylococcal poisoning than cream itself, usually as a result of poor hygiene during handling and temperature abuse.

### Bacillus Cereus

*B. cereus* is common in milk, and its endospores are able to survive pasteurisation. Some strains are also psychrotrophic, and capable of growth in refrigerated dairy products. Nevertheless, there are very few reports of B. cereus food poisoning associated with dairy products. There have been a small number of outbreaks associated with the consumption of pasteurised cream. In 1975 cream found to contain 5xl06 cfu B. cereus caused illness in several people. In 1989, two members of the same family became ill after consuming fresh single cream that was later found to contain B. cereus at levels of 3x107/g.

### Verotoxigenic Escherichia Coli (VTEC)

VTEC, particularly *Escherichia coli* O157, have been found in raw milk and have caused serious outbreaks of infection associated with consumption of raw or inadequately pasteurised dairy products. An outbreak of E. coli O157 infection was recorded in the UK in 1998, associated with consumption of raw cream from a small farm dairy.

Seven cases were recorded, with four requiring admission to hospital. These organisms are destroyed by properly applied pasteurisation, but if any opportunities for cross-contamination between raw and pasteurised cream exist, recontamination could potentially occur. It is likely that E. coli O157 could survive for prolonged periods in cream, but growth in the absence of temperature abuse is improbable. In view of the potentially serious nature of infections caused by VTEC, and the low infective dose, it is important to ensure that such cross-contamination does not occur, since, growth may not be required to cause infection.

### Viruses

Viral hepatitis is the most likely viral infection to be associated with dairy products. In 1975 in Scotland, an outbreak of hepatitis A infection occurred associated with cream consumption. The cause of the outbreak was handling of the cream by an infected cook during preparation.

❑❑❑

# Index